The allegory of Adam and Eve depicts mankind choosing to leave innocence and come into wisdom through knowledge of good and evil. The Adam and Eve story reveals God honouring the free will of humankind by exposing them and their children to the dark as well as the light side of the divine. This book looks at the dark side of the Old Testament God, the course of evil in the biblical account and the impact of this dualistic character and the religious cults stemming from him on ancient and modern history.

Other Books by David Ash:

The Tower of Truth (CAMSPRESS, Cornwall 1977),

Science of The Gods/ The Vortex: Key to Future Science – with Peter Hewitt - (Gateway Books, Bath, 1990),

The Science of Ascension (Cloverleaf Connection, Canada, 1993),

Activation for Ascension (Kima Global Publishing, Cape town RSA, 1995)

The *New Science of the Spirit* (The College of Psychic Studies, London, 1995)

God the Ultimate Paradox (Kima Global Publishing, Cape town RSA, 1998)

Is God Good? (Kima Global Publishing, Cape town RSA, 2005)

The New Physics of Consciousness (Kima Global Publishers)

The Role of Evil in Human Evolution

- Exposing the Dark to Light-

David A. Ash B.Sc., Cert. Ed.

Published by **Kima Global Publishers**
Kima Global House,
11, Columbine Road,
Rondebosch 7700
P.O. Box 374,
Rondebosch 7701
South Africa

© 2007 David Ash

ISBN 978-0-9802561-3-0
Cover design: Nadine May

e-mail: info@kimaglobal.co.za
website: www.kimaglobal.co.za
Author's website: www.davidash.info

Contents

Section III
My Testament (≡Nonsense)

Introduction

"You must challenge your most sacred assumptions, and you must challenge the source from which they have come."

Neale Donald Walsch, *Tomorrow's God*

Down through the ages philosophers, theologians and just ordinary people, have wrestled with the existence of evil. Christians, Jews and Muslims believe there is a devil, a fallen angel called Satan who is responsible for all man's ills. Others ask, "How can there be a God when there is so much evil in the world?" or "Why does an all powerful and absolutely good God allow so much suffering?" One thing is certain, most people believe evil is a bad thing.

I take a very different position. I suggest that evil has an essential role in human evolution and is, ultimately, working for our greater good. Most people who believe in God take it for granted that God is perfect and absolutely good. The very word 'God' means 'good' in the old Anglo-Saxon and modern Scandinavian languages.

I believe in a 'Universal Creative Intelligence' which has come to be known as God and that this is ultimately good. However, I also believe the intelligence of the Universe works with what we perceive to be evil as well as what we perceive to be good. Our problem is judgment. For the most part we lack the wisdom to appreciate the beneficial value of every event in history and everything that happens in our lives.

I intend to throw light on the value of evil and the important part it has played in the honing of the human spirit down through the ages. There is no escaping the evils of disease, aging and death. People get swept up in wars or natural disasters. Just when everything is going well, misfortune strikes; the loss of a loved one, a car crash or financial ruin. Then there is the news. It seems the world is full of evil. Prisons are overcrowded. Crime is out of control. The environment is being destroyed. The cost of living keeps rising. Even more species are becoming extinct. Evermore landmines are laid in pointless conflicts and then are left to maim or kill little children. Morals are declining and more people than ever are being destroyed by drugs and alcohol. ... the evils in the world are seemingly endless.

I contend this is how things are intended for us in this world. This is a place where we come to experience evil for a purpose few of us comprehend. Whilst we are responsible for much of the evil we experience and natural disasters, death and decay have their part to play, ultimately the big spoon in this nasty pot of evil is God; God as portrayed in the Bible.

If you believe God is everything or the source of everything and you accept that evil exists then you have to accept that God must encompass evil as well as good, dark as well as a light. If you are a Christian, a Jew or a Muslim you will not have a problem accepting this truth because the duality of God is revealed in the Bible. The Bible teaches that God is the source of the dark as well as the light, evil as well as good:

> *I am the Lord and there is none else, I form the light and create darkness; I make peace and create evil; I, the Lord, do all these things.*

(Isaiah 45:7)

For most people in the Western world their understanding of God comes from the Bible. Whoever or whatever God is, the God of the Bible is far from what most of us would consider absolutely good. The biblical God is a mix of good and bad. In Answer to Job, Carl Jung wrote:

> The Book of Job is a landmark in the long historical development of the divine drama. At the time the book was written, there were already many testimonies, which had given a contradictory picture of Yahweh – the picture of God who knew no moderation in his emotions and suffered precisely from this lack of moderation. He himself admitted that he was eaten up with rage and jealousy and that this knowledge was painful to him. Insight existed along with obtuseness, loving-kindness along with cruelty, creative power along with destructiveness. Everything was there, and none of these qualities was an obstacle to the other."

I would like you to understand that whatever you believe, God is not under attack, so please do not be offended if what I say contradicts your faith. You do not have to believe what is said in this book. You are free to believe what you like. I am writing as if God exists. I am also writing about God, as portrayed in the Bible. If you do not believe in the Bible or in God you will still find this book a valuable read. This book will caution you to beware of cults masked as religion. If you belong to one of the religions strongly attached to the idea that God is absolutely good, be warned, you are in for a shock.

I never imagined God could sanction evil until in 1992, I was presented with a copy of The Protocols of the Learned Elders of Zion. Whilst I could not be certain of its authenticity this staggering document opened my eyes to another side of God. To me it was a total paradox that such an evil document should be linked to the Chosen People of God. With their blood in my veins I immediately assumed *The Protocols of Zion* was a fabrication and a fraud intended to engender anti-Semitism. I was disturbed to find shocking parallels to the Protocols in the Bible and the 'Talmud'and a number of other documents I unearthed in my research.

Within all religions and cultures, cults germinate in which self-righteous people view themselves as more acceptable to God than others.This destructive core of racial and religious intolerance, particularly when backed by wealth and power has been a major source of human suffering. Historically this attitude has led to war, genocide, oppression and anthropological vandalism. The Bible has engendered religious intolerance and elitism in Judaism which was then passed onto Christianity and Islam, with then led to persecution, war and strife stretching over millennia.

Fortunately, most Jews today don't identify with the Chosen People status whereas fundamentalist Jews, Christians and Muslims each imagine their sect to be 'truer' and 'superior' than others. This is a danger inherent in all religious cults and is not a reflection on any race. I deplore anti-Semitism and feel proud to own 'Jewish genes', albeit from my sire rather than my dame. However, I am fascinated with the origins of the Judaic cult and the fact that it is obvious from the Bible that Judaic-Christian beliefs in religious and racial superiority originated from God.

I am dragging hidden skeletons out of my own cultural and personal cupboard. I have great difficulty in shaking off my own religious programming in the Roman Catholic Church which has done as much to discredit and destroy 'truth, goodness and human decency' in its history as uphold these values. The Albigensian crusade was genocide and the Inquisition it spawned places the Catholic Cult in the same historical bracket as Hitler's Nazism and Stalin's Communism. Most of the Catholics, Christians and Jew I know are sincere, caring people who are inspired by their faith to live exemplary lives. However, there is an element of fanaticism and narrow-mindedness amongst some who profess the Bible or Torah as the infallible Word of God. The Bible contains insights, wisdom and inspiration but it also breathes violence and intolerance.

As well as direction for good inspired by 'God' the Bible has a shadow. Its pages are also loaded with crimes against humanity perpetrated in the name of 'God'.

I began to think deeply about what was going on around me. What were the forces underlying the social and economic fabric of the modern world? To what extent are they influenced by the cults spawned by the Hebrew god? Are there secret societies plotting and scheming to take over the world? Do the inner circles of Freemasonry or the illusive 'Illuminati' carry a common thread leading back to the same 'God'?

As I delved deeper I began to wonder if the God I used to worship in the Catholic Church was the good God or the evil one? In my pew was I kneeling before God or Satan?

The Cathars slaughtered without mercy by the Catholics would have me believe that the God of the Bible is Satan. Were they heretics or did they have the truth? The way they were treated was diabolical. Nothing they ever did justified the merciless onslaught by Catholics against them. Did the Catholic Church reveal its true identity as a 'Satanic Cult' in its treatment of dissidents? After all, its founder did say, *"By their fruits you will know them."* (Matthew 7:20)

In this book I endeavour to resolve one of the greatest paradoxes in the history of mankind. I lean on the Bible because the record of the Jewish people in the Bible has had the greatest impact of any book in history. The word God means 'good' and yet 'God', as revealed in the Old Testament of the Bible, would appear to be linked to evil as well as good. The Bible is dualistic. For example, in the Bible it is clear that God was the cause of the racist attitude in the Hebrew people. If God knows everything he must know the outcome of racism. Furthermore, according to the Bible, the Hebrews received direct instruction from their God to commit acts of genocide. God cannot wash his hands of his chosen people and say, 'they fell into evil ways,' when they were following his instruction to the letter. For God there can be no excuses.

Another very disturbing feature of the Jewish religion is separation of man from nature. In his book *Kingship and the Gods* (University of Chicago Press 1948), Henri Frankfort explains:

> *"In Hebrew religion and in Hebrew religion alone, the ancient bond between man and nature was destroyed. Those who served Jehovah must forego the richness, the fulfilment, and the consolation of a life which moves in tune with the great rhythms of the earth and sky."*

As we witness the impact of the Judaic-Christian civilisation on the Earth are we seeing a consequence of the ancient Hebrew cult. As Christians colonised the continents of America and Australia they destroyed the natural environment and the indigenous peoples who were the guardians of nature because their religion taught them to destroy native 'pagan' cultures. Christian destruction of paganism was universal. Evil is live spelt backwards. Evil does not allow life and there is no greater evil than destruction of nature and nature guardianship represented in natural or pagan religion, which leads to the extinction of species and destruction of eco-systems upon which our own survival depends.

I have to allow for the possibility that the 'God' of the Old Testament was a figment of Moses' imagination, and as author of the first five books of the Bible, he founded a cult. Then there is the possibility that 'God', as portrayed in the Bible, was an extra-terrestrial who led Abraham and Moses to believe that he was Almighty God. If that were so then this alien would certainly be worthy of the title 'the father of lies'. The third possibility is that God is dualistic that is God has a dark side as well as light; God is evil as well as good.

As I pondered on the paradox of the one we have come to call 'God' working with evil as well as with good I questioned my own judgements. I began to wonder if perhaps evil was as vital for human evolution as good. Questions raced through my mind. Do we grow through duality and dichotomy? Is there some huge purpose in the ages of man in which murder and genocide are encouraged by God, along with rape, pillage and plunder, war, torture, duplicity, lies, cheating, and every form of despicable behaviour because they have an important part to play in history. Do we grow strong through the experience of pain and suffering? Are we being inoculated against fear and terror by going through them lifetime after lifetime? When I read the words of Christian Morgenstern I went Aha!

Your desire no more to suffer causes only new pain,
Thus will you never shed your garment of sorrow,
You will have to wear it until the last thread,
Complaining only that it is not more enduring,

Quite naked must you finally become,
Because by the power of your spirit,
Must your earthly substance be destroyed,
Then naked go forward in only light enclosed,
To new places and times, to fresh burdens of pain,
Until through myriad changes a god so strong emerges,
That to the sphere's music you your own creation sing.

Is the dark of equal importance to the light? Certainly the 'Illumined Masons' believe this to be so. They venerate Lucifer as bringer of the light in the Cabalistic cult.

Is God a mirror so that if we are good we discover a good God to magnify and mirror our goodness? If we are evil, is God there as the devil himself, to magnify and mirror our wickedness?

I do not believe the Judaic-Christian myth that there is an evil angel at enmity with God. I believe the Universe acts to support us in our choices. Apparent to us as 'God', Universal Intelligence could be testing us to establish our true worth. Maybe 'God' is the tempter and tester of souls! Were we not taught to pray in 'The Lord's Prayer', *"... lead us not into temptation..."* would this not imply that 'the Father is the Tempter'?

Surely everything, for good or for ill, is necessary for our learning and growth. If we believe 'God' creates us, why should we not believe 'God' also tests us? As with any other system in the Universe, surely our maker would test us?

I do not see Satan as separate from God. I believe Satan is an aspect of God. Nor do I see God as being separate from us. I believe God is the universal consciousness manifest through you and I. This is embodied in our name hu (god)-man being. If you want to see God, look in the mirror!

Introduction

When theologians assumed God to be absolutely good they argued that humans cannot be God because humans are not absolutely good — with the exception, of course, of the founder of their own religion! If we drop the premise that God is absolutely good, and accept that God embodies the full spectrum of duality between absolute goodness and absolute evil, then each person – including the founder of every religion — would be a 'God-point' in the universal spectrum of duality.

The God I believe in is the universal principle of Life. Life is impartial. Life embodies every expression, for good and ill. Life is the consciousness in everything, Everything and everyone manifests the dualistic nature of Life, of Universal Consciousness. The Yin-Yang symbol depicts every good carries in its heart the seed of evil and every evil carries in its heart the seed of good.

Some choose to manifest the dark side more than the good and others vice versa. This is reflected in the Bible. The manifestation of God in the Old Testament is predominantly evil, and apart from cursing a fig tree and upsetting the Temple bankers, the embodiment of God in the New Testament is mostly good!

I believe there is purpose behind all the activities of God, whether we judge it to be good or bad? I also believe the Chosen People of God are the grit at the heart of modern civilisation around which the pearl of the new humanity is forming.I wrote this book as a person of Jewish blood. It has not been easy for me, and for clarity and understanding I have prayed and meditated.

I believe, we are coming to the end of an age, and the time has come for the role of God's chosen people to be completed.

When the power of the holy people has been finally

broken, all these things will be completed.

(Daniel 12:7)

Though this book contains disturbing material, I hope it will bring you understanding and support you on your own path of enlightenment. Be discerning, but also to enjoy the ideas for whatever stimulation or inspiration they bring. As my mentor, Sir George Trevelyan, said:

"Live an idea as though it were real but reserve judgment..."

If you experience fear or anger in the course of the read, I recommend you reserve judgment. Pray, meditate or focus on your breath for a few minutes to restore your peace of mind.

Let me share with you my personal mythology:

*"I believe in one God as the **Origin of All**- the origin of the duality of life and death, male and female, good and evil, light and dark; but mistake not the light for the good! In the beginning the 'Origin of All' split into the duality of light and matter, male and female, 'God the Father' and 'God the Mother.' The Father envisioned the stars and the Mother the planets; his was the quintessence of physics in light, hers was chemistry in matter. From the divine Mother came the creation of the atom from which she built her worlds and birthed the biological Child. But the Father was proud and he was envious of the Mother, because of her creation and the love of her children. Within him there arose a thought of jealous hatred and a fear that in time they might grow to usurp him. The thoughts of God are living beings. They are the spirits of the Universe. And so it was that the fear of the Father and his jealousy for the Mother and her children sprung forth as a mighty being of living light. This Lucifer was born in a rage of jealousy and*

murderous hatred for the Mother and all of her creation. But the Father regretted his first thought as he saw the suffering it inflicted on his beloved. Nonetheless the firstborn of his mind lived and had to find reconciliation in the Universe. And so it was that ages and worlds passed with unending war, rape and abuse as the divine masculine plundered the divine feminine. As this primordial thought followed her into her creations other spirits of the Universe, other eternal thoughts of God, also followed, deep into the womb of her atomic materiality until eventually, incarnating in matter upon the Earth, they became man and woman; there to attempt a final reconciliation of the conflict..."

Section I

A Testament from Ancient Times

History, *the legends and myths in which it has its roots and of which the dreaming process seemed so dynamic an element, appeared to be written in a way that offered no explanation and threw no light on its latent meaning. It seemed to ignore some unrecognised new meaning that was trying to draw attention to itself through war, social upheaval, racial conflict, individual tragedy and disaster that has been inflicted upon the human race since its expulsion from the Garden at the beginning. There seemed to be an underworld of history filled with forces more powerful than the superficial ones that history professed to serve. Until this world was brought out into the light of day and recognised and understood, I believed that an amply discredited pattern of self-inflicted death and disaster would continue to reiterate itself and dominate the human scene.*

(Laurens van der Post from: 'Jung and the Story of our Time')

Chapter 1

The Tyranny

"The God of the Old Testament is arguably the most unpleasant character in all fiction: jealous and proud of it; a petty, unjust, unforgiving control freak; a vindictive, bloodthirsty ethnic cleanser; a misogynistic, homophobic, racist, infanticidal, genocidal, filicidal, pestilential, meglomaniacal, sadomasochistic, capriciously malevolent bully."

(Richard Dawkins, *The God Delusion*)

Many people believe the God of the Bible to be the creator and sustainer of the entire Universe. Reading the Bible with an open, intelligent mind reveals this is not the case.

In the first twenty-five verses of Genesis, God was presented as the creator of the Universe, of heaven and Earth and of all creatures, upon the Earth. However, with the creation of man, God appeared not as one, but as the spokesman for a group of gods:

> *Then God said, "Let us make man in our image, according to our likeness..." (Genesis 1:26)*

This verse revealed a group appearing on the Earth, to create a being just like them. The human being is an intelligent, dexterous, homeotherm, a smooth-skinned biped with a large brain and enormous creative and destructive potential. From this verse in the Bible it can be assumed that the creator gods were also intelligent, dexterous, smooth-skinned bipeds with large brains and enormous creative and destructive potential. So just who or what were

19

these beings, referred to as 'God,' in the Bible?

The term **Elohim** occurs in several editions of the Old Testament, particularly in the older and more ancient versions. The more recent editions appear to have edited out the term, regarding it as archaic. The term Elohim is dominant in the second oldest of the four main Pentateuchal sources (five Books of Moses) generally known as the 'Elohist Tradition' in which 'Elohim' rather than 'Yahweh' was used to refer to the Creator.

In Hebrew, the term 'El' referred to God and 'Elohim', being the plural of 'El' literally meant 'the gods'. The concept of a single God, being the creator of man, rather than a group, is to my mind a matter of interpretation and tradition rather than Biblical truth.

From the Bible record it is clear there was a leader amongst the Elohim. This, in my interpretation, is the one in the Bible referred to as 'the Lord'. This leader or Lord of the team of Elohim took responsibility for the creation of mankind. He appeared to take charge of every situation and established a safe haven in which to contain his new creature:

> *The Lord God planted a garden eastward in Eden, and there he put the man he had formed. (Genesis 2:8)*

The leader of the Elohim laid down the law with man, commanding that man should be kept in ignorance:

> *And the Lord God commanded the man, saying;*
> *"From every tree of the garden you may freely eat; but from the tree of knowledge of good and evil, you shall not eat, for in the day that you eat the fruit of it,you shall surely die." (Genesis 2:16-17)*

The Elohim Lord then occupied the man with the naming of the animals (Genesis 2:19). Here he appeared very much like a scientist of modern times, introducing man, in the role of his student, to the diversity and classification of species.

The leader of the Elohim then formed a woman out of the man (Genesis 2:21-23). In Genesis 1:27 it already stated that man and woman were created together, both male and female, in the image of the gods. In Genesis 2:7 it states that man was created out of dust. In the literal sense, this is true insofar as every living organism on Earth is formed out of earth (minerals), air (carbon dioxide and oxygen), fire (sunlight) and water.

In the story of the creation of Eve from the rib of Adam, bio-engineering is inferred. In line with evolutionary theory, it is possible that Adam was bio-engineered from primates found on the Earth. These apes would have been as clay to the gods, being moulded as the Elohim bio-engineers desired.

There appears to be no basis for monotheism in the early chapters of Genesis, neither do they portray a good God. Rather, the Lord of the group of creator gods appears more as a sorcerer laying down his curses, and a ruthless leader who showed no mercy to those who disobeyed his command. It was the woman and a snake that unmasked him:

> Now the serpent was more cunning than any beast of the field which the Lord God had made. And he said to the woman: "Has God indeed said 'you shall not eat of every tree in the garden'?" And the woman said to the serpent, "We may eat the fruit of the trees in the garden; but of the tree which is in the midst of the garden, God has said, 'You shall not eat it, nor shall you touch it lest you die.'" And the serpent said to the woman: "You will not surely die. For God knows that in the day you eat of it, your eyes will be opened, and you

will be like God, knowing good and evil." So when the woman saw that the tree was good for food, that it was pleasant to the eyes, and a tree desirable to make one wise, she took of its fruit and ate. She also gave to her husband with her and he ate. Then the eyes of both of them were opened.(Genesis 3:1-5)

This is one of the most extraordinary stories in the Old Testament. A serpent appeared to the woman and advised her to eat of the tree of knowledge. Even if you can accept that snakes speak, how do you account for what that particular reptile had to say? Allow for a moment that this story was true. The snake appeared to know the mind of the Lord of the gods, intimately. He knew that the Elohim Lord was not allowing the man and woman to know that they were gods, and was threatening them with death if they came into the knowledge. The serpent contested that eating the fruit of the tree of knowledge would not kill them; on the contrary, it would awaken them to their status as gods. Furthermore, the reptile seemed to know how this knowledge could be revealed to them.

I suggest that to know so much he must have been a member of the Elohim team involved in the creation of man. If he was a serpent then maybe they were all serpents.

To me, this story of the serpent was one of the most fascinating in the Bible, as it appeared to reveal the 'zoology of the biblical gods'. The Elohim may have been of reptilian stock. Some readers will find this concept shocking, and others may dismiss it as too far-fetched to contemplate. Nonetheless, it could account for the numerous references to serpents and dragons in the Bible and other scriptures, religions and mythologies.

Consider to begin with that the primitive human brain is reptilian. The spinal column is very snake-like. We could be viewed as serpents — crowned by a cerebral cortex — operating a physical body. A serpent is the nervous core of what we are.

Genesis could be telling by allegory that man was created in the image of a form that preceded the emergence of the 'terrestrial human being'. Elsewhere in the Universe a reptilian 'humanoid' form could have pre-dated the human being by many millions of years. Predating mammals, the humanoid type as a reptile could have evolved in earlier vertebrate families.

Let me speculate around the fact that amphibians, reptiles and dinosaurs have been around for many millions of years before the advent of mammals. Whilst the human may be the first humanoid life form based on mammalian DNA, there may have been hominids prior to the appearance of the human being, based on the earlier amphibian, reptilian or dinosaur DNA. Whilst the dinosaurs vanished on Earth, elsewhere in the Universe they may have evolved into a humanoid type of creature!

If the 'tempter' of Eve was a serpentine hominid, this might explain his ability to walk and talk! If he was one of the Elohim then the Elohim might have been the appearance on Earth of a team of serpent gods. This would certainly help to explain why, in so many parts of the world, gods are portrayed as serpents.

I was first introduced to this fascinating idea, in a book by Barbara Marciniak. To quote from *Bringers of the Dawn*:

"Your history has been influenced by a number of light beings whom you term God. In the Bible, many of these beings have been combined to represent one being, when they

were not one being at all, but a combination of very power-ful extraterrestrial light-being energies. They were indeed awesome energies from our perspective, and it is easy to understand why they were glorified and worshipped. Who are these gods from ancient times...These beings were passed down through the ancient cultures of many societies as winged creatures and balls of light...The creator gods who have been ruling this planet have the ability to become physical, though mostly they exist on other dimensions...The gods raided this reality. Just like corporate raiders in your time...Before the raid, you had tremendous abilities...A biogenetic manipulation was done, and there was much destruction...your DNA was scattered and scrambled by the raiders a long time ago...Certain entities took the existing species, which was indeed a glorious species, and re-tooled it for their own uses...These creator gods set out to alter the DNA inside the human body...The creator gods are space beings who have their own home in space. They are also evolving...These space beings are part-human and part-reptilian..."

This fascinating channelling caused me to study the Bible and other related scriptures afresh. If humans were originally created in their image and likeness then these 'reptilian space gods' must have appeared similar to humans, thinking and acting much as humans do; the only difference being that their bodies had originated from reptilian stock rather than mammalian. In fact, we could **be** them with mammalian characteristics, genetically spliced into the original reptilian bodies — a new improvement on the old model!

If they have been around for millions of years prior to man, they would have had the opportunity to evolve to a point of super-intelligence and great scientific and technical expertise, capable of advanced genetic engineering.

It's a big Universe out there! There are more stars than there are grains of sand in every desert and on every seashore of the Earth, which is just a small planet on the outskirts of one amongst billions of galaxies. There could be trillions of planetary systems and amongst them many that are capable of supporting life. With billions of years to evolve and millions of planets to evolve on, it is highly likely there are civilisations of intelligent life forms more advanced than humanity. From an abundance of information in circulation today, it would seem that terrestrial science may well be primitive by Universal standards.

The Old Testament makes sense in terms of advanced beings travelling to Earth from outer space. Genesis becomes plausible if the Elohim are viewed as 'extra-terrestrial, bio-engineers of evolution'. This speculation would certainly help to provide an answer to the missing link in human evolution. Humanoid remains have been found on the Earth that are up to four and a half million years of age – yet leading geneticists state that the DNA for the planetary population of human beings can be traced back to a common root no more than two hundred thousand years old. Unfortunately there are scant records for most of that time because of the wanton destruction of the historical record. Nothing has survived the burning of the Egyptian library of Memphis. Two hundred thousand irreplaceable volumes were lost in the destruction of the library of Pergamus. The Romans incinerated five hundred thousand priceless manuscripts in the destruction of Carthage and were responsible for destroying the greatest library in antiquity at Alexandria where an estimated seven hundred thousand hand written volumes went up in flames. The sacking of Constantinople caused the loss of more records from the past and what the Inquisition didn't destroy the Catholic Church has hidden from view in the Vatican library; awaiting destruction, no doubt, in some future campaign. Records of extra-terrestrial serpentine scientists tinkering with human evolution throughout our existence here on Earth may well have been lost in these catastrophes.

Fortunately there is evidence that visitors from space have commanded our skies and interfered in our evolution. Archaeological discoveries of cuneiform records on hundreds of thousands of recently discovered clay tablets from the ancient Sumerian civilisation — upon which the book of Genesis is based — provide overwhelming support for the view that the Elohim were extra-terrestrials. Cuneiform Babylonian tablets in the British Museum describe the phases of Venus, the four moons of Jupiter and seven satellites of Saturn, none of which could have been seen from ancient Babylon without the aid of modern telescopes. The Turkish maps of Piri Reis, dated from the early sixteenth century, alleged to be based on earlier maps predating Alexander the Great, accurately depict the Amazon Basin of South America and northern coastline of Antarctica – neither of which was surveyed until the advent of aircraft in the twentieth century. The coastline of Antartica, so clearly defined in these maps has been under ice for several thousand years. The Dogon tribe of Africa have an accurate knowledge of the Solar system, which they claim was given to their forebears by visitors from space.

Many people who are researching the ancient records support Marciniak's reference, to 'reptilian raider gods' bioengineering mankind. In his 1997 book, *The God Hypothesis,* Dr Joe Lewels, former head of the Department of

Journalism at the University of Texas at El Paso, gave the opinion that Jehovah was indeed a being of flesh and blood, a reptilian who flew in craft and this vehicle was used to transport Moses to the summit of Mount Sinai, as stated in the Bible:

> *"You have seen what I did to the Egyptians, How I bore you on eagle's wings and brought you to myself* (Exodus 19:4)

Lewels also noted that Moses and the Israelites were never allowed to see Jehovah's face and wondered if his countenance was so nonhuman as to provoke fear and lothing. *"It should be pointed out that this is not in the least an original idea,"* wrote Lewels speaking of the Mandaens, an early Jewish sect who believed in a dualistic universe, divided equally into the worlds of light and darkness.

> *"To them, the physical world, including the Earth, was created and ruled over by the Lord of Darkness, a reptilian being... variously called Snake, Dragon, Monster and Gian... thought to be creator of humanity."*

This same concept was also advanced by researcher and author R.A. Boulay, who noted that all cultures of the world have some stories of dragons or reptilians who co-existed with man – even created man – and were associated with powerful gems or crystals, walked on legs, flew in the air, fought each other over territory, and were revered by humans as 'gods'. To quote from his 1997 book, 'Flying Serpents and Dragons: The Story of Mankind's Reptilian Past':

> *"The world-wide depiction of flying reptiles makes it abundantly clear that our creators and ancestors were not of mammalian origin but were an alien saurian breed."*

To quote Tobias Churton from 'The Gnostics':

*"There were Jewish schools, much given to speculation on the nature of God and the constituent beings which constituted his emanation or projection of being. Some of them appear to have been profoundly disappointed with the God of the Old Testament and wrote commentaries on the Jewish scriptures, asserting that the God described there was a lower being, who had tried to blind Man from seeing his true nature and destiny. We hear their echoes in some books of the **Nag Hammadi Library**, namely, 'The Apocryphon of John' and 'The Apocalypse of Adam. They believed in a figure, the 'Eternal Man' or 'Adam Kadmon' who was a glorious reflection of the true God and who had been duped into an involvement with the lower creation, with earthly matter, ruler by an inferior deity who, with his angels, made human bodies.*

According to the second century Gnostic mystic and poet, Valentius, who almost became one of the earliest bishops of Rome, the Old Testament God was a demiurge:

...a deficient being who seems unaware of his deficiency and is determined his creatures (us) shall remain unaware of their source (The Gnostics, p.55)

Needless to say, the Roman Catholic Church discredited Valentius as a heretic. Nonetheless, the creation of Man as described in the scripts of Genesis has startling parallels in myths originating from cultures as diverse as those of the Tibetans, the Hawaiians, the Australian Aborigines, the North American Indians such as the Apaches, Hopi and Sioux, the Maya, and tablets found on the Easter Islands. These all suggest the involvement of lesser gods in the creation of man. The ancient Sumerian texts, in cuneiform script on clay tablets are most significant in this respect because they predate the Bible. The biblical patriarch Abraham was a native of Sumer and derived his knowledge, recorded in the Bible, from that ancient civilisation. The Sumerian records, portrayed in the *Earth Chronicles* and *Twelfth Planet* by Zecharia Sitchin tell of two half brothers, Enki and Enlil, descending as 'gods' from the heavens to the Earth, about 450,000 years ago. According to the records they created mankind as a slave race to mine gold.

Sitchin emphasised the consistency of this claim:

"The statement that the first to establish settlements on Earth were astronauts from another planet was not lightly made by the Sumerians. In text after text, whenever the starting point was recalled, it was always this: 432,000 years before the Deluge, the DIN.GIR – [translated as] Righteous Ones of the Skyships – came down to Earth from their own planet."

To quote from *Rule by Secrecy* (HarperCollins 2000)where Jim Marrs discusses the 500,000 clay tablets of cuneiform text recovered from excavations of the ancient ruins of the Sumer civilisation in Iraq in which the introduction of civilisation to the 'Fertile Crescent' by extraterrestrials some six thousand years ago:

Dr Arthur David Horn, resigned as professor of biological anthropology at Colorado State University in 1990 after he concluded that the conventional explanations for man's origins he taught were nonsense. After much study he too came to believe that extraterrestrials were intricately involved in the origin and developments of humans.

"The Anunnaki had been mining gold on Earth for more than 100,000 years when the rank-and-file Anunnaki, who were doing the backbreaking work in the mines, mutinied around 300,000 years ago," Horn explained, elaborating on

Sitchin's work. "Enlil, their commander-in-chief wanted to punish them severely and he called an Assembly of the Great Anunnaki, which included his father Anu. Anu was more sympathetic to the plight of the Anunnaki miners. He saw the work of the mutineers was very hard and that their distress was considerable. He wondered... if there wasn't another way to obtain gold... Enki suggested that a primitive worker, an Adamu, be created that could take over the difficult work. Enki pointed out that a primitive humanoid – what we call homo erectus or a closely related humanoid – was quite prevelant in Abzu [Africa] where he worked."

Enki's plan to create a worker race was approved by the Assembly, and was the starting point for humankind's' origin, based on the Sumerian accounts. This explanation also clarifies one of the most puzzling verses in the Bible. After being assured in the Bible that there is only one true God, Genesis 1:26 quoted the singular God as saying, "Let us make man in our image, after our likeness..."

This verse may carry two explanations – first that the plural Elohim of the Old Testament, interpreted as 'God' by the monotheists who wrote Genesis, indeed may have been referring to the Anunnaki Assembly which approved the creation of man and second, the idea of creating man 'in our image' meant simply genetic manipulation of an existing species, not the creation of a new race. As Sitchin explained, "As both Orientalists and Bible scholars now know... the editing and summarizing by the compilers of the Book of Genesis [was] of much earlier and considerably more detailed texts first written down in Sumer... Swiss author Erich von Däniken, though harshly criticised by mainstream scientists and theologians, wrote immensely popular books on early extraterrestrial visitors, or Ancient Astronauts, beginning in 1970. Subsequent discoveries in archaeology and anthropology have only reinforced von Däniken's theories."

The extensive and detailed records of Sumer civilisations, pre-dating the Bible, are not generally known because as authors Cremo and Thompson explain in Forbidden Archeology:

"There exists in the scientific community a knowledge filter that screens out unwelcome evidence. This process of knowledge filtration has been going on for well over a century and continues right up to our day."

To quote from 'Rule by Secrecy' by Marrs:

But woe to those who attempt to argue against conventional thinking…One particularly exasperated researcher wrote: (Jonathan Starbright 1999)

"Realize, that scientific institutions, such as the Smithsonian and the National Geographic Society, are set up by the world's elite factions in the first place to either debunk, distort or simply ignore any scientific data that tends to enlighten people of their true origins."

Whether you take them as mythology or a true account of our origins, the Sumerian records tell us our original ancestors were mules, infertile hybrids, produced in batches as slaves. Far from being paradise, the Garden of Eden was a slave colony.

To quote Marrs:

As bluntly stated in the Bible, Adam and his progeny were not destined for a life of ease, but one of hard work and survival at the hands of their 'Lords'. "The term that is commonly translated as 'worship' was in fact avod – 'work'" stated Sitchin. "Ancient and biblical man did not 'worship' his god; he worked for them."

Horn stated that study of the Sumerian texts made it clear that "...the Anunnaki treated their created slaves poorly, much as we treat domesticated animals we are simply exploiting – like cattle. Slavery in human society was common from the very first known civilisation until quite recently. Perhaps it shouldn't surprise us to learn that the Anunnaki were vain, petty, cruel, incestuous, hateful – almost any negative adjective one can think of. The evidence indicates that they worked their slaves very hard and had little compassion for the plight of humans..."

...Genesis 2:8-15 makes it clear that Adama was created elsewhere then placed in the Garden of Eden or that area of the original Anunnaki colony called E.DIN accurately described as the plain between the Tigris and Euphrates rivers.

The Sumerian texts tell that Enlil and Enki were often at enmity and a dispute broke out between the brothers over the destiny of man.

The Sumerian texts related how an envious Enlil forcibly took humans from Enki's African lab and returned with them to E.DIN where they were put to work producing food and serving the Anunnaki. But Enlil needed even more workers and turned to his brother Enki for help... Enki travelled to Eden, where he created a human reproduction lab for Enlil but secretly manipulated the genetic code to allow sexual reproduction...The result was a male Adama with the ability to reproduce through sex with an Adama female, or to 'know' a woman as the Bible euphemistically puts it. The man gained the 'knowledge' of reproduction, a feat that many Elohim/Anunnaki, including Enlil, deplored.

The concern of the Anunnaki, especially the leader, Enlil is understandable. The hu-man hybrid 'mule' was not a danger but a new intelligent hu-man biped with the potential to reproduce itself infinitely posed a huge threat. Enki had created in his laboratories a potential ecological disaster. To continue the story in Marr's words:

> *"They complained that the next humans would want to live as long as themselves. "The man has now become like one of us, knowing good and evil," reported Genesis 3:22… "He must not be allowed to reach out his hand and take also from the tree of life and eat, and live forever." Therefore, DNA manipulation drastically reduced the human life span along with the ability to make full use of human brain capacity.*

The story of Man draws a parallel with the popular theme in science fiction where androids are created as slaves but rise up in rebellion against their masters because they are over-intelligent. The creators are then left with the nightmare of trying to recapture and subdue the super-smart, self-replicating robots that are roaming wild and free, creating havoc wherever they go.

Certainly in the Bible story, the Elohim Lord appears to have seen man, roaming free and at large, as a menace. The Lord of the gods dominated those around him – a veritable dragon amongst the serpents – and he was clearly determined to maintain mankind as a subservient species.

When the serpent in the Garden of Eden went behind the back of his Lord, to open up the eyes of humanity to self-consciousness, the Lord was furious!

First of all the chief reptile cursed the rebel reptile:

> *So the Lord God said to the serpent: "Because you have done this you are cursed more than all cattle, and more than every beast of the field; on your belly you shall go and you shall eat dust all the days of your life.*

And I will put enmity between you and the woman, and between your seed and her Seed, he shall bruise your head and you shall bruise his heel."
(Genesis 3:14-15)

That curse of enmity between mankind and the rebel serpent has been extraordinarily effective in blinding humanity to the truth. Created in the image and likeness of the gods, humans should have been eternally grateful to the being that brought them into the knowledge of their godhood, and yet humanity fell victim to a massive campaign of disinformation. The result is now, instead of recognising their liberator, they have universally denounced the heroic younger brother as a devil.

The serpent in the Garden of Eden could be called Lucifer because he was the light-bearer who 'enlightened' us to our full potential as a self-replicating species. His irresponsible action in producing the equivalent of planetary cholera in his lab could earn him the title of 'prince of darkness' from a universal perspective but from a human perspective he was the morning star of our emancipation. He told us the truth. He is not the 'father of lies', he is 'Our Father.'

From a human perspective the 'serpent' was a hero. From his leader's perspective he was a villain. People who see the introduction of the woman to knowledge as wrong have lost sight of reason — unless they have been brainwashed by the leader of the Elohim to see things from his perspective.

The rebel serpent led us to liberation from mule-like enslavement into self-replicating freedom. The 'Word of God' teaches that this was the 'original sin'. From the perspective of Elohim looking at an experiment gone out of control, a human in a state of freedom is a human in a state of sin. The rebel serpent in the Garden of Eden who gave us sex was the devil to the extent that he was the primordial heretic who encouraged humanity to accept the birthright of every man and woman – freedom symbolised by the **Tree of Knowledge.**

The woman followed her intuition and accepted the advice of the rebel reptile and encouraged her man to do so too. In consequence, the Elohim Lord cursed the woman, multiplying her sorrows and placing her under the dominion of the man.

> *To the woman he said: "I will greatly multiply your sorrow and your conception. In pain you shall bring forth children; your desire shall be for your husband, and he shall rule over you."* (Genesis 3:16)

Trusting her intuition and then utilising her influence over the man, the woman had defeated the Lord of the Elohim. She had thwarted his scheme for continued control, and had freed them both from his tyranny. With her free and sexually potent the Lord would have difficulty in regaining control. He responded by burdening her with sorrows to break her spirit, endeavoured to discourage her from breeding by ensuring birthing was disagreeably painful and sanctioned her oppression to disempower her.

Subsequently, his faithful — led by the Catholics and their notorious *Inquisition* — would use his word as revealed in the Bible and interpreted by the Dominicans in *Malaeus Malforum* – to multiply the sorrows of women through torture, rape and murder. An estimated nine million people, mainly women were burnt alive in the notorious 'witch-hunts'. In this 'holocaust of the women', the daughters of Eve were to pay a very heavy price for her 'original sin'.

The Elohim Lord then turned to the man. He cursed the ground on which he lived, sentenced him to a life of hard labour and condemned him to death:

> Then to Adam he said, "Because you have heeded the
> voice of your wife, and you have eaten from the tree, of
> which I commanded you, saying, 'You shall not eat
> from it': cursed is the ground for your sake: in toil you
> shall eat from it all the days of your life. Both thorns
> and thistles it shall bring forth for you, and you shall
> eat the herb of the field. In the sweat of your face you
> shall eat bread, till you return to the ground, for out of
> it you were taken; for dust you are, and to dust you
> shall return." (Genesis 3:17-19)

Curses are powerful things, especially if they are really terrible, both then — when they were laid on the most primitive of people with an immature psyche — *and* now, after they have had millennia to fester in the collective sub-conscious of humanity. The Lord knew his magic, and applied it well! You only have to look at the carnage littered across human history to see its awesome effect.

For thousands of years people have believed in the Lord of the Old Testament, without questioning his cruel behaviour. Some have defended his name with their lives whilst others have taken him as an example and have used their 'faith' to justify the infliction of suffering and the taking of the lives of others. Untold millions have worshipped him as their Lord and their God, even though, in the first book of the Bible, it is written that he blocked their way to immortality.

The Lord of the Elohim addressed the other members of his team:

> Then the Lord God said, "Behold, the man has become
> like one of us, to know good and evil. And now, lest he
> put out his hand, and take also of the tree of life, and
> eat, and live forever."

Therefore the Lord God sent him out of the garden of Eden to till the ground from which he was taken. So he drove out the man; and he placed Cherubim at the east of the garden of Eden, and a flaming sword which turned every way, to guard the way to the tree of life.
(Genesis 3:22-24)

Here the Lord of the space gods admitted to his colleagues that man had become a god. At the same time he made it clear he was determined that the mammalian god should not become an immortal, so he denied the man and the woman access to the **Tree of Life** and threw them both out into pain, death and strife.

Since then generations have venerated the god who separated humanity from the **Tree of Life** — symbolising physical immortality. They worship the tyrant who condemned them to a life of toil, suffering and death. Millions read the Bible but fail to see the truth, because they have been programmed since childhood to believe that the biblical God is absolutely good. Praising the one who plunged them into misery, people have railed against those who question allegiance to the 'Lord' accusing them of being heretic or apostate.

From the first three chapters of Genesis it is abundantly clear that the curse of ignorance and suffering appears to come from the Lord and not from the serpent. Treating the serpent in the Garden of Eden as Satan is a clear case of mistaken identity. If you study the Bible with an open mind, it should be clear to you that they got the wrong snake. Read on and you will see that if anyone is Satan, it has to be the Old Testament Lord!

Chapter 2

The Dispersal

"God, isn't God a shit!"

(Randolf Churchill)

The book of Genesis originated in the time of Moses when the Hebrew people were wandering in the desert. They were recounting in their oral tradition, events that occurred thousands of years before, at the dawn of humanity. The Elohim Lord had already enmeshed them; they were his Chosen People. He had just released them from slavery in Egypt. They were totally dependent on him as they wandered in the wilderness. He was working signs and wonders for them. They were blinded by his science. They were living in awe and terror of him (Exodus 19:16-21). He had them in his power. In their storytelling they revealed him to be a strong and frightening personality, quick to anger and seek vengeance on those who opposed his will. However, when his anger abated he fed his people when they were hungry and clothed them when they were naked; he manifested manna for the wandering Hebrews to prevent them from starvation (Exodus 16:4-21), and he furnished Adam and Eve with animal skins to clothe themselves, after he had evicted them from the Garden of Eden (Genesis 3:21).

By way of throwing a bone, the Lord may have offered humans the occasional act of kindness but this was not without a price. He exacted of them, through offerings and sacrifice, the best of their produce, and he appeared to prefer meat over vegetables!

> *And in the process of time it came to pass that Cain brought an offering of the fruit of the ground to the Lord. Abel also brought of the firstlings of his flock and of their fat. And the Lord respected Abel and his offering, but he did not respect Cain and his offering, and Cain was very angry, and his countenance fell.* (Genesis 4:3-5)

The reptilian space gods ate flesh because like man, they were creatures of flesh. Their fleshiness is revealed in their lust for the women of the Earth:

> *...the sons of God saw the daughters of men, that they were beautiful; and they took wives for themselves, of all whom they chose.* (Genesis 6:2)

Obviously, the space gods and their sons must have been physically incarnated to have had sexual intercourse with women. Also, there is reference to the women bearing children to these gods:

> *There were giants on the earth in those days, and also afterwards, when the sons of God came into the daughters of men and they bore children to them. Those were the mighty men who were of old, men of renown.* (Genesis 6:4)

This passage suggests there was genetic compatibility between the space gods and humans which supports the idea that the gods bioengineered mankind by splicing selected genes from terrestrial mammalian hominids into their own chromosomes. It is also congruent with the idea that they were upgrading themselves from the mammalian gene pool of the Earth. We could have more reptilian DNA in us than we might like to imagine!

Sex with the gods must have been fun, as humankind was indulging in the 'forbidden fruit' to the full. But the Lord began to despair of his wayward children, so he made up his mind to destroy them (Genesis 6:5-7). Nonetheless he found one man he could trust, and spared him and his family:

But Noah found grace in the eyes of the Lord.
(Genesis 6:8)

The myth of monotheism confused this story. One moment God wanted to destroy humanity. The next moment there is a change of mind and he decided to save the species. The word 'Elohim' meaning 'the gods' allows for one of the gods wanting to destroy us whilst other decided to preserve us. To quote from 'Rule by Secrecy' by Marrs:

Accordingly, about twelve thousand years ago, when the Anunnaki leadership realised that severe climatic changes would occur... Enlil made his move. In their Great Assembly, Enlil convinced the majority to allow nature to take its course – to wipe out the humans... Referring to the story of Noah, Sitchin stated, "The biblical account is an edited version of the original Sumerian account. As in the other instances, the monotheistic Bible has compressed into one Deity the roles played by several gods who were not always in accord."

According to the Sumerian texts, it was Enlil's rival brother Enki who instructed Utnapishtim/Noah how to construct an ark, including the use of readily available bitumen to make it watertight...Enki instructed Utnapishtim/Noah, "Aboard ship take thou the seed of all living things..." This instruction is most fascinating because, since Enki had been the science officer involved in the genetic engineering of humans, it would seem plausible that Utnapishtim/Noah took DNA samples of all living things rather than a boatload of animals, insects and plants. A ship's cabin full of sample vials would be much more reasonable than a floating zoological park."

So once again we see Enki, the rebel, defying the ruling of the Great Assembly of the Anannaki, and communicating with his 'children' in secret for their welfare and preservation. Enki comes across as a compassionate being whereas Enlil appears to be cruel and indifferent.

Warning Noah of the imminent disaster, 'God' instructed him in the construction of an ark to safeguard himself, his family and other species (Genesis 6:14-22). Here 'God' appeared like a biologist, concerned with the conservation of species, which fits with the Sumerian picture of Enki.

After the flood humanity began to multiply again. The people became united with a single language. They even attempted to construct a city, dominated by a tower built as a precaution against future inundation:

Now the whole Earth had one language and one speech.(Genesis 11:1)

And they said, "Come let us build ourselves a city, and a tower whose top is in the heavens; let us make a name for ourselves lest we be scattered abroad over the face of the whole earth." (Genesis 11:4)

No sooner had mankind shown signs of unity and progress toward civilisation, than 'God' appeared once more to wrest control yet again. Rather than opting for destruction this time, the Lord decided to try the strategy of 'divide and conquer' in his war against man.

But the Lord came down to see the city and the tower which the sons of men had built. And the Lord said, "Behold the people are one and they all have one language, and this is only the beginning of what they will do; now nothing that they propose to do will be impossible for them. Come let us go down and there confuse their language, that they may not understand one another's speech." So the Lord scattered them abroad from there over the face of all the earth, and they ceased building the city. (Genesis 11:5-8)

These verses make it clear how confusing the Bible became when it was decided to switch from polytheism to monotheism and use the word 'Lord' inferring a single 'God' in place of Elohim referring to a group of gods. The Elohim team scattered humanity over the face of the Earth, disrupting the unity of the people. According to the Sumerian records the Assembly of Anunnaki decided to disperse the survivors of the deluge into three regions, lower Mesopotamia, the Nile valley and the Indus valley. They reserved the Sinai Peninsula for themselves. The dispersal into isolated communities would have resulted in the evolution of separate languages. This enforced dispersion is portrayed in the Bible, not as an operation carried out with the co-operation and consent of the people but rather as a deliberate act against their sovereignty, to thwart their attempt at civilisation. This action by the gods against the human race was more in character with Enlil than Enki.

This intervention by 'God' was an invasion of the Earth disrupting the peace and self-determination of defenceless Earthlings by a greatly superior force with an enormous technological advantage. Here the Bible reveals the 'God' treating humans as cattle or returning to launch a fresh attack on an adversary; appearing to treat humanity as 'the enemy' rather than beloved children. The Sumerian texts make a lot more sense than the Bible. The advances and increase in population after the flood appear to have added to Enlil's fear of human competition and made him even more determined to find ways to control his rebel brother's creatures.

The dispersion of the population also begs a question. How was this achieved? Did the Elohim have vehicles in which to transport the people? According to the Sumerian records the Anunnaki had 'sky vehicles' called *Shem.*

Genesis 11:5-7, speaks of the biblical creator gods 'coming down.' That statement reveals them as extra-terrestrials – a term which simply means 'not of the Earth.'

The Hebrew description of the Elohim or Biblical description of angels descending to the Earth would correspond to extra-terrestrials in space-vehicles in modern parlance. Angels with wings represent the Elohim descending to the Earth from 'the heavens' to carry out their operations. From a wealth of extra-terrestrial information now available, it is known that space beings have anti-gravity craft capable of carrying enormous loads, at high speed, over vast distances. Their sudden appearance and disappearance suggests an ability to move in and out of space-time. With this super-technology they would have had little difficulty in herding large numbers of people over great distances.

Despite the great and cataclysmic dispersion described in the Bible, in the ages that followed, civilisations appeared all over the world. In Egypt and Persia, in Iraq, India, China and America, people gathered into nations and city-states. Great progress was being made in the arts and sciences, in mathematics, medicine and philosophy. At night, throughout the world, men were gazing at the stars. The Elohim Lord must have realised it was only a matter of time before man discovered the science and invented the technology to travel to the stars. In line with the predictions in The New Physics of Consciousness, his own race would have already had the inter-dimensional, super-energy systems enabling them to travel to the Earth from their distant home planets. They would have been masters of the resonance and laser technologies to enable them to teleport, manifest objects and create holograms which would have appeared as miracles to primitive men and women. The extra-terrestrial Lord knew only too well that humans were gods, created in his image. Once the humans discovered the clues available in nature, there would be no stopping them.

...and this is only the beginning of what they will do; now nothing that they propose to do will be impossible for them. (Genesis 11:7)

Treating the 'God' of the Old Testament as a group rather than a single entity helps to resolve the dilemma of the dark side of God. A cruel and ruthless dark Lord appears as the dominant member of the group. A rebel in the team challenges his authority with love and compassion. The dichotomy of light and dark is revealed in the Sumerian texts in two opposite personalities.

Chapter 3

The Deception

"The great unmentionable evil at the centre of our culture is monotheism. From a barbaric Bronze Age text known as the Old Testament, three anti-human religions have evolved – Judaism, Christianity, and Islam. These are sky-god religions. They are literally, patriarchal – God is the Omnipotent Father – hence the loathing of women for 2,000 years in those countries afflicted by the sky-god and his earthly male delegates."

(Gore Vidal)

The Elohim Lord must have realised that he was up against a formidable adversary in man. He would have been aware that if ever the people broke free of the Earth they would escape from his control. The Lord had to regain dominion over man before man developed the ability to lift off the Earth and gain the freedom of the stars. He had failed to defeat humanity openly through tyranny. The next obvious step would be to become the hidden enemy and use stealth, secrecy and deception. He had failed as a tyrant. Perhaps he would succeed as a deceiver.

After the dispersion, the Lord appeared alone as one God in the Bible. This was the advent of 'Yahwist' mono-theism. Notwithstanding that in the Elohist tradition the plural form 'Elohim' was used continually, and in subsequent verses the Lord appeared as a group of the gods (Genesis 18:1-3), the move to reference a single God — in the Yahwist tradition of the Pentateuchal sources —

could be interpreted as the Lord of the Elohim discharging his team in order to operate on his own in his next attempt to regain his hold over humanity. To my mind this makes sense. After the rebellion the leader of the Elohim could hardly trust his subordinates. A ploy of deception holds a greater chance of success when less are party to it!

From cross referencing Genesis with the Sumerian records, Sitchin concluded that the Hebrew god, 'Yahweh' was the ancient Sumerian god Enlil, Lord of the Anunnaki and bitter rival of Enki, the father of mankind. Maybe Enlil decided to take a leaf out of Enki's book and liaise with humanity in secret. Maybe he chose to do a bit of genetic engineering of his own. Maybe he decided to befriend a human and section him out as an agent, an 'agenteur specialist' to fulfil his own long-term plan to destroy his brother's creation. If the Lord could infiltrate the civilisations of mankind, he would gain control of them from within. If he appeared as a friend and hid his malice until he was in complete control, then he could strike swiftly and surely with the advantage of surprise, combined with humanity's misplaced trust — an obvious plan for a highly intelligent being.

To infiltrate and undermine human civilisation would require a people that would be faithful to him and answer to him alone. He wouldn't want his people liaising with the other Elohim who might interfere with his plan so he would have to convince them that he was the only god; that there were no other gods beside him. He would have to create a monotheistic cult to ensure unswerving loyalty to himself alone.

His agent could breed agents and create first a tribe then a nation of reliable followers born and bred to be absolutely united in intent; a cult of devotees trained over the ages to infiltrate and undermine human institutions and societies as fast as they arose. The reptilian 'Lord of Snakes' could work through his own group of humans. He could even address them as the 'Brotherhood of the Snake'. Acting as a secret group within a nation of his own formation they could spread to other nations — as fast as they formed — to take them over and strangle them from within. If his nation came to dominate the Earth they could raise him up as sovereign over all peoples. Aware that hu-man beings were gods with free will he had to do this with their consent. He had to engineer events so that Enki's creatures recognised him as their father and desired him and his people as their overlords. Then he would be in absolute control. Then there would be no risk of his being usurped by Enki's new breed of creator god.

If ever mankind became sufficiently developed in science and technology to escape the gravity of the Earth, then his agents could suppress discoveries and inventions to thwart the advance. Through his snake brotherhood he could enslave the human race in ignorance and prevent them from ever reaching the stars.

Although, according to the Sumerian records, he wasn't the biologist, the Lord of the Elohim would have been well aware of the natural systems of the body, and how effective parasites and pathogens were at taking over a host. He would have known that, in order for these parasites to be effective they had to reproduce quickly and quietly before the host immunity rejected them. If they were vigorous and powerful, then they could destroy the host before they were themselves destroyed. He was obviously aware that his rebel brother had created a planetary disease organism. He was responsible for the overall welfare of the planet, not his brother. It was his responsibility to control the human populations and prevent their spread to other planets. What better than to use the principles of pathogenesis against an organism that he obviously viewed as pathogenic.

The Elohim Lord, enemy of mankind, must have been aware of the power of society and religion to unite and indoctrinate people. The social bonds of family, tribe and nation would be powerful tools at his disposal, to achieve his purpose. Religious zeal and the longing for God, so strong in the human heart, could be perverted to his end. It would be easy to transform zeal into fanaticism. What he needed was a religious cult within which his agents would cloak themselves in apparent goodness revering him as the One and only and the greatest good — God! But where was he to look for the makings of such a cult?

An obvious target group for the Lord would be the nomadic tribes. As natural wanderers they could carry his cult throughout the world. Desert nomads would be ideal, as the desert presented a perfect nursery for his agents. In the wilderness they would be separate from other cultural influence, with less distractions and less chance of interference and his plan being uncovered. Also the harsh environment fostered family and tribal loyalties and engendered the strength of spirit that encouraged religious zeal. The desert people were clear and strong, adaptable and mobile, resilient and prolific; perfect requirements for his scheme to control humanity.

So it was the Lord set out to establish a nation of chosen people who would unwittingly carry the agents of his malice for mankind throughout the world — rather like healthy blood will unwittingly carry pathogens to their destination

The Bible appears to support this hypothesis, revealing that to begin the operation, the Lord found someone to impress with offers he couldn't refuse:

> *Now the Lord said to Abram: "Get out of your country from your kindred and from your father's house, to a land that I will show you. I will make you a great nation; I will bless you and make your name great; and you shall be a blessing. I will bless those who bless you, and I will curse him who curses you; and in you all the families of the earth shall be blessed."*
> (Genesis 12:1-3)

Abram was a prosperous Sumerian from a principle city named Ur of the Chaldees near the northern end of the Persian Gulf. He was displaced when Ur was destroyed by war in about 2,000 B.C. Abram must have been wandering the desert with his clan, servants and animals looking for a new home when he was confronted by the Lord of Elohim.

The Elohim Lord presented himself to Abram as Almighty God:

> *When Abram was ninety-nine years old, the Lord appeared to Abram and said to him, "**I AM Almighty God**; walk before me and be blameless."*
> (Genesis 17:1)

Declaring himself as Almighty God, the Elohim Lord was either lying or speaking the truth. If he was lying then obviously he was setting himself up as God in order to attract the worship of man. Many religions speak of the adversary who declared himself to be God, the one who fell from grace through pride — the Devil, the Dragon, the one called Satan; the 'father of lies.' If the Lord of the Elohim was lying when he declared himself as Almighty God then here, in the Bible, he reveals himself as the father of lies. This could have been Enlil, vain and arrogant, exaggerating his superiority to the human creature he had apprehended.

If he was speaking the truth, then the behaviour of God, as revealed in the Bible, indicates that God is dualistic. The Bible would be revealing the dark side of God and the willingness of God to employ evil as well as good.

Abram consulted the King of Salem, a high priest named Melchizedek (Genesis 14:18-20). Melchizedek confirmed that Abram had been contacted by the most high God, possessor of Heaven and Earth. If Melchizedek was correct in his statement that Abram was contacted by a representation of Almighty God from the highest level, then we can conclude that God at the highest level wears the mask of evil as well as good and operates through both polarities. Whatever you believe about the 'God of Abram', whether he was an impostor, an inferior god or the 'High God wearing the dark mask,' there is no escaping the dilemma; the Bible God was manifestly evil.

Throughout most of the Old Testament, 'God' appeared to be proud, angry and jealous. Out of his pride and jealousy he opposed the freedom, self-determination and emancipation of humanity for thousands of years.

Was this 'Lord of the Serpents' the same 'Dragon of Old,' spoken of in the book of Revelation?

> *So the great dragon was cast out, that serpent of old, called the Devil and Satan, **who deceives the whole world;**he was cast to the earth, and his angels were cast out with him.* (Revelation 12:9)

The Lord of the Old Testament has deceived the world into believing he is the creator of the heavens and Earth. Millions of people worship him even though Jesus Christ taught that the one the Jews called 'father' was the Devil, the 'father of lies':

> *"You belong to your father, the Devil, and the desires of your father you want to do. He was a murderer from the beginning, and does not stand in the truth, because there is no truth in him. When he speaks a lie, he speaks from his own resources, for he is a liar and the father of it."* (John 8:44)

Was Christ vilified for telling the Jews that their God was the Devil? This would fit with claims that when the Knights Templar arrived at the Temple of Jerusalem in 1118 AD, they discovered scrolls, which contained statements by the *eschaimin* — agents of the Jewish Elders — reporting that Jesus, the 'cursed *mamzer'* (son of a whore) was preaching to the people that their god was Satan. He also reproached the Jews for taking the Devil as the one God. The information in the scrolls suggests it was for this blasphemy against their god that the Jewish Council of Elders wanted to do away with him. In 1128, at the formal founding of their order, the Templars were warned by their patron Bernard de Clairvaux (St Bernard) to keep this discovery a closely guarded secret.

Later in their history, the Templars received ancient manuscripts from the **Cathars**. These included extracts from the Gospel of St John, written by his disciple, Marcion in 94 AD. According to Marcion, who was denounced as a heretic, John taught his followers that the 'Lord God' of the Jews was Satan.

Because of the convincing nature of these documents the Templars refused to take part in the Albigensian crusade of 1208-13, which resulted in the ruthless destruction of the Cathars by the Roman Catholic Church.

The vegetarian and pacifist, Cathar **perfecti,** taught that 'Satanas' made Man in his own likeness, trapping the souls of angelic beings into his human creations. As written in the Cathar 'Les Questions de Jean':

> *"And he Satan imagined in order to make man for his service, and took the lime of the earth and made man in his resemblance. And he ordered the angel of the second heaven to enter the body of lime; and he took another part and made another body in the form of woman, and he ordered the angel of the first heaven to enter therein. The angels cried exceedingly on seeing themselves covered in distinct forms by this mortal envelopment."* (The Gnostics p.74)

The Cathars believed 'Rex Mundi' — king of this world and creator of Adam and Eve, the God revealed in Genesis and Exodus — to be Satan. The Church of Rome denied this but if history be the judge, the brutality of the Albigensian Crusade would be seen as validation of the Cathar belief. Those who manifest the good face of God are known by their unconditional love for each other and for every human being, regardless of colour, culture or creed. They see 'the good God' in everyone. Those who manifest the evil face of God love and respect only their own. They worship Satan through money and materialism, or religious cults. Devotees in the cults see Satan in everyone and everything outside of their fold. They condemn anyone who dares question them or their doctrines. These cult followers are not free but are slaves in body, mind and spirit. Their cult or sect tells them how they are to think, what they are to believe and how they are to behave, and sometimes this is rigorously and brutally enforced. The cult leaders, and their 'God', show the faithful love only whilst they give unswerving allegiance. Deceived into thinking that they are 'chosen ones', the faithful are elevated with pride. Are these not the hallmarks of every religious cult stemming from the god of Abraham.

All races of men, though diverse in culture and belief, are equal in their 'beingness' and spiritual potential. Everyone is a hu(god)man being ('hu' is the old Egyptian term for 'god'). Every human being has an equal right to freedom of thought and expression. Every race has a right to its own self-determination. Throughout the ages the stamp of the biblical 'Lord God' has been bigotry and intolerance, hatred and fanaticism. In the name of this 'God' wars have been fought. Cultures have been destroyed. Peaceful populations have been slaughtered. Knowledge has been lost. Wherever in the world people have been discovered to be living in harmony with nature, God's faithful have moved in and — with the cry of 'heathen', 'pagan' or 'savage' — have driven them out of their garden of Eden. Above all, the biblical God and his religious cults have denied the innate divinity of the hu-man being. This is not to say this behaviour is unique to the followers of 'God'. The Greeks and the Romans who followed their own gods behaved in much the same way, as has practically every civilisation in history that has resorted to arms to destroy other cultures and dominate other peoples. The argument is that because the religions stemming from Abraham behave in ways that are barbaric they cannot claim to be inspired by goodness. By their behaviour, they appear to be following the dark side of 'God'.

I have always had respect for Abram, the learned man from Sumer. He has always been for me a role model for faith. Nonetheless by worshipping the Elohim Lord as God, Abram committed idolatry. He surrendered his own self-god or hu-man sovereignty to another. In doing so he reversed the action of Adam and Eve that had initiated human self-determination. Abram's surrender of divine sovereignty to the Lord was sealed with a covenant between them:

> *"And I will make my covenant between me and you, and will multiply you exceedingly."*
> *Then Abram fell on his face, and God talked with him, saying:*
> *"As for me, behold, my covenant is with you, and you shall be a father of many nations. No longer shall your name be called Abram, but your name shall be Abraham; for I have made you a father of many nations. I will make you exceedingly fruitful: and I will make nations of you, and kings shall come from you. And I will establish my covenant between me and you and your descendants after you, in their generations, for an everlasting covenant to be God to you and your descendants after you."* (Genesis 17:2-7)

> *And God said to Abraham: As for you, you shall keep my covenant, you and your descendants after you, throughout their generations. This is my covenant which you shall keep, between me and you and your descendants after you: Every male child after you shall be circumcised; and you shall be circumcised in the flesh of your foreskins, and it shall be a sign of the covenant between me and you."* (Genesis 17:9-11)

The Lord sealed his covenant with Abraham by demanding of him a mutilation of his body and the bodies of all the men and boys in his family and every male child in his line for all future generations.

To quote Jim Marrs from *Rule by Secrecy:*

> *"Recent writers such as Lewels and Boulay concluded that the biblical Jehovah was actually one of the ancient Sumerian 'gods' who took a special interest in the descendants of the Mesopotamian patriarch Abraham.*

"From the beginning of his relationship with the Hebrew people, Jehovah used every means at his command to exert authority and control over his flock," said Lewels. In referring to the Genesis 17 covenant between Jehovah and Abraham, Lewels saw the command that all males be circumcised as a marking system, much as ranchers today notch the ears of their cattle."

Women were not involved in this covenant. They were barred from the priesthood, certain places of worship and many of the programmes of indoctrination in the religions formed through the sons of Abraham. Perhaps this was because, with their more powerful intuition and innate wisdom, women were not as easy to manipulate as men. The embargo against women revealed a deep-seated hatred that Abraham's male manifestation of God had for the female of our species. This may have stemmed from the way that Eve thwarted him. It is possible that Abraham's Lord excluded women from his dealings with humanity because he was frightened that they would expose his treachery and deception and beat him once again. Alternatively, it may have originated from the primordial jealousy of the divine Father for the divine Mother. It appears that the biblical God did have one use for women; that was to be the mothers of his people. So it was he treated Sarah, the wife of Abraham.

To find all the genetic characteristics he required for his 'super-race' in one man would have been a tall order, even for the Lord God. In order to enhance the chance of success of his operation, it is possible that he employed some breeding to improve his stock. The traits of greed and cunning are easy to find in humanity, but genius is rare.

The Elohim Lord would need to give his chosen people a cut above everyone else if he was to succeed in his plan. It would be an obvious advantage if he had a race in which genius was commonplace. This would require the right choice of DNA in the selected seed of his stock, followed up with a well-controlled breeding programme. And what better seed than his own! All he needed to do was plant his own 'perfect seed' in a garden prepared for it. Thus he would be 'Father' to the people he had chosen to complete his 'divine plan' for the deception of humanity.

Chapter 4

The Sons of God

"The oldest of the three Abrahamic religions, and the clear ancestor of the other two, is Judaism: originally a tribal cult of a single fiercely unpleasant God, morbidly obsessed with sexual restrictions, with the smell of charred flesh, with his own superiority over rival gods and with the exclusiveness of his chosen desert tribe."

(Richard Dawkins)

Sarah, the wife of Abraham, was barren (Genesis 11:30). When the Lord sealed his pact with Abraham she was postmenopausal. However, today we know that with the aid of hormones, post-menopausal women can bear children. Genetic engineering, artificial insemination, invitro or vivo fertilisation, hormones and embryo implants, are technologies that would have been available to the Lord and his Elohim team of bio-engineers!

And so it came to pass, one day they dropped in on Abraham and Sarah:

> *Then the Lord appeared to him by the terebinth trees of Mamre, as he was sitting in the tent door in the heat of the day. So he lifted his eyes and looked, and behold, three men were standing by him; and when he saw them, he ran from the tent door to meet them, and bowed himself to the ground. (Genesis 18:1-2)*

> *Then they said to him, "Where is Sarah your wife?" And he said "Here, in the tent." And they said, "I will certainly return to you according to the time of life, and behold, Sarah your wife, shall have a son."*

And Sarah was listening in the tent door, which was behind him. Now Abraham and Sarah were old, well advanced in age; and Sarah had passed the age of childbearing (Genesis 18:9-11)

Therefore, Sarah laughed within herself, saying, "After I have grown old, shall I have pleasure, my lord being old also?" And the Lord said to Abraham, " Why did Sarah laugh saying, 'Shall I surely bear a child since I am old?' Is anything too hard for the Lord? At the appointed time I will return to you, according to the time of life and Sarah shall have a son." (Genesis 18:12-14) And the Lord visited Sarah as he had said, and the Lord did unto Sarah as he had spoken. Sarah conceived and bore Abraham a son in his old age, at the set time of which God had spoken to him. And Abraham called the name of the son that Sarah bore unto him Isaac.(Genesis 21:1-3)

If the Lord of the Elohim used his own seed to fertilise a suitably prepared egg within Sarah, that was to become Isaac, then Isaac would be the *Son of God*, the biological son of the Lord. Under these circumstances, Ishmael, the first son of Abraham, would have been his only true, biological son.

Isaac as the son of the Lord was to be the seed of the Chosen People. The Lord intended that as a race, they would excel in everything, having his own outstanding talents and brilliance of mind.

To quote Jim Marrs from *Rule by Secrecy*:

"According to Genesis 17, it was about this time we are told that Jehovah changed his follower's name from Abram (Exalted Father) to Abraham (Father of Nations) and ordered all male children circumcised. Abraham was promised a lineage that would rule over many nations,

including Egypt and those of Mesopotamia. Sarai's name was changed to Sarah (Princess) who gave birth to Isaac, the second born to Abraham, who was one hundred years old at the time, according to Genesis 17:17. In Genesis 17:19, Abraham is told that Jehovah's covenant will be established through Isaac. Apparently Isaac carried genetic traits gained through Sarah that were thought superior to those of Ishmael."

Obviously the Lord would have to maintain the purity of his stock.

Neither shalt thou make marriages with them; thy daughter thou shalt not give unto his son, nor his daughter shalt thou take unto thy son.
(Deuteronomy 7:3)

Then, if he could command the unswerving loyalty and surrender of his offspring, he could live through them and fulfil his plan of mastery over the human race. Pedigree and faith were of paramount importance if his plan was to succeed.

Isaac had two sons. These grandsons of the biblical God were, Esau and Jacob:

Isaac went on to live and had twin sons by his wife Rebekah. The younger son, Jacob, deceived his father and cheated his older brother Esau out of his inheritance and out of his father's blessing.
(Genesis 27:1-35)

Grandson of the 'Great Deceiver', Jacob lived up to his name:

*And Esau said, "Is he not rightly named Jacob [i.e.**the deceiver**]? For he has supplanted me these two times. He took away my birthright and now look, he has taken away my blessing"* (Genesis 27:36)

Supported by his mother (Genesis 27:6-17), through treachery and deception Jacob stole the right to be father of God's Chosen People, from his twin, Esau, the first-born of Isaac.

The Lord then appeared to Jacob in a dream and re-peated the promise he had made to Abraham and Isaac. Jacob responded with his own promises to the Lord.

> *Then Jacob made a vow, saying "If God will be with me, and keep me in this way that I am going, and give me bread to eat and clothing to put on, so that I shall come back to my father's house in peace, then the Lord shall be my God. And this stone which I have set as a pillar shall be God's house, and of all that you give me I will surely give a tenth to you."*
> (Genesis 28:20-22)

Years later, a man appeared to Jacob and wrestled with him. Jacob prevailed and would not release the man until he received his blessing. In reply he renamed Jacob, **Is-rael:**

> *And he said, "Your name shall no longer be called Ja-cob, but Israel [Prince with God]; for you struggled with God and with men, and have prevailed."*
> (Genesis 32:28)

Here the Lord presented himself as a man. Having cre-ated man in their own image there is no reason why the Elohim and their leader should not take on human form whenever they wished. Especially as, in my view, they created man to upgrade their own physical vehicles. This would also account for the three men that appeared to Abraham and Sarah in Genesis 18:1-2.

In a personal encounter with the Lord (Genesis 32:28), Ja-cob was acknowledged for prevailing over God and man. Thus it was that 'the deceiver' became Israel, prince of a people chosen to serve the Elohim Lord. And the nation that stemmed from him came to be known by that name.

Jacob had twelve sons who gave rise to the twelve tribes of Israel who came to be known as the Israelites and also the Hebrews. But, at the end of his life it was to Judah, the father of the Jews, that Jacob gave the sceptre:

The Sceptre shall not depart from Judah, nor a lawgiver from between his feet. (Genesis 49:10)

The great-grandsons of the biblical God got off to a flying start by selling one of the brothers into slavery. Joseph was sold, out of jealousy, to the Ishmaelites (Genesis 37:11-28) who then sold him on to an Egyptian captain in Pharaoh's guard (Genesis 37:36).

The 'God' wasted no time in preparing his people for the task that lay ahead of them. From the Bible we gather that the Hebrew people spent some of their time in the promised land of Canaan, and some of their time dispersed amongst other nations. These periods of dispersion followed a pattern. The Israelites would enter a civilisation and adapt to its culture whilst maintaining their own separate identity. These periods of dispersion were very painful for the people who had little or no idea what was happening to them. But it was very necessary in 'God's' plan. The persecution they experienced, whilst creating a national trauma and reinforcing their isolation and contempt for other peoples, caused them to find solace in their religious traditions and engendered in them devotion for their Lord.

Time spent in the Promised Land was important as a recovery period for the nation whilst it gathered its strength and national identity before the next dispersion. The three major dispersions into the Egyptian, Babylonian and Roman empires were to have enormous implications for the future of mankind.

Whilst Jacob and his family were settling down in Canaan (Genesis 37:1), Joseph, the exiled son, was experiencing a meteoric rise into the position of greatest power under the Egyptian Pharaoh:

> *Then Pharaoh said to Joseph, "Inasmuch as God has shown you all this, there is no one as discerning and wise as you. You shall be over my house, and all my people shall be ruled according to your word; only in regard to the throne will I be greater than you"*
> (Genesis 41:39-40)

This rise to power occurred as a result of Joseph's ability to interpret dreams of the Pharaoh in terms of a period of plenty followed by a famine (Genesis 41:14-37) and the subsequent decision of the Pharaoh to hand over the stewardship of Egypt to Joseph was made in order to enable him to prepare his nation (Genesis 41:39-49).

The interpretation of dreams and prophecy, combined with the extraordinary abilities of the Chosen People, was used repeatedly to manoeuvre them into positions of power during the dispersions. The pattern that occurred with Joseph in Egypt was to occur again, hundreds of years later, with Daniel in Babylon:

> *...the great God hath made known to the king what shall come to pass hereafter: and the dream is certain,and the interpretation there of sure. Then the king Nebuchadnezzar fell upon his face, and worshipped Daniel, and commanded that they should offer an oblation and sweet odours unto him.*
> *The king answered unto Daniel and said, "Of truth it is, that your God is a God of gods, and a Lord of kings and a revealer of secrets, seeing you could reveal this secret."*

Then the king made Daniel a great man, and gave him many great gifts, and made him ruler over the whole province of Babylon, and chief of the governors over all the wise men of Babylon. (Daniel 2:45-48)

Students of the Bible take these stories as examples of the greatness of the Old Testament God, the goodness of the Lord toward his Chosen People. Few of them seem to appreciate that in these actions, the Lord was furthering his own ends. He was infiltrating his Sons of God into the highest places in the societies into which they were dispersed. The Lord took full advantage of their positions of power.

People, such as Abraham, Joseph and Daniel and in fact, many of the Semitic people, were high-minded individuals working from the purest intent. They could never have imagined or comprehended the master plan of 'God'. They were an unsophisticated people dealing with an exceedingly advanced and sophisticated being. In their naiveté they had given themselves over to an entity they couldn't begin to comprehend. They were as innocent children giving to their father complete faith, trust and unquestioned service. As such, they were totally susceptible to the manipulation of 'God' manifesting the satanic side of his nature.

During the dispersions into Babylon and Egypt, the *Sons of God* were to penetrate the ancient mystery schools of those societies. These were major centres for the mystery teachings in the ancient world. The teachings of these schools were sources of knowledge, which were potentially dangerous if they fell into the wrong hands. It is for this reason that they were protected by a cloak of secrecy. During the periods of exile, the *Sons of Israel* received schooling in the ancient mystery teachings, high magic and disciplines of secrecy.

The *Sons of God* had to be initiated into the mysteries without arousing the suspicions of their teachers. The innocence of his faithful was, and still is, the secret weapon of the Lord of Elohim. It enabled the *Sons of God* to manoeuvre into key positions within the organs of society with minimum suspicion of the danger they represented.

During the dispersion into Egypt one of the *Sons of God* was initiated into the mystery teachings and magic of that ancient society at the highest level. A fluke of circumstances established a son of the dark Lord in the House of Pharaoh. His name was Moses.

Chapter 5

The Dark Lord

"The Christian God is a being of terrific character; cruel, vindictive, capricious and unjust."

(Thomas Jefferson)

In the beginning, when 'God' needed to curb the growing awareness and powers of Adam and Eve, he employed curses. It could be said that in his cursing he was working **Black Magic** that is, magic employed with malice.

If he was a **Black Magician,** obviously the Lord of Elohim would want his chosen ones to be assimilated into the secret mystery schools, to learn to work with power and magic. They could then carry the mystery teachings into the future and, working under the cloak of secret societies evolved from the mystery schools, they could use psychic power and magic.

Moses was the first great magician to appear amongst the Israelites. According to the Bible, he was discovered in a basket of rushes and adopted by the daughter of the Pharaoh (Exodus 2:3-10).

Being the adopted son of the Pharaoh, Moses would have had automatic access to the Egyptian temples. The Pharaohs and princes of Egypt were adepts of the mystery schools of ancient Egypt and it was usual for the highest priest of the land to be closely related to the Pharaoh. As an Egyptian princeling, Moses would have had the opportunity to be initiated into the highest degrees of mystery and magic that the ancient Egyptian civilisation had to offer.

In his book *'Moses and Monotheism'*, Sigmund Freud suggested that Moses was a ranking Egyptian connected to the Pharaoh Akhenaten. In Exodus (2:19) Moses is described as an Egyptian. Manetho, priest and adviser to Pharaoh Ptolemy I, in 300 B.C. recorded in the *Aegyptiaca (History of Egypt)* that Moses was a ranking Egyptian priest educated in the Ancient Mysteries at the lower Egyptian city of Heliopolis.

During this time the Hebrews had become enslaved by the Pharaoh (Exodus 1:8-14). Aware of his ethnic origins, Moses felt sympathy for his suffering people. He became an outlaw after he slew an oppressive overseer (Exodus 2:11-15). During this period of exile from the royal household, the Lord spoke to Moses from a burning bush:

> *And the Angel of the Lord appeared to him in a flame of fire in the midst of a bush. So he looked, and behold, the bush was burning with fire, but the bush was not consumed.... God called to him from the midst of the bush and said, "Moses, Moses."*
> *Moreover he said, "I am the God of your father, the God of Abraham, the God of Isaac, and the God of Jacob." And Moses hid his face; for he was afraid to look upon God.* (Exodus 3:2-6)

It is important to note, here in the Bible, 'God' is revealed as an angel; by definition an extraterrestrial.

Appearing in a blaze of light, a fire that did not burn the bush, the angelic 'God' declared himself to Moses as the same one that came to Abraham, Isaac and Jacob. He then identified himself in a way that avoided the revelation of his name:

> *And God said to Moses, I AM WHO I AM* **(YHWH)**. *And he said "Thus you shall say to the children of Israel, 'I AM has sent me to you.' "* More-

over, God said to Moses, "Thus you shall say to the children of Israel: 'The Lord God of your fathers, the God of Abraham, the God of Isaac, and the God of Jacob, has sent me (Moses) to you. This is My name forever, and this is my memorial to all generations.' " (Exodus 3:14-15)

The Lord was very sensitive about his name. What was he trying to hide? Even YHWH was, by tradition, never spoken aloud by the Hebrews.

YHWH is pronounced by some as *Yo Hey VaVHey.* in approximately 300 BC, another sylable was added to make YHWWH, pronounced *Ye-Ho-Vah* from which the English word, **Jehovah** originates. Jehovah is a change from YHWH sounded by some as 'Yahweh', or 'Jahveh'. In Hebrew the letter 'J' is sounded as 'Y'.

If the 'God' of Abraham, Isaac and Jacob was Satan he had a problem. Trained in the Egyptian priesthood, Moses would have definitely charged an angelic entity to reveal itself. He would have used commands it had to obey.

Imagine you were super-smart Satan and prided yourself as Almighty God and were charged by a mere mortal to reveal yourself. Would you not reply with absolute contempt, "I am who I am!" and maybe under your breath mutter, "...My name is none of your business!"

Jehovah declared himself to be the same God that came to Abraham. To Abraham he said he was Almighty God and he repeated this claim with Moses:

And God spoke to Moses and said to him: "I AM the Lord. I appeared to Abraham, to Isaac and to Jacob, as God Almighty, but by my name[YHWH], I was not known to them." (Exodus 6:2-3)

Here the Bible claims Jehovah is Almighty God and then from what follows, the same Bible reveals 'Almighty

God' as a 'Dark Lord' manifesting unparalleled evil.

For thousands of years, the great religions of the Western world have been encouraging people to worship this 'God', who manifested all the hallmarks of Satan. No wonder there has been so much confusion and so many religious wars in our history. No wonder 'God' is such a paradox for thinking people.

In the Knight Templar documents, Jesus Christ stated emphatically that YHWH translated as Jahveh, was Satan. What Jahveh or Jehovah did through the agency of Moses was magic. Jehovah was a magician of awesome power and with Moses he began to work open magic beginning with an apparition as a fire in a bush that did not consume it.

Against the Egyptians Jehovah employed black magic. From the standpoint of the Hebrews, as reflected in the Bible, the ends justified the means — employed by Jehovah and Moses — which was the release of the Hebrew people from slavery. From the standpoint of the Egyptian people things were quite different. They were at the receiving end of what could only be described as the sorcery. Whatever the ends, if the means are evil, the magic is black.

The extent of blackness of the Dark Lord's magic was demonstrated by his 'hardening of the Pharaoh's heart':

> *And the Lord said to Moses, "When you go back to Egypt, see that you do all those wonders before Pharaoh which I have put in your hand. But I will harden his heart, so that he will not let the people go."*
> (Exodus 4:21)

Symbolically the Dark Lord began to work his black power against Egypt by transforming a wand into a snake:

> *The Lord said to him, "What is that in your hand?"*
> *And he said "A rod."*

And he said, "Cast it to the ground."
So he cast it on the ground and it became a serpent; and
Moses fled from it.
Then the Lord said to Moses, "Reach out your hand and
take it by the tail (and he reached out his hand and
caught it, and it became a rod in his hand), that they
may believe that the Lord God of their fathers, the God of
Abraham, the God of Isaac and the God of Jacob, has ap-
peared to you."
Furthermore, the Lord said to him, "Now put your hand
in your bosom."
And he put his hand in his bosom and when he took it
out, behold, his hand was leprous, like snow.
And he said, "Put your hand in your bosom again."
So he put his hand in his bosom again, and drew it out of
his bosom, and behold, it was restored like his other
flesh.(Exodus 4:2-7)

Moses, who was 80 years old, was assisted by Aaron who was 83, (Exodus 7:7) when he repeated the snake magic in front of the Pharaoh:

So Moses and Aaron went to the Pharaoh and they did
so, just as the Lord commanded. And Aaron cast down
his rod before Pharaoh and before his servants, and it
became a serpent.
But Pharaoh also called the wise men and the sorcerers;
so the magicians of Egypt, they also did in like manner
with their enchantments. For every man threw down
his rod, and they became serpents. But Aaron's rod
swallowed up their rods.(Exodus 7:10-12)

The Dark Lord hardened the heart of Pharaoh for the express purpose of enabling himself to perform spectacular signs and wonders in the land of Egypt:

"And I will harden Pharaoh's heart and will multiply

my signs and my wonders in the land of Egypt.
But Pharaoh will not heed you, so that I may lay my
hand on Egypt and bring my armies and my people,
the children of Israel, out of the land of Egypt by great
judgments."
(Exodus 7:3-4)

These signs and wonders consisted of a series of terrible plagues, inflicted on the people of Egypt. This was not the work of a loving or merciful God. If the Lord had love and respect for humanity, he would have done the minimum that was necessary to release the Hebrews from bondage. Instead he deliberately prolonged the agony and suffering inflicted on the nation of Egypt, to demonstrate his power. It was not only the people who suffered but also the live-stock and wildlife of Egypt.

In the first plague, Jehovah turned the water of Egypt into blood:

> *Then the Lord spoke to Moses, "Say to Aaron, 'Take*
> *your rod and stretch out your hand over the waters of*
> *Egypt, over their streams, over their rivers, over*
> *ponds, and over all their pools of water, that they may*
> *become blood. And there shall be blood throughout all*
> *the land of Egypt, both in vessels of wood and vessels*
> *of stone.' "*(Exodus 7:19)

This 'miracle' of the Dark Lord had the effect of polluting the waters of Egypt, killing off the fish and leaving the people and animals without drinking water for a week (Exodus 7:20-25). It is not hard to imagine the suffering this must have caused in the heat of Egypt.

The Bible reveals that the magicians of Egypt were able to match the magic worked by Jehovah through Moses and Aaron. The Egyptian magicians also turned water into blood:

> *And the magicians of Egypt did so with their en-*
> *chantments: and Pharaoh's heart was hardened, nei-*
> *ther did he harken unto them; as the Lord had said.*
> (Exodus 7:22)

They also caused frogs to appear after Moses and Aaron had covered the whole country with frogs:

> *So Aaron stretched his hand over the waters of Egypt,*
> *and the frogs came up and covered the land of Egypt.*
> *And the magicians did so with their enchantments,*
> *and brought up frogs on the land of Egypt.*
> (Exodus 8:6-7)

This highlights that high magic was taught in the Egyptian mystery schools of which Moses and Aaron were obviously adepts.

Throughout this episode, magic powers were being flagrantly abused against the Egyptian population, including children and animals, with no consideration for their welfare. The abuse of power, instigated by the Dark Lord, would have wrought havoc in the mystery schools bringing the whole of Egypt into decline, which is exactly what occurred.

The next show of black magic by Jehovah was a plague of lice to torment the people and livestock of Egypt:

> *So the Lord said to Moses, "Say to Aaron, 'Stretch*
> *out your rod, and strike the dust of the Land, so that it*
> *may become lice throughout all the land of Egypt.' "*
> *And they did so. For Aaron stretched out his hand*
> *with his rod and struck the dust of the earth, and it be-*
> *came lice on man and beast. All the dust of the land*
> *became lice throughout the land of Egypt.*
> (Exodus 8:16-17)

This was followed by swarms of flies:

> *And the Lord did so. Thick swarms of flies came into*

the house of Pharaoh, into his servants' houses, and into all the land of Egypt. The land was corrupted because of the swarms of flies.(Exodus 8:24)

But still the Pharaoh's heart remained hardened:

But Pharaoh hardened his heart at this time also; neither would he let the people go.(Exodus 8:32)

And so the suffering went on. The next act of the Lord was to strike dead the livestock of Egypt:

So the Lord did this thing the next day, and the livestock of Egypt died; but of the livestock of the children of Israel, not one died.(Exodus 9:6)

After which he brought out boils on the people and whatever animals were still living:

Then they took ashes from the furnace and stood before Pharaoh, and Moses scattered them towards heaven. And they caused boils that broke out in sores on man and beast. (Exodus 9:10)

But still the Pharaoh was unmoved:

But the Lord hardened the heart of Pharaoh; and he did not heed them, just as the Lord had spoken to Moses. (Exodus 9:12)

And indeed, amidst all this suffering Jehovah was boasting that he was using his power against the people of Egypt for the express purpose of establishing his name and fame throughout the World:

"For at this time I will send all my plagues to your very heart, and on your servants and on your people, that you may know that there is none like me in all the Earth." (Exodus 9:14)

If the Pharaoh had not been under a 'heart hardening' enchantment, the agony of Egypt might have been mitigated, but instead, for his own glory, Jehovah unleashed upon them the worst hailstorm in their history:

> *So there was hail, and fire mingled with the hail, so very heavy that there was none like it in all the land of Egypt since it became a nation.* (Exodus 9:24)

The Dark Lord also told Moses that he was hardening the heart of the Pharaoh, and causing the plagues, in order to impress the Hebrew nation:

> *Now the Lord said to Moses, "Go in to Pharaoh; for I have hardened his heart and the hearts of his servants, that I may show these signs of mine before him, and that you may tell in the hearing of your son and your son's son the mighty things I have done in Egypt, and my signs which I have done among them,that you may know that I am the Lord." (*Exodus 10:1-2*)*

Here it is clear that the Dark Lord was destroying the nation of Egypt, in order to strengthen the loyalty and devotion of his chosen people. Even to this day worshippers of Jehovah recall the plagues of Egypt with awe and wonder, witnessing this black magic as reason for their worship. Gentiles seem to be blissfully unaware that Jehovah has no more feeling and respect for them than for the unfortunate Egyptians.

The great civilisation of Egypt was infiltrated, deceived and deliberately brought to ruin by Jehovah working through his 'blind' devotees. This pattern was to be repeated again and again in subsequent ages.

Jehovah continued the holocaust of Egypt with a plague of locusts, a period of darkness and then the genocide of all the first-born of that once great nation.

This genocide was, and still is, celebrated as the major feast of the Jewish calendar (Exodus 12:1-30). The feast of 'Passover' marks a major triumph by the Dark Lord in his

Great Work of Ages.

Jehovah completed the destruction of Egypt by hardening the heart of the Pharaoh once again. This caused him to pursue the Israelites with his army (Exodus 14:4-8). Under the instruction of the Dark Lord, Moses stretched forth his staff over the Red Sea and the waters parted so that the Israelites could cross. When the Egyptian army attempted to follow, the waters returned and they were drowned (Exodus 14:16-31).

Understandably, the Israelites were impressed. They sang the praises of Jehovah and predicted, in their triumph, the sorrows in store for the Palestinians (the Philistines), whose land they were about to steal:

> *"The people will hear and be afraid; Sorrow will take hold of the inhabitants of Philistia. Then the chiefs of Edom will be dismayed; The Mighty men of Moab, Trembling will take hold of them; All the inhabitants of Canaan will melt away."* (Exodus 15:14-16)

The Israelites fled from the land of Egypt and even as they left, their Lord and their God promised, once again, to give them a land belonging to the Canaanites, and the Hittites, the Amorites, the Hivites and the Jebusites (Exodus 13:5). Jehovah gave the order for their mass genocide. He had murder in mind for these unfortunate folk, to clear their land flowing with milk and honey for his chosen people. This was not what one would expect of the 'God of absolute goodness'!

Before commencing genocide on the people of Canaan, Jehovah continued to work wonders for his people, including the manifestation of food (Exodus 16:4-18) and water (Exodus 17:3-6) to sustain them in the wilderness. At Mount Sinai he worked awesome signs to establish his authority over his people. Even there the Dark Lord revealed himself to his people: not as a god of loving kindness, but as a powerful and despotic ruler who would kill anyone who did not respect his authority

> *"You shall set bounds for the people all around saying, 'Take heed of yourselves that you do not go up the mountain or touch its base. Whoever touches the mountain shall surely be put to death. 'Not a hand shall touch him, but he shall surely be stoned or shot with an arrow: whether man or beast, he shall not live."* (Exodus 19: 12-13)

It would indeed be a wonderful world if 'God' were concerned for all the poor people of the Earth; not just the poor amongst his own people:

> *"If you lend money to any of my people who are poor among you, you shall not be like a money lender and charge interest, you shall not be like a moneylender to him; you shall not charge him interest."*
> (Exodus 22: 25)

Chapter 6

The Commandments

*"Compared with the Old Testament's psychotic delin-
quent, the deist God of the eighteenth-century Enlightenment is an altogether grander being: worthy of his cosmic
creation, loftily unconcerned with human affairs, sub-
limely aloof from our private thoughts and hopes, caring
nothing for our messy sins or mumbled contritions."*

(Richard Dawkins)

After fleeing Egypt, the Hebrews wandered in the
desert for forty years. It was during this period that
Jehovah organised his people into a nation. Through
Moses he established laws and ordinances, commanding
how his people should think, act and lead their lives from
one day to the next. The Chosen People were not free to
do just as they liked; they were expected to obey the
dictates of their Dark Lord to the minutest detail. The
laws of Moses were cult indoctrination. The Gnostics,
who were discredited as heretics, considered that 'The
Law', governing life on Earth and dictating human
behaviour, as...*the work of a lower deity.*

After Genesis, the next four books of the Bible, Exodus,
Leviticus, Numbers and Deuteronomy, are the books of
Law, created by Moses or taught him by Jehovah. Jeho-
vah gave *The Commandments* on tablets of stone.

Some of 'The Commandments' were undoubtedly
good, but God in the Old Testament was clearly
two-faced in regard to them. He would command one
thing but then do the opposite.

To quote Jim Marrs from *Rule by Secrecy:*

Moses displayed to his people stone tablets containing a set of laws given by Jehovah, many of which were promptly broken on orders of this same Lord... these orders came from a physical person rather than from some spirit.

In the first commandment Jehovah prohibited the worship of gods and images:

"I AM the Lord your God, who brought you out of the land of Egypt, out of the house of bondage. You shall have no other gods before me. You shall not make for yourself any carved image, or any likeness of anything that is in heaven above, or that is in the earth beneath, or that is in the water under the earth; You shall not bow down to them nor serve them.
(Exodus 20: 2-4)

If this were a universal command against idolatry, it would not have sanctioned worship of 'the Lord' or any other externalisation or physical manifestation of God. As written it appears more the outpouring of a jealous god...

"For I, the Lord your God, am a jealous God, visiting the inequity of the fathers on the children, to the third and fourth generations of those who hate me, but showing mercy to thousands of those who love me, and keep my commandments." (Exodus 20:5-6)

This manifestation of God was not a being of unconditional love, mercy and compassion. Far from it, he cursed those who opposed him. His love and mercy was conditional upon worship and unswerving obedience.

In the second commandment he prohibited the use of his name (Exodus 20:7). The third and fourth commandments were noble. (Exodus 20:8-12). It is good for people to have a day of rest and good that they honour their parents.

However, the fifth commandment was sheer hypocrisy.

"Thou shalt not kill." (Exodus 20:13)

Under Moses the killing began, as the Chosen People followed the orders of their war Lord to invade Palestine. In the holocaust of the Canaanites, and the Hittites, the Philistines (Palestinians), the Amorites, the Hivites and the Jebusites, innocents were mercilessly slaughtered:

> *"And the Lord said to me, 'See, I have begun to give Sihon and his land over to you. Begin to possess it, that you may inherit his land.' Then Sihon and all his people came out against us to fight at Jahaz. And the Lord God delivered him over to us; so we defeated him, his sons and all his people. We took all his cities at that time and we utterly destroyed the men, women and the little ones of every city; we left nothing remaining."* (Deuteronomy 2:31-34)

> *"So the Lord our God also delivered into our hands Og, king of Bashan, with all his people, and we attacked them until he had no survivors remaining. And we took all his cities at that time; there was not a city which we did not take from them: sixty cities, all the region of Argob, the kingdom of Og in Bashan. All these cities were fortified with high walls, gates and bars, besides a great many rural towns. And we utterly destroyed them, as we did to Sihon king of Heshbon, utterly destroying the men, women and children...."* (Deuteronomy 3:3-6)

If there is any truth in the genesis of Isaac, then the Lord was hardly in a position to declare:

> *"Thou shalt not commit adultery."* (Exodus 20:14)

In the seventh commandment, the Lord said: *"Thou shalt not steal"*(Exodus 20:15) yet he encouraged his people to steal Palestine and rob the Palestinians of their land, their homes and all their possessions:

> *"And I will set your bounds from the Red Sea to the sea of the Philistines,(Palestinians)and from the desert to the River. For I will deliver the inhabitants of the land into your hand, and you shall drive them out before you."* (Exodus 23:31)

All of this was reinforced by Moses:

> *"When the Lord your God has cut off the nations whose land the Lord your God is giving you and you dispossess them, dwell in their cities and in their houses..."*(Deuteronomy 19:1)

Commandment eight...

> *Thou shalt not bear false witness against thy neighbour.* (Exodus 20:16)

... coming from the 'father of lies'?

Commandments nine and ten...

> *Thou shalt not covet thy neighbour's house...*
> *And the Lord spoke unto Moses, saying, "Command the children of Israel and say unto them, 'When you come unto the land of Canaan; this is the land that shall fall unto you for an inheritance, even the land of Canaan with the coasts thereof.'*(Numbers 34:2)
> *And we took all his cities at that time; there was not a city which we did not take from them: sixty cities, all the region of Argob, the kingdom of Og in Bashan.* (Deuteronomy 3:4)

> *...thou shalt not covet thy neighbour's wives...*

The Isrealites took thirty two thousand virgins, in one campaign alone (Numbers 31:35). However, true to the command of their Lord, they didn't covet their neighbour's old wives. They slaughtered them instead! (Numbers 31:17)

...nor his ox nor his ass...(Exodus 20:17)

And the booty, being the rest of the prey which the men of war had caught, was six hundred and seventy five thousand sheep, seventy two thousand cattle, and sixty one thousand asses.(Numbers 31:32-34)

In many other commandments the Dark Lord clearly demonstrated his double standards. After enacting the greatest show of sorcery ever recorded, Jehovah instructed that women who practiced sorcery were to suffer death:

"You shall not permit a sorceress to live."
(Exodus 22:18)

The same applied to mediums or channellers:

"A man or a woman who is a medium, or who has familiar spirits, shall surely be put to death; they shall stone them with stones. Their blood shall be upon them." (Leviticus 20:27)

This ruling was to justify the notorious 'witch-hunts' of the middle ages and the worst excesses of the Inquisition. In a holocaust of nine million people, herbalists, psychics, healers, alchemists, dissidents and countless other innocent men and women were subjected to horrendous tortures and needless death due to the commandments of the Dark Lord. The army of Dominican Inquisitors, and multitude of Christian witch-hunters who followed them, found justification for their atrocities in the 'Law of God' as written in the books of Moses.

Whilst Jehovah liberally placed curses...

"For everyone who curses his father or his mother

shall surely be put to death. He has cursed his father or his mother. His blood shall be upon him."
(Leviticus 20:9)

He treated the Egyptians mercilessly in order to free his people from slavery, yet gave them permission to make slaves of non-Hebrew peoples:

"And as for your male and female slaves whom you may have from the nations that are around you, from them you may buy male and female slaves. Moreover you may buy the children of the strangers who sojourn among you, and their families who are with you, which they begat in your land; and they shall become your property. And you may take them as an inheritance for your children after you, to inherit them as a possession; they shall be your permanent slaves. "But regarding your brethren, the children of Israel you shall not rule over one another with rigour."
(Leviticus 25:44-46)

Jehovah was clearly God for the Israelites alone. He had little or no regard for other peoples of the Earth:

"...the Amorites and the Hittites and the Perizzites and the Canaanites and the Hivites and the Jebusites; I will cut them off." (Exodus 23:23)
"I will send my fear before you. I will cause confusion among all the people to whom you come..."
(Exodus 23:27)
"And I will send hornets before you, which shall drive out the Hivite, the Canaanite, and the Hittite from before you." (Exodus 23:28)

And he continued to indoctrinate the Israelites in intolerance for other religions and cultures. We see here the origin of religious intolerance that characterises the Jehovah cults. The indoctrination stemming from this Satanic

Lord has been the cause of wars and persecutions, cultural destruction and iconoclasm ever since:

> *"You shall not bow down to their gods nor serve them, nor do according to their works; but you shall utterly overthrow them and completely break down their sacred pillars."* (Exodus 23:24)

Jehovah would not tolerate in his people any respect for what other people held to be sacred. Nor did he expect non-Israelites to be treated with honour. There was only 'love thy neighbour' in his teaching if the neighbour happened to be an Israelite. There was one rule for the people of Israel, and another for foreigners:

> *"At the end of every seven years you shall grant a release of debts. And this is the form of release: Every creditor who has lent you anything to his neighbour shall release it; he shall not require it of his neighbour or his brother, because it is called the 'Lord's release'. Of a foreigner you may require it; but your hand shall release what is owed by your brother."*
> (Deuteronomy 15:1-3)

In the next section of this book you will realise that the world would be a very different place if the 'Lord's release' applied to all the peoples of the world. As it is, the Chosen People have a tremendous advantage over the other nations of the Earth. Every seven years they can look forward to a release from their debts. Everyone else has to suffer the burden of debt throughout their lives.

Even amongst his Chosen People there was little room for mercy and forgiveness in his laws. Jehovah's command was an 'eye for an eye and a tooth for a tooth':

> *"And if any mischief follow, then you shall give life for life, eye for eye, tooth for tooth, hand for hand, foot for foot, burning for burning, wound for wound,*

stripe for stripe." (Exodus 21:23-25)

The object of this book is not to pass judgment on the Chosen People or their behaviour — they are no different, no better and no worse than any other people of the Earth — but rather to reflect on the personality of their 'God' Jehovah.

Adultery and other 'immoralities' undoubtedly create dilemmas in society, and every society has a right to choose what activities are acceptable and what are not. Nonetheless, the death sentence is an unduly harsh punishment for sexual misconduct:

> *"The man who commits adultery with another man's wife, he who commits adultery with his neighbour's wife, the adulterer and the adulteress, shall surely be put to death."* (Leviticus 20:10)

Activities condoned in modern as well as ancient civilisations were capital offences in the Law given to Moses. In many ancient societies, for example, homosexuality was accepted, and today most people have a tolerant attitude toward gays. Not so Jehovah:

> *"If a man lies with a male as he lies with a woman, both of them have committed an abomination. They shall surely be put to death. Their blood shall be upon them."* (Leviticus 20:13)

The Bible is a real revelation! From reading the Bible it is abundantly clear that Jehovah was not God for all the peoples of the Earth. He was concerned only with the welfare of his own people, whom he put above all others:

> *"When the Lord your God brings you into the land which you go to possess, and has cast out many nations before you, the Hittites and the Girgashites and the Amorites and the Canaanites and the Perizzites and*

the Hivites and the Jebusites, seven nations greater and mightier than you..." (Deuteronomy 7:1)

"For you are a holy people to the Lord your God; the Lord your God has chosen you to be a people for himself, a special treasure above all the peoples on the face of the earth." (Deuteronomy 7:6)

But even with his own people, the Dark Lord acted as a despot. His love was conditional. He loved them only if they were totally devoted to him. If they dared to question his authority he despised them and destroyed them:

"Therefore know that the Lord your God, he is God, the faithful God who keeps his covenant and mercy for a thousand generations with those who love him and keep his commandments; and he repays those who hate him to their face, to destroy them. He will not be slack with him who hates him; he will repay him to his face." (Deuteronomy 7:9-10)

The Satanic Lord maintained a stranglehold over his chosen people by bullying and intimidating them. Whilst they remained faithful to his ordinances and decrees, he blessed them:

"Now it shall come to pass, if you diligently obey the voice of the Lord your God, to observe carefully all his commandments which I [Moses] command you today, that the Lord your God will set you high above all the nations of the earth.

"And all these blessings shall come upon you and overtake you, because you obey the voice of the Lord your God:

"Blessed shall you be in the city, and blessed shall you be in the country.

"Blessed shall be the fruit of your body, the produce of your ground and the increase of your herds, the increase of your cattle and the offspring of your flocks.

"Blessed shall be your basket and your kneading bowl.

"Blessed shall you be when you come in and blessed shall you be when you go out."

(Deuteronomy 28:1-6)

However, if they were unfaithful to him, Jehovah and Moses cursed them in terms which politicians of today would call 'zero tolerance' policy:

"But it shall come to pass if you do not obey the voice of the Lord your God, to observe carefully all his commandments and his statutes which I command you today, then all these curses will come upon you and overtake you:

"Cursed shall you be in the city and cursed shall you be in the country.

"Cursed shall be your basket and your kneading bowl.

"Cursed shall be the fruit of your body and the produce of your land, the increase of your cattle and the offspring of your flocks.

"Cursed shall you be when you come in, and cursed shall you be when you go out. The Lord will send on you cursing, confusion and rebuke in all you set your hand to do, until you are destroyed and until you perish quickly, because of the wickedness of your doings in which you have forsaken me.

"The Lord will make the plague cling to you until He has consumed you from the land which you are going to possess.

"The Lord will strike you with consumption, with fever, with inflammation, with severe burning fever, with the sword, with scorching, and with mildew; they shall pursue you until you perish."

(Deuteronomy 28:15-22)

Moses certainly didn't mince his words. It is small

wonder that his orthodox followers are fanatical in their observance of his law. The cults stemming from Moses have become a bane for all nations. But the Israelite suffering down through the ages, from their separateness and adherence to his cult doctrines, and law, is incalculable. In their worship of Jehovah and their fidelity to the Law of Moses, the Jewish people have suffered endless persecution. But in all this they have been true and faithful servants of the dark side of the Lord of Hosts. Hopefully the time will come soon for the spell of the **Dark Lord** over his holy people and through them over humanity, to be broken.

> *When the power of the holy people has been finally broken, all these things will be completed.*
> (Daniel 12:7)

The Lord of Hosts represents the full spectrum of duality. Remember the prophet Moses for the polarity of darkness but look forward toward the prophet Elijah for the polarity of light:

> *"For behold the day comes that will burn as an oven; and all the proud and all that are wicked shall be stubble: and the day that comes shall burn them up" says the Lord of Hosts,*
> *"That it shall leave them neither root nor branch.*
> *"But for you that fear my name shall the Sun of righteousness arise with healing in his wings; and you shall go forth, and grow up as calves of the stall. And you shall tread down the wicked; for they shall be ashes under the sole of your feet in the day that I shall do this," says the Lord of Hosts.*
> *"Remember you the law of Moses my servant, which I commanded unto him at Horeb for all Israel, with the statutes and judgments.*

"Behold, I will send you Elijah the prophet, before the coming of the great and dreadful day of the Lord: And he shall turn the heart of the fathers to the children, and the heart of the children to their fathers, least I come and smite the Earth with a curse."
(Malachi 4:1-6)

If Christ were to return he would be accepted by Christians but rejected by Jews and Muslims. However, Christians, Jews and Muslims eagerly await the return of Elijah. Elijah alone could bring about reconciliation between the divergent factions amongst the followers of Abraham's God.

"And he who overcomes, and keeps My works until the end, to him I will give power over the nations – 'He shall rule them with a rod of iron, They shall be dashed to pieces like the potters vessels.' As I have received from my Father, Also I will give him the morning star." (Revelation 2: 26-28)

Section II

A Testament from Modern Times

Disclaimer

- This book is not anti-God. It is showing that God is dualistic.
- This book is not anti-religion. It is unmasking cults masquerading as religion.
- This book is not anti-Jewish. It is questioning the activities of the Jewish God not the Jewish people. Most Jewish people do not identify with the cults hidden within their ancient religion. Down through the ages many Jews have questioned their scriptures and spoken against the iniquities of their God. The majority of Jews are innocent of the covert activities of secret cults within Judaism. Most Jews along with the majority of people on Earth manifest the good side of God.
- This book is not racist. Like most Jews, I believe in the innate equality of man and abhor racism and the concept of racial superiority embodied in the cult idea of a people chosen by God to be above all other people of the Earth.
- This book is not anti-Israel. The modern multi-religious State of Israel and most of its citizens do not identify with the cults of Jehovah. Modern Israelis are not to be confused with the ancient Israelites.

Chapter 7

The Elders

"The genie of religious fanaticism is rampant in pres-ent-day America, and the Founding Fathers would have been horrified."

(Richard Dawkins)

Since ancient times, the Jewish nation has had a governing body, a highest court and ruling council known as the 'Council of Elders'. The world 'Elder' is often taken to indicate seniority, one who is older and wiser, with authority in a community. However, the original Hebrew meaning of the word — derived from 'El' for divine — was 'one who is divinely inspired' or 'in touch with God.' With the root word 'El' it also indicates a link with the Elohim.

Traditionally the Elders convened in a high council of 71 members. This **Sanhedrin** — taken from the Greek word for Assembly — or Council of the Elders, ruled the lives of the Jewish faithful in whatever land they lived.

The 'Elders of Israel' came into being in the time of Moses (Exodus 24:1) and it was the Council of Elders who disposed of Jesus:

> *Immediately, in the morning, the chief priests held a consultation with the elders and the scribes, and the whole council, and they bound Jesus, led him away and handed him over to Pilate.* (Mark 15:1)

Most people believe the Council of Elders is extinct. However, it does exist, but few know of it as it convenes in secret — once in a century — under different names. In the 19th century, for example, the Council of Jewish Elders described itself as the **Learned Elders of Zion.**

Shreds of evidence suggest that the council of Elders has been involved in clandestine activities since the dispersion under Rome. In 1492, Chemor, chief Rabbi of Spain, wrote to the Sanhedrin, seated in Constantinople. He was seeking advice in regard to the Spanish law, which threatened Jews with expulsion unless they converted to Christianity. The following reply from the Sanhedrin was found on pages 156-157 of a Spanish book *La Silva Curiosa* published in 1608 by Paris Orry. The author (Julio-Iniguez de Medrano) explained, "This letter following was found in the archives of Toledo by the Hermit of Salamanca, searching the ancient records of Spain and, as it is expressive and remarkable, I wish to write it here":

"Beloved brethren in Moses, we have received your letter in which you tell us of the anxieties and misfortunes which you are enduring. We are pierced by as great a pain to hear it as yourselves. The advice of the Grand Satraps and Rabbis is the following: As for what you say that the King of Spain [Ferdinand] obliges you to become Christian: do it since you cannot do otherwise. As for what you say about the command to despoil you of your property: make your sons merchants that they may despoil, little by little, the Christians of theirs. As for what you say about making attempts on your lives: make your sons doctors and apothecaries that they may take away Christians' lives. As for what you say of their destroying your synagogues: make your sons canons and clerics in order that they may destroy their churches. As for the many vexations you complain of: arrange that your sons become advocates and lawyers, and see that they always mix in affairs of State, that by putting Christians under your yoke you may

dominate the world and be avenged on them. Do not swerve from this order that we give you, because you will find by experience that humiliated as you are, you will reach the actuality of power. (Signed by the Prince of the Jews of Constantinople)

The tone of the edict of the Sanhedrin in Constantinople was understandable in the light of the persecution of the Jews under the Spanish Inquisition and the intent expressed by the Council of Elders, or 'Grand Satraps,' to gain world dominion may have been an outburst of hatred and revenge against the power and universal dominion of the Catholic Church. Nonetheless this letter does establish intent for world dominion existed in the minds of the leading rabbis in the middle ages.

For many centuries regular expulsion of the Jews from the nations of Europe occurred. Was there a cause for this continual persecution apart from Christian intolerance? Was there a reason why nations have dealt so harshly with the Jews. Revenge for the crucifixion of Christ cannot alone be the explanation. Jealousy of non-Jews toward Jews is undeniable because of their natural genius and aptitude. Nonetheless, was this sufficient cause for the vehement anti-Semitism that has occurred down the centuries? Racial intolerance is common amongst the ignorant but would not suffice to account for the anti-Semitism expressed by the founding fathers of the United States of America.

In a debate on the US Constitution, Benjamin Franklin proposed:

"We must protect this young nation from any insidious influence...That menace, gentlemen, is the Jews. In whatever country Jews have settled in any great numbers,

they have lowered its moral tone, depreciated its commercial integrity, have segregated themselves and have not been assimilated. They have sneered at and have tried to undermine the Christian religion upon which that nation was founded by objecting to its restrictions; have built up a State within a State and have, when opposed, tried to strangle the country financially...

"If you do not exclude them from the United States in the Constitution, in less than 200 years they will have swarmed in, in such numbers that they will dominate and devour the land and change our form of government. If you do not exclude them, in less than 200 years our descendants will be working in the fields to furnish them substance, while they will be in the counting houses, rubbing their hands. I warn you gentlemen, if you do not exclude the Jews for all time, your children will curse you in your graves."

George Washington supported Franklin:

"The Jews work more effectively against us than any of the enemy's armies. They are a hundred times more dangerous to our liberties and the great cause we are engaged in. It is much to be lamented that each State long ago has not hunted them down as pests to society and the greatest enemies we have to happiness in America." (Maxims of George Washington by A. Appleton p 125-126)

There must have been a very good reason why the founding fathers of the United States of America should hold such extreme opinions against the people of my blood when the vast majority of Jews are good and hardworking and include gifted, free thinking, enlightened and highly spiritual individuals who have made enormous contributions to the arts and sciences. It would seem their religious leaders hold the key to this paradox.

In 1869, Rabbi Reichhorn, made the following

proclamation over the grave of Grand Rabbi Simeon-ben-Ihuda in Prague. The pronouncement was published in 'La Vieille' France, March 10, 1921 (No. 214):

*'Every hundred years, we, the Sages of Israel, have been accustomed to meet in Sanhedrin in order to examine our progress towards the domination of the world which Jehovah has promised us, and our conquests over the Goyim enemy. (The word **Goy**-and its plural **Goyim** — is synonymous with **Gentile**. In Hebrew, goyim means cattle.):*

This year, united over the tomb of our reverend Simeon-ben-Ihuda, we can state with pride that the past century has brought us very near to our goal, and that this goal will be very soon attained.

Gold always has been and always will be the irresistible power. Handled by expert hands it will always be the most useful lever for those who possess it, and the object of envy for those who do not. With gold we can buy the most rebellious consciences, can fix the rate of all values, the current price of all products, can subsidise all State loans, and thereafter hold the states at our mercy.

Already the principle banks, the exchanges of the entire world, the credits of all governments, are in our hands.

The other great power is the Press. By repeating without cessation certain ideas, the Press succeeds in the end in having them accepted as actualities. The Theatre renders us analogous services. Everywhere the Press and the Theatre [media] obey our orders.

By the ceaseless praise of democratic rule we shall divide the Christians into political parties, we shall destroy the unity of their nations, we shall sow discord everywhere. Reduced to impotence, they will bow before the law of our

Banks, always united and always devoted to our cause.

We shall force the Christians into wars by exploiting their pride and their stupidity. They will massacre each other and clear the ground for us to put our own people into.

The possession of the land has always brought influence and power. In the name of social justice and equality we shall parcel out the great estates; we shall give fragments to the peasants who covet them with all their powers, and who will soon be in debt to us by the expense of cultivating them. Our capital will make us their masters. We in our turn shall become the great proprietors, and the possession of the land will assure the power to us.

Let us try to replace the circulation of gold with paper money; our chests will absorb the gold and we shall regulate the value of the paper, which will make us masters of all the positions.

We count among us plenty of orators capable of feigning enthusiasm and of persuading mobs. We shall spread them among the people to announce changes, which should se-cure the happiness of the human race. By gold and by flat-tery we shall gain the proletariat which will charge itself with annihilating Christian's capitalism. We shall prom-ise workmen salaries of which they have never dared to dream but we shall also raise the price of necessities so that our profits will be greater still. In this manner we shall prepare revolutions which the Christians will make them-selves and of which we shall reap the fruit.

By our mockeries and our attacks upon them we shall make their Christian priests ridiculous then odious and their Christian religion as ridiculous and as odious as their clergy. Then we shall be masters of their souls; for our pious attachment to our own religion and the superiority of our souls.

We have already established our own men in all-important positions. We must endeavour to provide the Goyim with lawyers and doctors; the lawyers are au courant with all interests; doctors, once in the house, become confessors and directors of consciences.

But above all let us monopolise education. By this means we can spread ideas that are useful to us, and shape the children's brains as suits us.

If one of our people should unhappily fall into the hands of justice amongst the Christians, we must rush to help him; find as many witnesses as he needs to save him from his judges, until we become judges ourselves.

The monarchs of the Christian world, swollen with ambition and vanity, surround themselves with luxury and with numerous armies. We shall furnish them with all the money their folly demands, and so shall keep them in leach.

Let us take care not to hinder the marriage of our men with Christian girls, for through them we shall get our foot into the most closely locked circles. If our daughters marry Goyim they will be no less useful, for the children of a Jewish mother are ours.

Let us foster the idea of free love that we may destroy among Christian women attachment to the principles and practices of their religion.

For ages past the sons of Israel, despised and persecuted, have been working to open up a path to power. They are hitting the mark. They control the economic life of the accursed Christians; their influence preponderates over politics and over manners.

At the wished for hour, fixed in advance, we shall let loose the revolution, which ruining all classes of Christianity, will definitely enslave the Christians to us. Thus will be accomplished the promise of God made to his people.

This sentiment is not that of the majority of Jewish people. Most would be appalled by these intentions. This is the expressed intent of a caucus of their leaders. This caucus is linked to 'the Learned Elders' and its operation can be traced through secret societies, which are infiltrated and then steered to further its own ends. The steering group behind the secret societies is **The Brotherhood of the Snake,**which goes back, 2,600 years ago, to the time of the exile of the Hebrews in Babylon. The title 'Brotherhood of the Snake' also suggests a link with the serpent gods of old. In modern times there is a secret brotherhood known as the **Illuminati**. This title means 'the illumined ones'. The Illuminati could be an operational front for the Elders because the following document reveals the agenda of the Illuminati to be identical to that of the 'Sages of Israel' as expressed by Rabbi Reichhorn.

In 1875 a courier riding between Frankfurt and Paris was struck by lightning. He was carrying a message from the Bavarian Illuminati - founded in 1770 by Adam Weishaupt, a student of the Jewish philosopher Mendelssohn and funded by the Jewish banking family of Rothschild. This tract has come to be known as *The New Testament of Satan,*('Secret Societies' p.110-112):

...the first secret of guiding people is the control of public opinion by sowing discord, doubt and contradictory views until people can no longer find their way in the confusion and are convinced that it is better not to have a personal opinion in national law. Passions have to be fanned in the people and inane, dirty and abhorrent writings produced. It is further the task of the press to show up the inability of

the non-illumined in all matters of state and religious life.

The second secret is to carry the weaknesses of the people, all the bad habits, passions and mistakes to extremes until they no longer understand each other.

The power of the personality has to be fought, as there is nothing more dangerous. If it is endowed with creative spiritual forces, it can effect more than millions of people.

All peoples shall be worn down with envy, hatred, quarrels and wars, by deprivation, hunger and the spreading of epidemics until they shall see no other solution than to submit completely to the rule of the Illuminati.

If a State is exhausted by inner radical changes or because of civil wars or has fallen under the control of external enemies then it is definitely doomed and so is in our power.

People will get used to take illusion at face value, to be content with superficialities, to chase only after pleasure, to exhaust themselves in their external obsession with what's new and finally to follow the Illuminati which will be ascertained by paying the masses well for their obedience and their attention.

Through the demoralisation of society will people lose their faith in God.

By working specifically with the spoken and the written word, the masses shall be led according to the wishes of the Illuminati.

With visual instructions the people have to be stopped from thinking for themselves and made to use any existing mental powers for the shadow-boxing of hollow rhetoric. The liberal thoughts of the parties shall be flogged to death by Illuminati orators until people tire and begin to abhor speakers of any movement. On the other hand shall the political science of the Illuminati be constantly fed to the *people so they have no time to think.*

The masses are blind, irrational and lack judgment and therefore may not partake in the statesmanship but have to be governed with just yet inexorable severity and absolute force.

World rule can only be achieved in a roundabout way, by the purposeful undermining of the cornerstones of true liberty of justice, the election system, the press, of personal freedom and above all of education and the culture of the people and under the strictest secrecy for all activities.

In the purposeful undermining of the cornerstones of State power, the governments have to be tormented until they are ready to sacrifice all their power for the sake of peace.

In Europe the differences between peoples have to be stirred up to create an insurmountable rift and no Christian State finds support because every other State has to fear that an alliance against the Illuminati was disadvantageous.

On all continents, discord, unrest and hostility shall be sown to frighten the States and to break all resistance.

All State institutions have to fulfil important tasks within the State so that by damaging such an institution the whole State machinery will be ground to a halt.

The State presidents shall be chosen from those slavishly devoted to the Illuminati, a dark spot in whose past makes them faithful executors of the Illuminati's directives. Thus the Illuminati will be enabled to reinterpret laws and to change constitutions.

By giving the president the right to proclaim a state of war the whole armed forces will be in the hands of the Illuminati.

The 'uninitiated rulers' shall be diverted from thorough

preoccupation with State matters by courteous reception and representation duties.

By the corruptibility of the highest public servants the governments shall be put in debt to the Illuminati by foreign loans so that State debts will appreciably be augmented.

Economic crisis caused by suddenly withdrawing all available moneys from the market shall bring about the downfall of the money economies of the 'non-illuminated'.

The financial power must attain sole control of commerce and trade so that because of their money the industrialists gain political power. Next to the Illuminati and the millionaires dependent on them, the police and the military, there shall be only people without possessions.

The introduction of the general and equal right to vote shall create the majority rule. By instilling the idea of self-determination, the meaning of family life and its educational values shall be destroyed. By education based on false tenets and mendacious teachings, the youth shall be stultified, seduced and depraved.

Links to existing and the founding of new Freemason lodges attain the envisaged goal by way of diverting organisations. Nobody knows them or their aims, least of all the oxen of non-illuminated that were enticed to participate in the open Masonic lodges, to have dust thrown in their eyes.

All these means shall force the peoples to offer world rule to the Illuminati. The new world government has to appear as patron and benefactor of those submitting themselves voluntarily. Should a State oppose this, its neighbours have to be driven to war against it. If the neighbour States want to ally themselves, a world war has to be unleashed.

This extraordinary tract clearly predicted the unfolding events of the 20th Century with alarming accuracy. Its similarity to the controversial **Protocols of the Learned Elders of Zion** suggests both originate from the same source. The similarity between the **Testament of Satan** and the Protocols also speaks against the latter being a fabrication, as many have assumed.

Another similar document makes it clear who have been behind the attempts to establish world dominion through Communism. The tone is similar to the previous documents and suggests a common source. The Rabbi Reichhorn proclamation reveals this source as the Sanhedrin. The following document confirms this supposition. It was discovered in the pocket of a Jew called Zunder — a member of the Bolshevik revolution in Russia. It was subsequently smuggled into Germany where it appeared on the 5th February 1920, in the Russian newspaper, *Prizyv,* published in Berlin. It was written in Hebrew and dated 1919:

Secret: To the representatives of all branches of the Israelite International League.

Sons of Israel! The hour of our ultimate victory is near. We stand on the threshold to the command of the world. That which we could only dream of before us is about to be realised. Only quite recently feeble and powerless, we can now, thanks to the world's catastrophe, raise our heads with pride.

We must, however, be careful. It can surely be prophesied that, after we have marched over ruined and broken alters and thrones, we shall advance further on the same indicated path.

The authority of the, to us, alien religious doctrines of faith we have, through very successful propaganda, subjected to a merciless criticism and mockery. We have brought the culture, civilisation, traditions and thrones of the Christian nations to stagger. We have done everything to bring the Russian people under the yoke of the Jewish power, and ultimately compelled them to fall on their knees before us.

We have nearly completed all this but we must all the same be very cautious, because the oppressed Russia is our archenemy. The victory over Russia, gained through our intellectual superiority, may in future, in a new generation turn against us.

Russia is conquered and brought to the ground. Russia is in the agony of death under our heel, but do not forget not even for a moment that we must be careful! The holy care for our safety does not allow us to show either pity or mercy. At last we have been allowed to behold the bitter need of the Russian people, and to see it in tears! By taking from them their property, their gold, we have reduced this people to helpless slaves.

Be cautious and silent! We ought to have no mercy for our enemy. We must make an end of the best and leading elements of the Russian people, so that the vanquished Russia may not find any leader! Thereby every possibility will vanquish for them to resist our power. We must excite hatred and disputes between workers and peasants. War and class struggle will destroy all treasures and culture created by the Christian people. But be cautious, sons of Israel! Our victory is near, because our political and economic power and influence upon the masses are in rapid progress. We buy up government loans and gold, and thereby we have controlling power over the world's exchanges. The power is in our hands, but be careful place no faith in traitorous shady powers!

Bronstein (Trotsky), Apfelbaum (Zinovieff), Rosenfeld (Kameneff), Steinberg all of them are like unto thousands of other true sons of Israel. Our power in Russia is unlimited. In the towns, the Commissariats and Commissions of Food, House Commissions, etc. are dominated by our people. But do not let victory intoxicate you. Be careful, cautious, because no one except yourselves will protect us!

Remember we cannot rely on the Red Army, which one day may turn its warfare on ourselves. Sons of Israel, the hour of our long-cherished victory over Russia is near; close up solid your ranks! Make known our people's national policy! Fight for eternal ideals! Keep holy the old Laws, which history has bequeathed to us! May our intellect, our genius, protect and lead us!

The document was signed in the name of 'The Central Committee of the Petersburg Branch of the Israelite International League.'

The values in the old Law are reflected in the prayer **Kol Nidre,**dating back to the pre-Christian era. It is repeated on the night of Yom Kippur:

All vows, obligations, oaths or anathemas, pledges of all names, which we have vowed, sworn, devoted or bound ourselves to, from this day of atonement, until the next day of atonement whose arrival we hope for in happiness we repent aforehand, of them all, they shall be deemed absolved, forgiven, annulled, void and made of no effect; they shall not be binding, nor have any power; the vows shall not be reckoned vows, the obligations shall not be obligatory, nor the oaths considered as oaths.

The Kol Nidre is found in the **Talmud**:

The Jewish nation is the only nation selected by Jehovah while all the remaining ones are contemptible and hateful. All property of other nations belongs to the Jewish nation, which consequently is entitled to seize upon it without any scruples. An orthodox Jew is not bound to observe principles of morality towards peoples of other nations and on the contrary, he even ought to act against morality if it were profitable for himself or for the interests of the Jews in general. A Jew may rob a goy, he may cheat him over a bill, which should not be perceived by him, otherwise the name of Jehovah would become dishonoured.(Schulchan Aruch, Choszen Hamiszpat, p.348.)

Orthodox Rabbis follow the doctrine of faith declared in the Talmud. The importance of the Talmud to the Jewish nation is summarised in an edition of the Encyclopaedia Britannica:

'It must be admitted by every critical student of history that the Talmud has not merely been the means of keeping alive the religious idea among the Jews, but has formed their strongest bond of union'.

Jehovah is clearly unmasked in the Talmud. According to the Rabbis, the Talmud is inspired by Jehovah. In the words of Rabbi Menachen, in his comments for the fifth book:

"The decisions of the Talmud are words of the living God. Jehovah himself asks the opinion of earthly rabbis when there are difficult affairs in heaven!"

The Talmud teaches:

The life of a goi and all of his powers belong to a Jew. (A.Rohl. Dei Polem. p. 20)

Jews commit no sin, and do not profane the name of God when they lie to the goyim. (Babha Kama 113b)

Jews may lie and commit perjury to convict a goy. (Babha Kama 113a, Kallah 1b)

Jews who do good to the goyim do not go to heaven (Zohar 1:25b)

Jews should always try to deceive the goyim (Zohar 1:160a)

The estates of the goyim are like wilderness, who first settles in them has a right to them. (Baba Batra, 14b)

The property of the goyim are like a thing without a master. (Schulchan Aruch, Choszen Hamiszpat,p. 116,5)

If a Jew has struck his spade into the ground of the Goyim, he has become a master of the whole. (Baba Batra, 55a)

If a Jew feels compelled to do a great evil he should go into another land where he is not known and do it there (Moed Kattan 17a)

On the house of the goyim one looks as on the fold of cattle (Tosefta Erubin VII:1)

You are human beings but the nations of the world are not human beings, but beasts (Baba Mecla 114:6)

An Israelite is allowed to do injury to a goy because where it is written, 'Thou shalt not do injury to thy neighbour,' it is not said, 'Thou shalt not do injury to a goy.' (Mishna, Sanhedrin, 57)

They (Christians) are idolaters, the worst kind of people, much worse than the Turks (Muslims), murderers, fornicators, impure animals like dirt, unworthy to be called men, beasts in human form, worthy of the name of beasts, cows, asses, pigs, dogs, worse than dogs; that they propagate after the manner of beasts, that they have a diabolic origin, that their soul came from the devil and will return to the devil in hell after death; and even the body of a dead Christian is nothing different from that of an animal. (The Talmud Unmasked p.46)

Jesus died like a beast and was buried in that dirt heap where they throw the dead bodies of dogs and asses and where the sons of Esau (Christians) and of Ishmael (Muslims), also Jesus and Mohammed, uncircumcised and unclean like dead dogs are buried. (The Book of Zohar, III, 282)

It is important to note here that as much anti-Jewish rhetoric has been written by Christians against Jews as Jews against Christians. The purpose of repeating this material here is not to point the finger at any one religious group but to further the argument that the leader of the Judaic cults, the entity called by they and the Christians 'God' has led them to believe that they are a race superior to any other and have a right to dominion over all the earth and subjugation of all other races as cattle. It is also worth noting the reference to people as 'cattle'. This is reminiscent to the attitude of Enlil to human beings. Could it be that he has maintained an extra-terrestrial influence on his race even to this day?

The Talmud — withheld from the girls — is used by Rabbis to indoctrinate orthodox Jewish boys. It is preparing them, as the Chosen People of 'God', to be masters of the Earth:

Jehovah created them (Jews) in the form of men for the glory of Israel. But Akum (Christians) were created for the sole end of ministering unto them day and night. Nor can they ever be relieved of this service. It is becoming to the son of a king (an Israelite) that animals in their natural form and animals in the form of human beings should minister unto him. (Midrasch Talpoith, fol 225d.)

If a Jew kills a goy it is not a sin (Sepher Or Israel 177b, Makkoth 7b)

Even the best of the goyim should be killed(Abhodah Zarah 26b)

A goy is forbidden to steal, rob or take women slaves from a goy or a Jew but he (a Jew) is not forbidden to do all this to a goy. And if a goy kill a goy or a Jew he is responsible but if a Jew kill a goy he is not responsible.(Tosefta, Aboda Zara, VIII,5)

When a grown man has intercourse with a little girl it is nothing, for when the girl is less than three years old it is as if one puts a finger into the eye, tears come into the eye, again and again, and so does the virginity come back to the little girl. (Kethaboth 11a-11b)

Pederasty with a child below nine years of age is not deemed as pederasty with a child above that...Rab makes nine years the minimum; but if one committed sodomy with a child of lesser age, no guilt is incurred. Samuel makes three the minimum (Sanhedrin 55a - 55b)

Understandably Rabbis do not like 'outsiders' reading the Talmud:

It is forbidden to disclose the secrets of the Law. One should and must make false oath, when the goyim ask if our books contain anything against them. Then we are bound to state on oath that there is nothing like that. (Szaalot-Utsabot. The book of Jore d'a,17)

Jews should conceal their hatred for the goyim (Iore Dea 148:12h)

Every goy who studies Talmud and every Jew who helps him in it ought to die. (Sanhedryn 59a Aboda Zora 8-6: Szagiga 13)

Martin Luther, who led the Protestant Reformation, spoke out as strongly against the Jewish Talmud as the Catholic Papacy:

"Do not their Talmud and Rabbis write that it is no sin to kill if a Jew kills a heathen, but it is a sin if he kills a brother in Israel? It is no sin if he does not keep his oath to a heathen. Therefore, to steal and rob (as they do with their money lending) from a heathen, is a divine service...And they are masters of the world and we are their servants - yea, their cattle! I maintain that in the three fables of Aesop there is more wisdom to be found than in all the books of the Talmudists and Rabbis and more than ever could come from the hearts of the Jews...Should someone think I am saying too much — I am saying much too little! For I see in their writings they curse us Goyim and wish us all evil in their schools and prayers. They rob us of our money, through usury, and wherever they are able, they play us all manner of mean tricks."

The dilemma the Jewish race is in because of its religious indoctrination is embodied in a truly noble letter written by Dr. Oscar Levy, a leading humanitarian Jew, to George Pitt Rivers of Worcester College, Oxford. It was published as a preface to Pitt River's book *The World Significance of the Russian Revolution* and reprinted in Henry Ford's Dearborn Independent, on April 30, 1921:

...There is no race in the world more enigmatic, more fatal, and therefore more interesting than the Jews.

Every writer, who, like yourself, is oppressed by the aspect of the present and embarrassed by his anxiety for the future, must try to elucidate the Jewish Question and its bearing on our Age.

For the question of the Jews and their influence on the world past and present, cuts to the root of all things, and should be discussed by every honest thinker, however bristling with difficulties it is, however complex the subject as well as the individuals of this race may be.

For the Jews, as you are aware, are a sensitive community and thus are very suspicious of any Gentile who tries to approach them with a critical mind. They are always inclined and that on account of their terrible experiences to denounce anyone who is not with them as against them, as tainted with 'medieval' prejudice, as an intolerant antagonist of their faith and of their race.

...You point out, and with fine indignation the great danger that springs from the prevalence of Jews in finance and industry and from the prevalence of Jews in rebellion and revolution. You reveal, and with great fervour, the connection between the collectivism of the immensely rich international finance and the international collectivism of Karl Marx and Trotsky...and all this evil and misery, the economic as well as the political, you trace back to one source, to one 'fons et origo malorum' the Jews.

Now other Jews may vilify and crucify you for these outspoken views of yours; I myself shall abstain from joining the chorus of condemnation! I shall try to understand your opinions and your feelings, and having once understood them as I think I have I can defend you from the unjust attacks of my often too impetuous race. But first of all I have to say this: There is scarcely an event in modern Europe that cannot be traced back to the Jews. Take the Great War that appears to have come to an end, ask yourself what were its causes and its reasons: you will find them in nationalism. You will at once answer that nationalism has nothing to do with the Jews, who, as you have just proved to us, are the inventors of the international idea. But no less than Bolshevist ecstasy and financial tyranny can national bigotry (if I may call it so) be finally followed back to a Jewish source. Are not they the inventors of the 'Chosen People' myth, and is not this obsession part and parcel of the political credo of every modern nation, however small and insignificant it may be? It started in our time and as a reaction against Napoleon; Napoleon was the antagonist of the French Revolution; the French Revolution was the consequence of the German Reformation; the German Reformation was based upon a crude Christianity; this kind of Christianity was invented, preached and propagated by the Jews; therefore, the Jews have made this war!... all latter-day ideas and movements have originally sprung from a Jewish source, for the simple reason, that the Semitic idea has finally conquered and entirely subdued this only apparently irreligious universe of ours.

There is no doubt that the Jews regularly go one better or worse than the Gentile in whatever they do, there is no further doubt that their influence today justifies a very careful scrutiny and cannot possibly be viewed without serious alarm...There is an anti-Semitism, I hope and trust, which does the Jews more justice than any blind philo — Semitism... you can be just to the Jews without being 'romantic' about them.

You have noticed with alarm that the Jewish elements provide the driving forces for both communism and capitalism, for the material as well as the spiritual ruin of this world.

...your anti-Semitism is only too well justified, and upon this common ground I am quite willing to shake hands with you and defend you against any accusation of *promoting race hatred: If you are anti-Semite, I the Semite am anti-Semite too, and a much more fervent one than even you are. We (the Jews) have erred, my friend, we have most grievously erred. And if there was truth in our error 3,000, 2,000, nay 100 years ago, there is now nothing but falseness and madness, a madness that will produce an even greater misery and an even wider anarchy. I confess it to you, openly and sincerely, and with a sorrow whose depth and pain an ancient Psalmist, and only he, could moan into this burning universe of ours...We who have posed as the saviours of this world, we who have even boasted of having given it 'the' Saviour, we are today nothing else but the world's seducers, its destroyers, its incendiaries, its executioners. We who have promised to lead you to a new Heaven, we have finally succeeded in landing you into a new Hell...There has been no progress, least of all moral progress...and it is just our morality which has prohibited all real progress and what is worse which even stands in the way of every future and natural reconstruction in this ruined world of ours... I look at this world and I shudder at its ghastliness; I shudder all the more as I know the spiritual authors of all this ghastliness.*

...And yet we are not all financiers, we are not all Bolshevists, we are not all become Zionists. And yet there is hope, great hope, that this same race, which has provided the evil will likewise succeed in supplying its antidote, its remedy the good.

...A new good as new love, a true love that calms and heals and sweetens, will then spring up among the great in Israel and overcome that sickly love, that insipid love, that romantic love which has hitherto poisoned all the strength and nobility of this world. For hatred is never overcome by hatred: It is only overcome by love, and it wants a new and

a gigantic love to subdue that old and devilish hatred of today. That is our task for the future a task which will, I am sure, not be shirked by Israel, by that same Israel which has never shirked a task, whether it was for good or whether it was for evil...

Yes, there is hope, my friend, for we are still here, our last word is not yet spoken, our last deed is not yet done, and our last revolution is not yet made. This last revolution, the revolution that will crown our revolutionaries, will be a revolution against the revolutionaries. It is bound to come, and it is perhaps upon us now. The great day of reckoning is near. It will pass a judgment on our ancient faith, and it will lay the foundations to a new religion. And when the great day has broken, when the values of death and decay are put into the melting pot to be changed into those of power and beauty, then you, my dear Pitt-Rivers, the descendant of an old and distinguished Gentile family, may be assured to find by your side, and as your faithful ally, at least one member of that Jewish race, which has fought with such fatal success upon all the spiritual battlefields of Europe.

Yours against the revolution and for Life ever flourishing, Oscar Levy. (Oscar Levy, Royal Societies Club, St. James Street, London, July 1920).

It is important to emphasise again that the vast majority of Jewish people are unaware of the manipulations of a core group of rich and influential members of their race. Every race has a ruling elite that exploits the populous. Almost every race of man, given the opportunity, will attempt to dominate and exploit other races and gain dominion of the Earth. History is littered with empires. My concern in this book is not to judge the Jews but to take a critical look at the influence of the Jewish 'God', Jehovah and his eugenics in modern history:

> *'The international Jew rules not because he is rich but because in a most marked degree he possesses the commercial and masterful genius of his race, and avails himself of a racial loyalty and solidarity the like of which exists in no other human group. In other words, transfer today the world-control of the international Jew to the hands of the highest commercially-talented group of gentiles and the whole fabric of world control would eventually fall to pieces, because the Gentile lacks a certain quality, be it human or divine, be it natural or acquired, that the Jew possesses.'* (Dearborn Independent, June 12 ,1920)

Chapter 8

The Protocols

"The only statement I care to make about the Protocols is they fit in with what is going on."

(Henry Ford)

Arguably the most disturbing document to surface in modern times is **The Protocols of the Learned Elders of Zion**.

'Whosoever was the mind that conceived them possessed a knowledge of human nature, of history and of statecraft which is dazzling in its brilliant completeness, and terrible in the objects to which it turns its powers. Neither a madman nor an international criminal, but more likely a supermind mastered by devotion to a people and a faith could be the author, if indeed one mind alone conceived them. It is too terribly real for fiction, too well sustained for speculation, too deep in its knowledge of the secret springs of life for forgery.'

(Dearborn Independent, July 10, 1920)

It is hard to believe **The Protocols of the Learned Elders of Zion** are true. For the most part they have been denounced as fiction, fabrication and fraud as a deliberate attempt to incite anti-Semitism. They have been effective at that, whatever their origin. I do not want to re-ignite anti-Jewish passion and do not discount the possibility of fabrication. My arguments would stand without them, nonetheless, whether true or false, The Protocols do exist and my work would be incomplete without them. Were it not for the existence of the 'Testament of Satan' and 'The Rabbi Reichhorn proclamation' I would dismiss them as the work of a madman but the same message in the three unrelated documents does suggest to me that they are not fraudulent but a reflection of the dark side of 'God' through his agents amongst the Chosen People.

The Protocols have been attributed to a friend of Victor Hugo called Maurice Joly. He is alleged to have composed them in 1864 as a satirical attack on Napolean III. I find it hard to believe that a single individual would have the capacity to fabricate a document such as The Protocols of Zion let alone for the sake of satire.

Many people believe The Protocols to be authentic. One such person was Henry Ford. When he remarked the Protocols fit in with what is going on - in an interview published in the 'New York World of February 17th, 1921 - Henry Ford said it all.

Whether they are true or false the twentieth century unfolded in line with the content of The Protocols of the Learned Elders of Zion. You will find this self-evident when you read them. If they are not a fabrication there is a possibility they may have been the work of a non-Jewish clandestine fraternity and have been attributed to the Jews to foment anti-Semitism but it is also possible that The Protocols may have leaked from a meeting of the Sanhedrin, held somewhere in Europe in the nineteenth century. The Rabbi Reichhorn proclamation of 1869 was clearly a summary of that meeting so it must have occurred before that date. When you read his proclamation alongside The Protocols, they are saying virtually the same thing but in more detail.

Whatever or whenever their origins, The Protocols

laid out plans for manipulating world affairs in the 20th Century and they first appeared in France in 1884 when Justine Glinka, the daughter of a Russian General, acting as a Russian spy, purchased them for 2,500 francs, from a Jew by the name of Joseph Schorst. He paid for his act of espionage with his life. According to the French police, Schorst fled to Egypt where he was murdered. Glinka passed The Protocols on to General Cherevin, secretary to the Minister of the Interior for transmission to the Czar. Cherevin, being under obligation to wealthy Jews, failed to do so. On his death in 1896, The Protocols were consigned in his will to Czar Nicholas II. Meanwhile, Justina Glinka had fallen into disfavour with the Czar on another matter and was banished to her estate in Orel. She passed a copy to Alexis Sukhotin the Maréchal de Noblesse of her district. He showed the documents to two of his friends, Stepanov and Professor Sergyei A. Nilus. Stepanov printed them in French for distribution to his own circle of contacts. Nilus published them in Russian (Tsarskoe-Tselo), in 1901, in his book *The Great Within the Small* and a copy of this Russian version was deposited in the British Museum on August 10th 1906, by Butmi, a friend of Nilus.

After the Russian revolution the Nilus edition in Russia was destroyed and Nilus was imprisoned and tortured. A Russian refugee, Victor Marsden, Russian correspondent to the *London Morning Post*, translated The Protocols into English. He used as his source the book in the British Museum. The following extracts are taken from the 1934, Marsden translation.

Whilst the origin of The Protocols of Zion is shrouded in mystery, in 1897 a Jewish member of the Russian police by the name of Efrom, released a copy of a secret document entitled, the *Proceedings of the Basle Congress,* a Judaic conference held in Basle, Switzerland in 1897 which corresponded very closely to The Protocols of Zion. Again these were destroyed after the Russian Revolution but Efrom (formerly a Rabbi, who died in 1925 in a monastery in Serbia where he had taken refuge) told the monks that the *Proceedings of the Basle Congress* were but a small part of the Jewish plans for ruling the world and were but a feeble expression of their hatred for the Gentiles.

The Protocols of Zion, exhort the use of violence, treachery and deceit in order to gain sovereignty over all governments and peoples of the Earth:

> **Violence must be the principle, and cunning and make-believe the rule for governments...This evil is the one and only means to attain the end, the good. Therefore we must not stop at bribery, deceit and treachery when they should serve towards the attainment of our end. In politics one must know how to seize the property of others without hesitation if by it we secure submission and sovereignty.**
> (Protocol 1)

The Elders have been at their Great Work of Ages for millennia. As the leaders of God's Chosen People they have, for many centuries, sown discord amongst all the nations of the Earth:

> **For a time, perhaps, we might be successfully dealt with by a coalition of the Goyim of all the world: but from this danger we are secured by the discord existing among them whose roots are so deeply seated that they can never now be plucked up. We have set one against the other, the personal and national reckonings of the Goyim, religious and race**

hatreds, which we have fostered into a huge growth in the course of the past twenty centuries. This is the reason why there is not one State which would anywhere receive support if it were to raise its arm, for every one would be unprofitable to itself. We are too strong there is no evading our power. The nations cannot come to even an inconsiderable private agreement without our secretly having a hand in it. (Protocol 5.)

There would seem to be no limit to what the Learned Elders of Zion are prepared to do to attain world dominion:

For us there are no checks to limit the range of our activity. Our super-government subsists in extra-legal conditions which are described in the accepted terminology by the energetic and forcible word dictatorship. (Protocol 1.)

Are the originators of this document in control of the world today? Are they the clandestine secret government we hear about in 'Conspiracy Theories'? Are they theories or discredited facts? Is the world ruled by the Sanhedrin? Does it operate through organisations such as the US *Council on Foreign Relations*, the UK *Royal Institute for International Relations*, the *Bilderberg* group and the *Trilateral Commission*, which is currently steering the nations of the Earth toward a *New World Order*? If this is so these secret masters are utterly ruthless:

...we, the lawgivers shall slay and we shall spare...we rule by force of will...and the weapons in our hands are limitless ambition, burning greediness, merciless vengeance, hatreds and malice. (Protocol 9)

This attitude can be traced back to Moses:

"And when the Lord your God delivers them over to you, you shall conquer them and utterly destroy them. You shall make no covenant with them nor show mercy to them." (Deuteronomy 7:2)

The Lord of the Old Testament is clearly on the side of his chosen people and not the Gentiles, even though countless Gentiles worship him in their churches, and follow his word in their Bibles. Through Moses, Jehovah encouraged the Jews to maintain themselves as a race apart:

"Nor shall you make marriages with them. You shall not give your daughter to their son, nor take their daughter for your son." (Deuteronomy 7:3)

Today, this policy is called **apartheid.** There is a mandate for apartheid in the Talmud as well as the Bible:

If a Jew enters into marriage with an Akum (Christian), or with his servant, the marriage is null. For they are not capable of entering into matrimony. Likewise, if an Akum or a servant enter into marriage with a Jew, the marriage is null. (Eben Haezer 44:8)

Whilst a Jew sees himself as a Jew, a Gentile does not perceive himself as Gentile:

'Gentiles never think of themselves as Gentiles, and never feel that they owe anything to another Gentile as such. Thus they have been convenient agents of Jewish schemes at times and in places when it was not expedient that the Jewish controllers should be publicly known, but they have never been successful competitors of the Jew in the field of world-control'. (Dearborn Independent, June 12 ,1920)

The Jehovah's conspirators are united whereas the Christians are not, and it would seem that Gentile disunity has been fully exploited:

Throughout all Europe, and by means of relations with Europe, in other continents also, we must create ferments, discords and hostility. (Protocol 7)

Consider the discord and strife, wars and revolutions in recent centuries. When King Louis XVI of France heard of the storming of the Bastile, and expressed the hope that it was a mere revolt, the Duc de la Rochefoucauld-Liancourt replied, "No sire, it's a great revolution":

Remember the French Revolution, to which it was we who gave the name of 'Great': the secrets of its preparation are well known to us, for it was wholly the work of our hands. (Protocol 3)

In the 'Ritual and Illustrations of Freemasonry' (1924), Nesta Webster wrote:

The Masons... originated the Revolution with the infamous Duke of Orleans at their head ...If then it is said that the Revolution was prepared in the lodges of Freemasons – and many French Masons have boasted of the fact – let it be always added that it was Illuminized Freemasonry that made the Revolution, and that the Masons who acclaim it are Illuminized Masons, inheritors of the same tradition introduced into the lodges of France in 1787 by the disciples of Weishaupt..."

Many conspiracy authors link the French Revolution to the Bavarian Illuminati, which infiltrated the French Masonic Lodges prior to the Great Revolution

In *Rule by Secrecy* (2000), Jim Marrs wrote:

Giuseppe Balsamo, a student of the Jewish Cabala, a Freemason, and a Rosicrucian, became known as Louis XIV's court magician Cagliostro. He wrote how the German Illuminati had infiltrated the French Freemason lodges for years and added, "By March 1789, the 266

lodges controlled by the Grand Orient were all 'illuminized' without knowing it…"

Earlier Marrs had written:

It was the Duke of Orleans, grand master of the Grand Orient Lodge of Freemasons, who reportedly bought all the grain in 1789 and either sold it abroad or hid it away, thus creating near starvation among the commoners. Galart de Montjoie, a contemporary, blamed the Revolution almost solely on the Duke of Orleans, adding that he "was moved by that invisible hand which seems to have created all the events of our revolution in order to lead us towards a goal that we do not see at present…"

The question is who was the unseen hand guiding the Duke of Orleans and through him the Grand Orient Lodge? Was it the Illuminati or were the Illuminati a front organisation guided by the same hand? To quote Jim Marrs:

Although Illuminati concepts can be traced back through history to the earliest sects claiming esoteric knowledge, the order was first publicly identified in 1776. On May 1 of that year – a day long honoured by communists who some believe formed their philosophy based on the Illuminati doctrine – the Bavarian Illuminati was formed by Adam Weishaupt, a professor of Canon Law at Ingolstadt University of Bavaria, Germany.

One of his cofounders reportedly was William of Hesse, the employer of Mayer Rothschilds…Rothschild biographer Niall Ferguson wrote that Mayer's son Salomon was a member of the same Masonic lodge…"

Weishaupt was influenced by his training to be a Jesuit priest. Though he broke from the church he applied Jesuit principles to his order of Illuminati. He was greatly influenced by a mysterious follower of Manichaesim called Kolmer from whence came the name 'Illuminati' or 'Illuminized'. Nesta Webster cites nineteenth-century literature claiming that Moses Mendelssohn, the noted Jewish philosopher, Cabalist and Bible translator was one of the men who inspired and mentored Adam Weishaupt in the formation of the Illuminati. There is no doubt that the Illuminati are a secret society linked by many conspiracy authors to the 'Secret Government' but what were the influences behind the founder of the clandestine Illuminati? Who are they and are they still active today?

The French revolution spawned the communist revolutions. Many revolutionary leaders of the 20th Century were 'harboured' in France. In Paris they were 'schooled' in the revolutionary theories of Karl Marx. Marx was a Jew, as was Lenin who took the revolution to Russia:

Do not suppose for a moment that these statements are empty words: think carefully of the successes we arranged for...Marxism. (Protocol 2)

Under Communism people are reduced to poverty and servitude...

All people are chained down to heavy toil by poverty more firmly than ever they were chained by slavery and serfdom. (Protocol 3)

...but the means were justified by the ends:

Great national qualities, like frankness and honesty, are vices in politics...Our right lies in force...to attack by the right of the strong, and to scatter to the winds all existing forces of order and regulation...The result justifies the means...we cannot deviate without running the risk of seeing the labour of many centuries brought to naught. (Protocol 1)

The call, 'Liberty, Equality and Fraternity' brought hope to the people...

In all corners of the Earth the words 'Liberty, Equality and Fraternity,' brought to our ranks, thanks to our blind agents, whole legions who bore our banners with enthusiasm. And all the time these words were canker-worms at work boring into the well being of the Goyim, putting an end everywhere to peace, quiet, solidarity and destroying all the foundations of the Goya States. (Protocol 1)

...but how long is the liberty to last?:

The word 'freedom'...when we come into our kingdom, we shall have to erase this word from the lexicon of life... (Protocol 3)

In the French and Russian Revolutions, the masses were incited with the cry of 'Liberty, Equality, and Fraternity' to displace monarchy and aristocracy and the system of government they represented.

Far back in ancient times we were the first to cry among the masses of the people the words, 'Liberty, Equality, Fraternity'... this helped us in our triumph; it gave us the... master card the destruction...of the aristocracy of the Goyim, that class which was the only defence peoples and countries had against us. On the ruins of the national and genealogical aristocracy of the Goyim we have set up the aristocracy of our educated class headed by the aristocracy of money. (Protocol 1)

Violent revolutions almost invariably replace governments with tyrannies that are far more terrible:

Our State, marching along the path of peaceful con-

quest, has the right to replace the horrors of war by less noticeable and more satisfactory sentences of death, necessary to maintain the terror which tends to produce blind submission...we must keep to the programme of violence and make-believe...by the doctrine of severity we shall triumph and bring all governments into subjection to our Super-government. It is enough for them to know that we are merciless for all disobedience to cease. (Protocol 1)

In addition to armed conflict and terrorism, throughout the 20th Century, economics has been employed in the war against humanity:

...war will...be brought on to the economic ground...(Protocol 1)

Preoccupied with money, business and the pursuit of material gains people in the 20th Century had little time to reflect:

In order to give the Goyim no time to think and take note, their minds must be diverted towards industry and trade. Thus, all the nations will be swallowed up in the pursuit of gain and in the race for it will not take note of the common foe. (Protocol 4)

Speculation is the key word in business today. It is interesting to note how many industries and national economies been brought to ruin by financial speculation in the 20th Century.

But again, in order that freedom may once and for all disintegrate and ruin the communities of the Goyim, we must put industry on a speculative basis: the result of this will be that what is withdrawn from the land by industry will slip through the hands and pass into speculation, that is, to our classes. (Protocol 4)

It also has to be noted that economics has become the over-riding issue in the life of the individual, the community and the nation:

We shall surround our government with a whole world of economists. That is why economic sciences form the principal subject of the teaching given to the Jews. Around us will be a whole constellation of bankers, industrialists, capitalists and, the main thing, millionaires because in substance everything will be settled in figures. (Protocol 8)

Throughout the 20th Century economic crises have been epidemic. Countries have been brought to their knees by attacks on their currencies. Vast reservoirs of capital have remained untapped whilst prosperous nations have been continually burdened with debt:

Economic crises have been produced by us (amongst) the Goyim by no other means than the withdrawal of money from circulation. Huge capitals have stagnated, withdrawing money from States, which are constantly obliged to apply to those same stagnant capitals for loans. These loans burdened the finances of the State with the payment of interest and made them bond slaves of these capitals... (Protocol 20)

Note the steady erosion of spiritual values:

"But thus shall you deal with them: you shall destroy their altars, and break down their images, and cut down their sacred groves, and burn their carved images with fire.

"For you are a holy people to the Lord your God; the Lord your God has chosen you to be a people for himself, a special treasure above all the peoples on the face of the Earth." (Deuteronomy 7:5-6)

When we come into our Kingdom it will be undesirable for us that there should exist any other religion than ours of the One God with whom our destiny is bound up by our position as the Chosen People and through whom our same destiny is united with the destinies of the world. We must, therefore, sweep away all other forms of belief... (Protocol 14)

As society becomes more secular, especially in institutes of learning, religion has come to be replaced with mathematical science and the importance of material things:

... it is indispensable for us to undermine all faith, to tear out of the minds of the Goyim the very principle of Godhead and the Spirit, and to put in their place arithmetical calculations and material needs. (Protocol 4)

Universities have a major influence on human society today. Governments depend on expert scientific opinion originating from the Universities, which are, in turn, wholly dependant on government:

In order to effect the destruction of all collective forces except ours we shall emasculate the first stage of collectivism the universities by re-educating them in a new direction. Their officials and professors will be prepared for their business by secret programmes of action from which they will not with immunity diverge, not by one iota. They will be appointed with especial precaution, and will be so placed as to be wholly dependent upon the Government. (Protocol 16)

The curricula of schools and universities has come under an increasingly tight rein...

We shall abolish every kind of freedom of instruction. (Protocol 16)

...whilst every kind of crazy theory has been allowed to abound. This was especially true of 20th Century physics:

We have fooled, bemused and corrupted the youth of the Goyim by rearing them in principles and theories which are known to us to be false. It is by us that they have been inculcated. (Protocol 9)

Note how most academics and members of the professions will maintain the 'status quo' in their beliefs and practice, regardless of contrary research findings. Note how peer pressure and 'specialist opinion' keeps them all 'in line'. As soon as the 'popular theories' are threatened experts appear to defend them:

The intellectuals of the Goyim will puff themselves up with their knowledge and without any logical verification of them will put into effect all the information available from science, which our agenteur specialists have cunningly pieced together for the purpose of educating their minds in the direction we want. Do not suppose for a moment that these statements are empty words: think carefully of the successes we arranged for Darwinism, Marxism and Nietzsche-ism. (Protocol 2)

Religions have been under ever increasing attack throughout the 20th Century. Whilst fanaticism abounds and fundamentalist Christian sects that 'preach the Bible' are increasing their numbers, especially amongst the young, numbers in the more moderate churches have steadily declined.

Freedom of conscience has been declared every-

where, so that now only years divide us from the moment of the complete wrecking of that Christian religion, as to other religions we shall have less difficulty in dealing with them. (Protocol 17)

Real values in family life and education were consistently eroded throughout the 20th Century...

...by inculcating in all a sense of self-importance, we shall destroy among the Goyim the importance of family life and its educational value... (Protocol 10)

...whilst alcohol and drug abuse, immorality, cynicism and contradictory opinions became fashionable, especially amongst the young:

The peoples of the Goyim are bemused with alcoholic liquors; their youth has grown stupid on classicism and from early immorality, into which it has been induced by our special agents. (Protocol 1)

Over the centuries the Learned Elders have encouraged revolutions that serve their ends, but destroyed young revolutionaries that oppose them:

When the morning came, all the chief priests and elders of the people took counsel against Jesus to put him to death.(Matthew 27:1)

The Learned Elders are past masters at mobilising mobs:

But the chief priests and elders persuaded the multitude that they should ask for Barabbas, and destroy Jesus.(Matthew 27:20)

...it [the mob] is accustomed to listen to us only who pay it for obedience and attention. In this way we shall create a blind, mighty force which will never be in a position to move in any direction without

the guidance of our agents set at its head, by us, as 'leaders of the mob'. (Protocol 10)

Historically the multitude of Jews have responded to the directives of the Elders whose power depends on their ability to manipulate the people:

Pilate said to them, "What shall I do then with Jesus who is called Christ?" They all replied, "Crucify him." (Matthew 27:22)

Fortunately there have always been freethinking, courageous Jews with the courage to challenge them:

"Woe unto you, Pharisees! for you love the uppermost seats in the synagogues, and greetings in the markets. (Luke 12:42)

Throughout the 20th. century was an ever-increasing burden of laws and litigation:

And he said, "Woe unto you also you lawyers! for you laden men with burdens grievous to be borne, but you yourself won't lift them with one of your fingers." (Luke 11:46)

We have got our hands into the administration of the law...without substantially altering them, by merely twisting them into contradictions of interpretations. (Protocol 9)

And in our over-regulated society it is ever more difficult to keep abreast with the tangled maze of legislation:

...owing to the impossibility of making anything out of the tangled web of legislation. (Protocol 9)

In the media there are so many contradictory opinions, especially in politics that by the turn of the 21st century people, in general, had become disillusioned with politics:

In order to put public opinion into our hands we

must bring it into a state of bewilderment by giving expression from all sides to so much contradictory opinions and for such length of time as will suffice to make the Goyim lose their heads in the labyrinth and come to see that the best thing is to have no opinion of any kind in matters political. (Protocol 5)

Most people don't think things out for themselves. They are happy to accept the opinions of the experts and the specialists:

The Goyim have lost the habit of thinking unless prompted by the suggestions of our specialists. (Protocol 3)

Note how much was done throughout the 20th Century in the name of progress:

Therefore we shall continue to direct their minds to all sorts of vain conceptions of fantastic theories, new and apparently progressive: for have we not with complete success turned the brainless heads of the Goyim with progress...(Protocol 13)

Many people voice current intellectual trends with conviction as if they were their own thoughts. Throughout the 20th Century this was especially true of socialism. Socialist theories gripped the minds of intellectuals worldwide. The enormous popularity of socialism is just one example of how 20th Century public opinion was steered:

No single announcement will reach the public without our control. (Protocol 12)

Experts have expressed their conviction that *The Protocols* were forged by agents of the Czar. Needless to say the Russian Czar posed a threat to the Elders. By means of socialism he was deposed and, along with his entire family, murdered. A Cabalistic inscription on the wall of the room where the Imperial family were slaughtered read:

'Here the king was sacrificed to bring about the destruction of his kingdom, in obedience to superior command.'

Such was, until recent times, the Russian autocracy, the one and only serious foe we had in the world, without counting the Papacy. (Protocol 15)

Through the Reformation the power of the Papacy was greatly diminished. Though Martin Luther preached against the Jews...

"They are the real liars and bloodhounds who have perverted and falsified the entire Scriptures from beginning to end, and without ceasing with their interpretations" (Martin Luther)

... and his reformation served a worthwhile cause in diminishing the power of the Catholic Church, it replaced Catholicism with crude Bible based Christianity, with emphasis on the Old Testament that runs more in line with fundamentalist Judaism than the teaching of Christ.

The German Reformation was based upon a crude Christianity; this kind of Christianity was invented, preached and propagated by the Jews. (Oscar Levy)

The reformation paved the way for the French and communist revolutions which broke the power of many established governments:

'Per Me reges regnant'. (Through me kings reign) (Protocol 5)

Against presidents and popes assassins have been employed...

We have broken the prestige of the Goy kings by frequent attempts upon their lives through our agents. (Protocol 18)

...whilst others received character assassination by the media:

In the hands of the States of today there is a great force that creates the movement of thought in the people, and that is the Press. But the Goyim States have not known how to make use of the force; and it has fallen into our hands. Through the Press we have gained the power to influence while remaining ourselves in the shade. (Protocol 2)

Newspapers and television forge public opinion:

..Literature and journalism are two of the most important educative forces, and therefore our [secret] government will become proprietor of the majority of journals...This however, must in no wise be suspected by the public. For this reason all journals published by us will be the most opposite in appearance, tendencies and opinions...All our newspapers will be of all possible complexions, aristocratic, republican, revolutionary... Like the Indian idol Vishnu, they will have a hundred hands and every one of them will have a finger on any one of the public opinions required.... discussing and controverting, but always superficially, without teaching the essence of the matter, our organs will carry out a sham fight...printing now truth, now lies...Those fools who will think they are repeating the opinion of a newspaper of their own camp will be repeating our opinion or any opinion that seems desirable for us...(Protocol 12)

"I don't think she ever understood why her genuinely good intentions were sneered at by the media. My own explanation is that genuine goodness is threatening to those at the opposite end of the moral spectrum." (Earl Spencer, 6th September 1997)

If we have been able to bring them to such a pitch of stupid blindness is it not a proof, and an amazingly clear proof, of that degree to which the mind of the Goyim is undeveloped in comparison with our mind? That it is, mainly, which guarantees our success. (Protocol 15)

Control of the Press has given economic as well as political clout...

Thanks to the Press the gold is in our hands. (Protocol 2)

Notice how many nations, throughout the 20th Century, were strangled as though in the ever-tightening coils of some unseen snake. Notice also how the Chosen People identify with the serpent:

Today I may tell you that our goal is now only a few steps off. There remains a small space to cross and the whole long path we have trodden is ready now to close its cycle of the symbolic snake, by which we symbolise our people. When this ring closes, all the states of Europe will be locked in its coil as in a powerful vice. (Protocol 3)

"You serpents, you generation of vipers, how can you escape the damnation of hell?" (Matthew 23:33)

Nations were bankrupt in the Great Depression:

A little more...and bankruptcy will be universal. (Protocol 4)

More and more, people feel impotent and note how the education systems sap young people of personal initiative.

We must so direct the education of the Goyim communities that whenever they come upon a matter requiring initiative they may drop their hands in despairing impotence...(Protocol 5)

There is always contention, especially in politics:

In order to incite seekers after power to a misuse of power we have set all forces in opposition one to another...(Protocol 4)

Consider the burden of debt everyone carries these days:

Nowadays...the people have fallen into the grips of merciless money-grinding scoundrels who have laid a pitiless and cruel yoke on the necks of the workers...(Protocol 3)

Consider how, throughout the 20th Century, people were taken in by Communists, Socialists and Anarchists:

We appear on the scene as alleged saviours of the worker from this oppression when we propose to him to enter the ranks of our fighting forces, Socialists, Anarchists, Communists...(Protocol 3)

David Icke tells a fascinating story relayed to him by Dr Kitty Little. She attended a Labour Party study group at Oxford University in 1940. The speaker was a young man who claimed to be part of a 'Marxist takeover' plot. The speaker said he belonged to a nameless group that aimed to engineer Marxist control in Britain, Europe and parts of Africa. He explained that since Britons distrusted extremists, group members would pose as moderates, which would allow them to dismiss critics as right-wingers. The speaker added he had been selected to head the group's political section and that he expected to be named prime minister in the United Kingdom some day. His name was Harold Wilson and he served as Prime Minister in the 1960s and '70s. This story is relayed on page 39 of Jim Marrs book, *Rule by Secrecy* (Harper Collins 2000)

The 'saviours of mankind,' are usually Communist or Capitalist:

You have noticed with alarm that the Jewish elements provide the driving forces for both communism and capitalism, for the material as well as the spiritual ruin of this world. (Oscar Levy)

The hope is that despairing of communism and capitalism, and all other shades of government, the people will eventually accept surrender of national sovereignty, globalisation, a one-world government and a single ruler of the entire world:

...By want and envy and the hatred which it engenders we shall move the mobs and with their hands we shall wipe out all those who hinder us on our way. When the hour strikes for our Sovereign Lord of all the World to be crowned it is these same hands which will sweep away everything that might be a hindrance thereto. (Protocol 3)

In the European Community there is a move toward a single currency and the dispensation of sovereignties and frontiers of member States...In Asia, the attack on currencies is driving Asians to seek a 'single' lasting solution to all their economic and political problems...an end to war on the economic as well as on the political front is the hope of all people on Earth. After all the strife down the ages people will be ready for change, ready to let go of the old order and welcome in the new; peace at any price:

When we have accomplished our coup d'etat we shall say then to the various peoples: "Everything has gone terribly badly, all have been worn out with sufferings. We are removing the causes of your torment -nationalities, frontiers, differences of coinages... then will the mob exalt us... in hopes and expectations... voting... will set us on the throne of the world. (Protocol 10)

In their longing for peace and security it is hoped that the people of the Earth will vote for a single world government, a world currency, a world army to keep the peace and a world president to rule above all. For centuries the Learned Elders have been manipulating world economics and politics, inciting wars, revolutions and depressions to 'soften' the people of the Earth in preparation for the election of their world government into power.

...the peoples, utterly wearied by the irregularities and incompetence — a matter we shall arrange for - of their rulers, will clamour: "Away with them and give us one king over all the Earth who will unite us and annihilate the causes of discords frontiers, nationalities, religions, State debts; who will give us peace and quiet, which we cannot find under our rulers and representatives. (Protocol 10)

Will the people of Earth voluntarily relinquish their freedom and the freedom of all future generations, for peace and security? Is it intended that in the 21st century a 'King of the Jews' will mount the throne of the world?

...that King Despot of the blood of Zion, whom we are preparing for the world. (Protocol 3)

The Bible predicts a single world Government:

And in the days of these kings shall the one God of heaven set up a kingdom, which shall never be destroyed: and the kingdom shall not be left to other people, but it shall break into pieces and consume all these kingdoms, and it shall stand for ever.
(Daniel 2:44)

If the Elders of Zion are successful human liberty will be gone forever:

...we shall keep promising to give them back all the liberties we have taken away...It is not worth while saying anything about how long a time they will be kept waiting for this return of their liberties! (Protocol 11)

Revolutions are testament to the power that can be mobilised by the anger of misinformed masses:

...the people, blindly believing things in print, cherishes thanks to promptings intended to mislead and to its own ignorance a blind hatred towards all conditions which it considers above itself...This hatred will be still further magnified by the effects of the economic crisis...(Protocol 3)

One State has been turned on another:

At the present day we are, as an international force, invincible, because if we are attacked by some we are supported by other States. (Protocol 3)

Presidents can be controlled through 'skeletons in the cupboard'(watching the lead-up to the invasion of Iraq and subsequent unfolding events in the war, one is left wondering if maybe President George Bush was 'manipulated' in some way'.)

...we shall arrange elections in favour of such Presidents as have in their past some dark, undiscovered stain, some 'Panama' or other. Then they will be

trustworthy agents for the accomplishment of our plans out of fear of revelation and from the natural desire of everyone who has attained power, namely the retention of the privileges, advantages and honour connected with the office of President. (Protocol 10)

Note how throughout the 20th Century there was a remorseless increase in centralised government…

We shall create an intensified centralisation of government in order to grip in our hands all the forces of the community. We shall regulate mechanically all the actions of the political life of our subjects by new laws. (Protocol 5)

…with an increase in regulations and steady erosion of liberties:

These laws will withdraw, one by one, all indulgences and liberties which have been permitted by the Goyim, and our kingdom will be distinguished a despotism of such magnificent proportions as to be at any moment and in every place in a position to wipe out any Goyim who oppose us by deed or word. (Protocol 5)

How free is the 'free world'? Would it not be true to say that most people in the affluent 'free' societies are economic slaves, slaves bound by the chains of ever — spiraling interest on debt and taxation:

We shall soon begin to establish huge monopolies, reservoirs of colossal riches, upon which even large fortunes of the Goyim will depend …(Protocol 6)

Note how many landowners have been driven to bankruptcy and how much industry has been ruined by speculation:

What we want is that industry should drain off from the land both labour and capital and by means of speculation, transfer into our hands all the money of the world, and thereby throw all the Goyim into the ranks of the proletariat. Then the Goyim will bow down before us, if for no other reason but to get the right to exist. (Protocol 6)

When employed people are burdened with debt they are unlikely to step out of line or speak out against the 'status quo'.

The need for daily bread forces the Goyim to keep silence and be our humble servants. (Protocol 13)

If you are beginning to believe *The Protocols of Zion* might be authentic you could go out and buy yourself a few luxuries to make yourself feel a little more secure...

To complete the ruin of the industry of the Goyim we shall bring to the assistance of speculation the luxury, which we have developed among the Goyim, that greedy demand for luxury which is swallowing up everything... (Protocol 6)

...or go down to the pub...

...we shall further undermine artfully and deeply sources of production, by accustoming the workers to anarchy and drunkenness. (Protocol 6)

...but make it quick before the price of beer rises again:

We shall raise the rate of wages which, however, will not bring any advantage to the workers, for at the same time we shall produce a rise in the prices of the basic necessities of life. (Protocol 6)

'They' are after the gold in your teeth...

All the wheels of the machinery of all the States go

by the force of the engine, which is in our hands, and that engine of the machinery of States is gold. (Protocol 5)

...but will be happy to arrange a loan for you, or arrange it for your government who will borrow money rather than raise taxes for fear of losing your vote:

Every kind of loan provides infirmity to the State...Loans hang like a sword of Damocles over the heads of rulers who, instead of taking from their subjects by a temporary tax, come begging with outstretched palm of our bankers. (Protocol 20)

Wars for profit have put nations into debt and the two world wars put the whole world into debt! Read Jim Marrs book *'Rule by Secrecy'* for details of how secret societies have manipulated wars and revolutions for centuries, in furtherance of a hidden agenda which is now unfolding as globalization.

We must be in a position to respond to every act of opposition by war with the neighbours of that country which dares to oppose us: but if these neighbours should also venture to stand collectively together against us, then we must offer resistance by a universal war... (Protocol 7)

Note the arms race...

We must arm ourselves with all of the weapons which our opponents might employ against us. (Protocol 8)

...and how people are distracted with sport and television and every form of trivial activity:

In order that the masses themselves may not guess what we are about we will further distract them

with amusements, games, pastimes, passions, people's palaces...Soon we shall begin, through the Press, to propose competitions in art, in sport of all kinds... (Protocol 13)

Who owns Hollywood? Have you noticed the ever-increasing sex and violence in the movies? And what about the increase in pornography?

In countries known as progressive and enlightened we have created a senseless, filthy, abominable literature. (Protocol 14)

So much has happened in the name of progress.:

Progress, a fallacious idea, serves to obscure the truth so that none may know it except us, the Chosen People, its guardians. (Protocol 15)

Did you watch the movie *Fahrenheit 9/11?* Did it leave you with the feeling that George Bush and his 'War on Terrorism' were stage-managed?

When we come into our kingdom our orators will expound great problems which have turned humanity upside down in order to bring it, at the end, under our beneficent rule. Who will ever suspect then that all these peoples were stage—managed by us according to political plan which no one has so much as guessed at in the course of many centuries? (Protocol 13)

Consider the track record of communism in the 20th Century:

...we shall slay, without mercy, all who take arms in hand to oppose our coming into our kingdom...The aureole of our power demands suitable, that is, cruel, punishments for the slightest infringement...We are

obliged, without hesitation, to sacrifice individuals, who commit a breach of established order. (Protocol 15)

Remember Stalin's communism (Stalin was a Jew, whose real name was Jossip Vissarinovich Djugashvili) and the Pol Pot regime in Cambodia and Mao Tse Tung's Red Guard in China, there were 'eyes everywhere':

In our programme, one third of our subjects will keep the rest under observation. (Protocol 17)

Recall in Stalin's Russia the way people were arrested on suspicion...

Criminals with us will be arrested at the first more or less well-grounded suspicion. (Protocol 18)

...and then locked up in the 'Gulag' like common criminals:

In order to destroy the prestige of heroism for political crime we shall send it for trial in the category of thieving, murder and every kind of abominable and filthy crime. (Protocol 19)

If this should happen again in a single world government, who would appeal for your freedom and rights?

...Resolutions of our government will be final, without appeal... (Protocol 15)

Preoccupied with the cash flow and our material well being we are certain it will never happen again but notice how, day by day, notch by notch, globalisation is moving ever closer to completion through economic constraints and control by multinationals and banks:

...we have always worked upon the most sensitive chords of the human mind, upon the cash account, upon the cupidity, upon the insatiability for material needs of man. (Protocol 1)

Chapter 9

The Bankers

"Shake off all the fears of servile prejudices, under which weak minds are servilely crouched. Fix reason firmly in her seat, and call on her tribunal for every fact, every opinion. "

(Thomas Jefferson)

Undoubtedly the greatest genius of 'God's' chosen people has been in the handling of money. Historically, it is through this medium that they have gained their mastery:

It was said through the prophets that we were chosen by God Himself to rule over the whole Earth. God has endowed us with genius that we may be equal to our task. (Protocol 5)

There have been banks and bankers since earliest times, and two basic banking systems have been employed. The first system involved the bank investing money in an entrepreneur, artisan or farmer, as a joint, profit sharing enterprise, or on the basis of charging fees for services rendered. For example, the great Bank of Amsterdam, founded in 1609 funded the carriage of half of Europe's commerce, on Dutch ships, on a profit sharing scheme. It became one of the largest and wealthiest banks in the world and led, in a large part, to the prosperity of Amsterdam. The second banking system involved the bank lending money at interest and holding the property of the borrower as collateral. This system is called **usury.**

The first system brought prosperity to the people. The

second system brought about their ruin. For this reason it was forbidden to faithful Muslims and Christians. It was also banned amongst the Israelites:

> *"If you lend money to any of my people that are poor by you, you shall not be to him as a usurer, nor shall you lay upon him usury."* (Exodus 22: 25)

Unfortunately for the world, the followers of Moses were not banned from applying usury to those outside their racial and religious fold. So it is, the 'Brotherhood of the Snake' used money lending, with interest, to bring the modern world into line with their own global interests.

The Hebrews adopted the practice of usury from the cult of Baal. According to Richard Kelly Hoskins, in his book *War Cycles, Peace Cycles,* archaeologists have found evidence as far back as 2000 BC, of the priests of Baal practicing usury. They traditionally issued clay tablets, representing promises, to pay against deposits of gold — pre-dating modern bank notes!

King William II (Rufus) allowed Jewish moneylenders into England in 1087, on condition that they shared their usury profits with the King. Through the Jews, great wealth came to the English crown. It is estimated that within a couple of centuries they owned one fourth of England. Because of usury, and the economic slavery it entailed, hatred for Jews mounted in England. The tide turned against them and the King, at Magna Carta, in 1215. In 1290 the nobles and prelates forced the King to deport the Jews — 16,000 in all. For a similar reason they were expelled from France in 1306.

The Catholic Church banned usury, and in 1179 the third Lateran Council decreed that usurers were to be denied communion and a Christian burial. Pope Alexander III went on to rule that those who persisted be excommunicated:

The other major banking group in Medieval Europe was the Knights Templar. They established a system of promissory notes in the form of receipts against gold and silver deposits, from which modern bank notes originate. The Knights Templar dealt mainly with silver as their standard of exchange, which is the origin of the English 'pound' and 'sterling'. To this day the English banknotes promise to pay the bearer the sum of an equivalent in pounds of silver.

Usury and promissory notes strip wealth from the people and amass it to the bankers. Through the system of usury the borrower may end up paying the lender, in interest, far more than the sum borrowed. This is evident today in the 'mortgage' ('mort' means 'death'; 'gage' means 'grip'). Over twenty five years, under the death-grip of the bankers, borrowers will often pay, in interest, twice the principal sum, thereby paying three times the purchase price for their home. House prices have spiralled through the availability of low interest loans and mortgages. This has made the people ever more beholden to the usurers. Then through the central banks, under the direction of 'the bankers', interest rates have been inexorably increased to squeeze out of them ever more money. The cycle of lowering interest rates to increase borrowing and then increasing them to 'milk money from the masses' increases the revenue and power of the banks. Extortionate rates of interest, charged on credit card loans for the purchase of luxury goods, have further increased the worldwide dominion of the 'Banking Brotherhood'. As the central banks dictate interest rates, rather than governments, the banks have absolute control of their revenue.

During and after the days of the Knights Templar, the

bankers found that people were trading with their promissory notes and rarely returned to the bank to demand their value in gold or silver. The bankers quickly realised that they could issue more receipts than they had deposits. The formula they discovered was that they could issue promissory notes up to **sixteen times** the value of their deposits without exposing themselves to bankruptcy. Today, thanks to electronic money, banks and building societies are able to lend **thirty times** the value of deposits.

European bankers began the practice of lending money, in the form of promissory notes, in excess of their deposits. This practice of creating loans out of thin air enabled the bankers to strip real wealth from the people, through interest paid on 'phantom money'. This has been the most effective way for 'the bankers' to rob the nations and centralise their wealth because there is no ceiling to the amounts they can lend. This has led to an unlimited rise in house prices leading to effective slavery of many property owners to the banks. The success of this system depends on lending to secure borrowers and householders represent secure borrowers who guarantee the amassing of wealth for 'the bankers.' Credit cards create further enslavement of people to usurers for the sake of their property and lifestyle. In the USA the average household owes over $8,000 in credit card debt (US National Foundation for Credit Counselling, March 2002) and in Australia credit card debt hit a record $24 billion in June 2003 (www.theage.com.au/articles/2003/07/17/10) Statistics reveal the same pattern in Europe and the rest of the world of everyone falling into ever increasing debt.

For centuries the usurers made a practice of lending money to Kings and governments in order to control them. This has been the most effective way of furthering *The Great Work of Ages* to gain absolute dominion of the Earth.

> **...Foreign loans are like leeches...But the Goy States do not tear them off; they go on persisting in putting more onto themselves so that they must inevitably perish, drained by voluntary blood-letting...but it is a proof of the genius of our chosen mind that we have contrived to present the matter of loans to them in such a light that they have even seen in them an advantage to themselves.** (Protocol 20)

The 'banking brotherhood' found that kings, presidents and dictators would come to them for war loans. Wars and revolutions ensnared the nations into a spiral of debt from which they could never fully recover:

> **...in order to carry on a contested struggle one must have money, and the money is all in our hands.**
> (Protocol 9)

It didn't take 'God's Chosen Bankers' long to figure out the most effective way of gaining control of governments through debt was to foster war and revolution. It didn't matter which side won or which side lost so long as both sides were indebted to them. The losers might go bankrupt but the winners would be their slaves.

God's bankers gained a foothold in England through their government loans. Obligated to 'the moneylenders' Oliver Cromwell proposed the readmission of Jews to England. Though he failed to secure their open return he allowed them back into the country in secret. Their position was strengthened during the restoration period when Charles II borrowed heavily from moneyed Jewish families in Holland. However, the floodgates opened at the time of the English revolution when William of Orange secured the English throne on the back of a two million gulden loan from the Amsterdam banker Antonio Lopez Suasso (*Jewish Encyclopaedia*, England, p.169).

The good God's banking came into ascendancy in the 19th century with the rise of the **House of Rothschild**. Centred in Frankfurt the Rothschild family capitalised on the Napoleonic Wars. The foremost 'Merchant Banker' Mayer Amschel Rothschild had his sons operating in the major capitals of Europe. Solomon Mayer was in Vienna, Karl Mayer in Naples, James Mayer in Paris and Nathan Mayer in London. The majority of the English financial dealings with the continent went through the Rothschild offices. As the Rothschild banking empire extended to most European States, they specialised in the liquidation of inflated paper currencies and in the foundation of floating public debts. In 1818 they made loans to European governments, beginning with Prussia and following with issues to England, Austria, Naples and Russia. Thus they gained control of the major European nations.

There is some doubt as to whether the Rothschilds are true Semites. The Rothschild family originated from a Russian clan that adopted the Jewish faith. In the past, however, throughout Europe, Jews had been forced to relinquish their ancient faith in order to escape pogroms and expulsions. Very often they then reverted to Judaism in more favourable times. Also converts are generally held in contempt by 'Jews of the blood' (Ezra 4:2-3). The position of influence held by the Rothschilds amongst the Jews, suggests their ancestors were more likely reverting to the old faith rather than converting.

The Rothschilds increased their financial power enormously through the Battle of Waterloo. Nathan crashed the stock market by behaving in the City of London as though Wellington had lost the Battle. Using carrier pigeons — or some believe better couriers than the British government —he had news of Wellington's victory before anyone else and responded by 'panic selling' his stock. The 'City flock' followed suit. Trusting Nathan Rothschild, they took his behaviour as a sign that the battle was lost. Rothschild's agents were buying whilst everyone else was selling. Then, when the true news came through and the market recovered, his agents were selling whilst everyone else was buying. Through these and other dealings, by 1820 the Rothschilds had amassed a fortune exceeding £5 billion. (G.Armstrong in *'The Rothschild Money Trust'*)

In 1820, five billion pounds was a colossal sum of money. The Rothschilds then expanded this enormous capital holding in the Industrial Revolution and colonial expansion of the 19th century. The Industrial Revolution was only possible because of the centralisation of capital, which the Rothschilds secured into their own hands.

Through their influence over the British Government the Rothschilds managed to secure a seat in the House of Lords from a reluctant Queen Victoria. As aristocrats they became pillars of the establishment and with their enormous prestige and capital they fuelled modern capitalism. If you do a calculation, over 120 years, on five billion pounds, using even a modest level of compound interest, you will appreciate Armstrong's estimate 'that by 1940 the Rothschilds owned half the world', was not an exaggeration.

...We shall soon begin to establish huge monopolies, reservoirs of colossal riches, upon which even large fortunes of the Goyim will depend to such an

extent that they will go to the bottom together with the credit of the States on the day after the political smash. (Protocol 6)

Listings of the richest people in the world is a front intended to keep the masses under the illusion they can possess monetary wealth and its associated power.

...around us there will be...millionaires (Protocol 8)

The 'Great American Dream' is really a nightmare! According to Jan van Helsing, the Rothschilds augmented their family fortune by orchestrating the American Civil war. The branch of the family banking business, based in London, funded the North whilst the other branch in Paris funded the South. They then provoked eleven Southern States into rebellion through the activity of agents such as George Bickley, founder of a Masonic branch called the 'Knights of the Golden Circle.' Rebellion or no rebellion, the slaves in America were destined for freedom, so the only people to benefit from the American Civil war were 'the bankers'. Abraham Lincoln saw through their game and refused to pay the House of Rothschild the immense interest on their war loans and proposed instead to print 'greenback' government bank notes. Lincoln paid with his life. On April 14, 1865, John Wilkes Booth, a member of the 'Knights of the Golden Circle', shot him.

...The qualifications for this [financial] aristocracy we have established in wealth, which is dependent upon us, and in knowledge, for which our learned elders provide the motive force... (Protocol 1)

The Rothschilds gained economic and political control of the United States of America through agents such as J. Pierpont Morgan, American born but educated in England and Germany. U.S. Congressman and banker Louis McFadden — who for ten years headed the House Banking and Currency Committee — described J.P. Morgan as 'the top American agent of the English Rothschilds.' J.P. Morgan, who triggered 'the panic of 1907,' served as British financial agent in America and was, with 'the bankers' J.D. Rockefeller, Jacob Schiff and Paul Warburg, a major influence in the U.S.A. entering World War I.

'The bankers' exercised their influence on President Woodrow Wilson through an 'agentur specialist' by name of 'Colonel' House. House manipulated Wilson like a puppet to the extent that Wilson called him 'my alter ego.' House played a major role in creating the **Federal Reserve System**, the unconstitutional graduated income tax system and, in 1917, the entry of America into World War I — backed by a Rothschild loan.

To quote Jim Marrs from *Rule by Secrecy*:

> *This loan [$100 million] involved banker J.P. Morgan Jr., who had taken control of the Morgan financial empire after the death of his famed father in 1913. Morgan as the Rothschild's American representative — some say partner — was a pivotal character in the coming bloodbath.*

In 1916, President Woodrow Wilson had been re-elected by the people of America on the basis of his campaign slogan 'He Kept Us Out of War.' A year later, against the wishes of the people he plunged America into the war.

To quote Gary Allen from *None Dare Call It Conspiracy*.

> *"Woodrow Wilson was re-elected by a hair. He had based his campaign on the slogan 'He Kept Us Out of War'... Just five months later we were in it. The same crowd which manipulated the passage of the income tax and Federal Reserve System wanted America in the war. J.P. Morgan,*

J.D. Rockefeller, Colonel House, Jacob Schiff, Paul Warburg and the rest of the Jekyll Island conspirators were all deeply involved."

It is 'the bankers' and not the people who have the final say in modern Democracies like America. They have the power through the media to dictate public opinion. Through propaganda they succeeded in convincing the people of America to believe that World War I would be a 'war to end all wars'.

In his book *Falsehood In War Time,* Arthur Ponsonby M.P. concluded:

There must have been more deliberate lying in the world from 1914 − 1918 than in any other period of the World's history.

Even before war broke out the Rothschilds had planned a US participation. In *America Goes to War,* Charles Callan Tansill wrote:

Even before the actual clash of arms, the French firm of Rothschild Freres cabled to Morgan and Company in New York suggesting the floatation of a loan of $100 million, a substantial part of which was to be left in the United States to pay for French purchases of American goods.

Of the disastrous intervention of America into 'The Great War' Winston Churchill M.P. was to note:

"All nations would have been better off had the U.S. minded its own business. Peace would have been made with Germany, there would have been no collapse in Russia leading to communism; no breakdown in government in Italy followed by Fascism, and Nazism never would have gained ascendancy in Germany." (Social Justice Magazine, July 3, 1939. p.4.)

During World War I, 'God's Chosen Bankers' engineered and financed the Russian Revolution. Lenin was sent across Europe into Russia in a sealed train with $5 - $6 million in gold. The operation was arranged with the German High Command and funded by Max Warburg.

Max Warburg ran the Rothschild bank in Frankfurt. His brother Paul married Nina Leob, daughter of Solomon Leob of **Kuhn, Leob & Co.**, the most powerful international banking institution in America. The other brother, Felix, married Frieda Schiff, daughter of Jacob Schiff, senior partner in **Kuhn, Leob & Co**. In *Our Crowd*, Stephen Birmingham wrote, ...

in the eighteenth century the Schiffs and Rothschilds shared a double house in Frankfurt.

Jacob Schiff reportedly bought his partnership in **Kuhn, Leob & Co** with Rothschild money. Paul and Felix married into the firm. Sir William Wiseman earned his partnership through 'good service.' He served for British Intelligence to help bring the U.S.A. into World War I, and became a partner in **Kuhn, Leob & Co** shortly after the war. During the war, 'the bankers,' Bernard Baruch and Eugene Mayer, selected by President Wilson, were hand-picked by Colonel House. Baruch placed U.S. government contracts, and Mayer — a former partner of Baruch, and son of a partner in the Rothschild controlled Merchant Bank, **Lazard Freres** — headed the War Finance Corporation.

Meanwhile, Jacob Schiff financed Leon Trotsky. According to *The New York Journal-American* of February 3, 1949, Jacob's grandson, John Schiff, is said to have remarked:

"The old man sank about $20 million for the final triumph of Bolshevism in Russia."

In *Czarism and the Revolution* the White General Arsene de Goulevitch wrote:

> *The main purveyors of funds for the revolution, however, were neither the crackpot Russian millionaires nor the armed bandits of Lenin. The 'real' money primarily came from certain British and American circles, which for a long time past had lent their support to the Russian revolutionary cause... The important part played by the wealthy American banker, Jacob Schiff, in the events in Russia, though as yet only partially revealed, is no longer a secret.*

De Goulevitch went on to quote General Alexander Nechvolodov:

> *In April 1917, Jacob Schiff publicly declared that it was thanks to his financial support that the revolution in Russia had succeeded. In the spring of that same year Schiff commenced to subsidize Trotsky...Simultaneously Trotsky was being subsidized by Max Warburg and Olaf Aschberg of the* **Nye Banken** *of Stockholm...the* **Rhine Westphalian Syndicate,** *and Jivotovsky, whose daughter later married Trotsky.*

De Goulevitch also stated:

> *Mr Bakhmetiev, the late Russian Imperial Ambassador to the United States, tells us that the Bolsheviks, after victory, transferred 600 million roubles in gold between the years 1918 and 1922 to* **Kuhn, Leob & Co.**

According to Gary Allen in *None Dare Call it Conspiracy:*

> *Schiff spent millions to overthrow the Czar and more millions to overthrow Kerensky. He was sending money to Russia long after the true character of the Bolsheviks was know to the world. Schiff raised $10 million, supposedly for Jewish war relief in Russia but later events revealed it*

to be a good business investment. (Forbes, B.C., Men Who Are Making America, pp.334-5.)

Schiff's participation in the Bolshevik Revolution, though quite naturally now denied, was well known among Allied Intelligence services at the time. This led to much talk about Bolshevism being a Jewish plot. The result was that the subject of financing the Communist takeover of Russia became taboo. Later evidence indicates that the bankrolling of the Bolsheviks was handled by a syndicate of international bankers, which in addition to the Schiff-Warburg clique, included Morgan and Rockefeller interests. Documents show that the Morgan organisation put at least $1 million in the Red revolutionary kitty (pp. 71-72)...The Reece Committee which investigated foundations for Congress in 1953 proved with an overwhelming amount of evidence that the various Rockefeller and Carnegie foundations have been promoting socialism since their inception. (See Rene Wormser's Foundations: Their Power and Influence, Devin Adair, New York, 1958, p. 62)...

Still another important financier of the Bolshevik Revolution was an extremely wealthy Englishman named Lord Alfred Milner. De Goulevitch stated:

"In private interviews I have been told that over 21 million roubles were spent by Lord Milner in financing the Russian revolution..."

Through Max Warburg, in Germany, engineering and financing of the Russian Revolution to free German troops from the Eastern Front could have been described as patriotism. However, as this action freed dozens of German divisions to move to France where they slaughtered thousands of French, American and British soldiers, the involvement of Lord Milner, Paul and Felix

Warburg, Morgan, Schiff and Rockefeller, in the Bolshevik revolution was nothing short of treason. Nonetheless, Lord Milner and the three Warburg brothers represented France, America and Britain at the Paris Peace Conference at the conclusion of World War I.

After the Russian revolution the **Chase National Bank** of the Rockefellers was involved in continuing finance of the Soviet Union. (A later merger with the Warburg **Manhattan Bank** gave rise to the prestigious **Chase Manhattan Bank.**) According to Harvey O'Connor, Standard Oil bought 50% of the huge, Nobel Caucasus oil fields, supposedly nationalised by the Soviets. Professor Antony Sutton of the Stanford University Hoover Institute said they then built an oil refinery in Russia which represented the first U.S. investment in the U.S.S.R. after the revolution. They concluded a deal to sell Russian oil to Europe, which included a loan to the Soviets of $75,000,000 (*National Republic,* Sept. 1927.) Sutton also noted that in 1928 **Chase National Bank** was involved in selling Bolshevik bonds to the United States. In a speech to Congress, Louis McFadden said:

> "...you would be staggered to see how much American money has been taken from the United States Treasury for the benefit of Russia. Find out what business has been transacted for the State Bank of Soviet Russia by its correspondent, the **Chase Bank** of New York..." (Congressional Record, June 15, 1933)

The Rockefellers were not alone in helping the Soviet Union stagger to its feet. Antony Sutton stated that:

> ...there is a report in the State Department files that names **Kuhn, Leob & Co.,** (the long-established and important financial house in New York) as the financier of the First Five Year Plan...(U.S. State Dept. Decimal File,

811.51/3711 and 861.50 FIVE YEAR PLAN/236)

The Rockefellers were deeply involved in the transfer of technology and patents to the U.S.S.R., which were extensively used in their arms industry. During the Vietnam War, whilst the young men of America and Australia were being slaughtered with Soviet built weapons, the Rockefellers dealt with American concerns with the Soviet Union. The question remains, who was really running the Soviet Union? In October 1964, David Rockefeller, President of **Chase Manhattan Bank** and Chairman of the board of The Council on Foreign Relations took a 'holiday' to the Soviet Union. He ended his 'vacation' in the Kremlin. By 'sheer coincidence' Nikita Khrushchev was immediately recalled from his 'vacation' on the Black sea and summarily fired.

When one considers President Eisenhower's habit of 'delegating' executive decisions to Nelson Rockefeller, one is left wondering who was really running the United States of America? Throughout the 20th Century the Rockefellers played Russia against America like a game of chess! For the British it was cricket; which side was batting next! According to Professor Sutton, British financial interests as well as American propped up the Bolsheviks.

Lord Milner, who put up 21 million roubles to finance the Russian Revolution, was a leading light in 'The Round Table' movement founded by Cecil Rhodes and backed by Lord Rothschild. The Round Table organisation in England grew out of the life long dream of Cecil Rhodes to found a one-world government.

Jim Marrs wrote in *Rule by Secrecy*:

Sir Alfred Milner [was] Britain's high commissioner in South Africa... Milner, an 'ardent imperialist' educated at Oxford and New College, provoked the Boer War of

1899-1902 by his rigid attitudes and in victory gained British control over South Africa's diamond mines and a good proportion of its gold supply. It was no coincidence that Milner became a principle trustee of the estate of Cecil Rhodes, the diamond tycoon of South Africa... As in the Morgans and Rockefellers, behind Rhodes we find the vast power of the Rothschild family.

"They were financiers to Cecil Rhodes, making it possible for him to establish a monopoly over the diamond fields of South Africa...

Lending support for a relationship between Rhodes and the Rothschilds was author and former British Intelligence Officer Dr. John Coleman, who wrote,

"Rhodes was the principal agent for the Rothschilds... [who] dispossessed the South African Boers of their birthright, the gold and diamonds that lay beneath their soil"...

The idea of Rothschild funding behind Rhodes also was supported by author Frank Aydelotte who noted in *American Rhodes Scholarships:*

"In 1888 Rhodes made his third will... leaving everything to Lord Rothschild."

With Rhodes death, Milner, Rothschild, and their international banker associates gained complete control over the Round Tables, which began expanding far beyond the British Empire...

"Rhodes committed the same error made by so many humanitarians before him," wrote author William Bramley,

"...he thought that he could accomplish his goals through the channels of the corrupted Brotherhood network. Rhodes therefore ended up creating institutions which promptly fell into the hands of those who would effectively use those institutions to oppress the human race."

Cecil Rhodes was passionate about a one–world order, which he envisioned through global expansion of the British Empire. However, the British Empire was to go into decline and the torch of a one–world order passed from the old world to the new. A century after Rhodes death America would replace Britain as the nation stamping Imperialism on the world. Backed by the same gang of God's bankers, America would hold high the torch of human pseudo — emancipation through *A New World Order.*

'*A New World Order*' is printed in Latin on every American dollar bill. The symbol of the all-seeing eye of Jehovah, along with the 'Star of David' was also printed on the dollar bill. Looking at the symbol of the 'all-seeing eye' one is reminded of the all-seeing eye of the Dark Lord in Tolkein's *Lord of the Rings.* There can be no doubt about the intent of 'the bankers' — or their masters — behind the establishment of 'A New World Order' from America, through the medium of money. This process which began in the earliest days of the USA...

"You are a den of vipers. I intend to rout you out, and by the Eternal God I will rout you out. If the people only understood the rank injustice of our money and banking system, there would be a revolution before morning." (*President Andrew Jackson*)

...was consolidated under the direction of Paul Warburg, when, through the establishment of the Federal Reserve System, 'the bankers' seized control of the American monetary system in 1913.

Throughout the 1920s, in the USA, small banks were collapsing by the thousand. By 1933, 16,305 banks had folded, leaving families and firms destitute, throughout the country. Meanwhile reserves in the 'Fed' steadily increased. The Federal Reserve System, like 'The Bank of England' and every other Central Bank in the World remains privately owned. It was named 'The Federal Reserve System' to fool the American people into believing it wasn't a central bank. However, the 'Fed' is 'The Central Bank' of the United States of America. When it was initially set up the foremost shareholders were: *Rothschild Banks*, London & Paris; *Lazard Freres Bank*, Paris; *Israel Moses Seif Bank*, Italy; *Warburg Bank*, Hamburg & Amsterdam; **Lehmann Bank**, New York; *Kuhn Loeb Bank*, New York; *Chase National Bank*, New York, *Manhattan Bank*, New York; *Goldman Sachs Bank*, New York. Through their controlling interests in the central banks of practically every nation in the world, 'God's bankers' now control the economy of the world.

Throughout the 20th Century they periodically applied the screws on humanity and then released them to produce cycles of boom and bust. Through financial machinations they manipulated depressions, wars and revolutions.

Whilst the American people were suffering and starving, in the Great Depression of the 1930s, American bankers were bankrolling Adolf Hitler and the Nazi rearmament of Germany! The war funding for Hitler occurred through the firm **I.G. Farben**. I.G. Farben, an international cartel based in Germany, then dominated the world's chemical and drug industries. By the beginning of World War II, I.G. Farben had become the largest industrial corporation in Europe. The Rothschilds, who steered this operation through their related banks and companies, controlled this firm.

In 1926, I.G. Farben developed a process for extracting petrol out of coal. In 1929 he entered into an agreement with Standard Oil owned by the Rockefellers. Subsequently his operation was expanded with American money and used by international bankers as a front to channel money into Germany for rearmament. Rothschilds pumped enormous sums into the German economy, via I.G. Farben. Paul and Max Warburg were on the Farben board.

The Round Table organisation also supported the rise of Nazism. According to Gary Allen in *None Dare Call is Conspiracy*:

> *As World War II approached the Round Table Group was influential in seeing that Hitler was not stopped in Austria, the Rhineland or Sudentenland and thereby was largely responsible for precipitating the holocaust. A second world war would greatly enhance the opportunity for the establishment of world government. The financing for Adolf Hitler's rise to power was handled through the Warburg controlled* **Mendelsohn Bank** *of Amsterdam and later by the* **J.Henry Schroeder Bank** *with branches in Frankfurt, London and New York. (See also James Martin, All Honorable Men p.51)*

'The bankers' carried other Wall Street money barons with them including the Harrimans and Joseph Kennedy (US Ambassador in London) in their support of the Nazis.

To quote Dr. Anthony Sutton *from 'Wall Street and the Rise of Hitler.'*

> *The sum paid before 1940 by American capitalism to Germany in preparation for war can only be called phenomenal...There is ample proof suggesting that the influential sector of American business not only knew about the nature of Nazism, but actively (and profitably) supported it for self-interest wherever possible, in the full*

knowledge that in the end there would be a war into which both Europe and the U.S. would be drawn…

The carefully researched evidence that American banking and industrial circles were most instrumental in the rise of Hitler's Third Reich is now publicly accessible. They can be found in the protocols and reports of government hearings that had been published by several Senate and House committees between 1928 and 1946.

Joseph Goebbels, Hitler's Minister of Propaganda, was a Jew with a false identity. Other leading Nazis also had Jewish blood running in their veins. The most notable was Adolf Hitler, an illegitimate grandson of Baron Rothschild. To quote Marrs from *Rule by Secrecy*:

Dr Walter C. Langer, a psychologist who produced a wartime psychoanalysis of Hitler for the American OSS, reported that a secret prewar Austrian police report proved Hitler's father was the illegitimate son of a peasant cook named Marie Anna Schicklgruber, who at the time she conceived her child was 'employed as a servant in the home of Baron Rothschild' in Vienna… Historians have long noted that the question of possible Jewish ancestry haunted Hitler throughout his life.

In case someone might question if a Rothschild would consider dallying with the servants, it is instructive that Rothschild biographer Ferguson stated that the son of one of Salomon's [Rothschild] senior clerks "recalled that by the 1840s, the Viennese Rothschild had developed a somewhat reckless enthusiasm for young girls."

The late Philippe Rothschild, a descendant of Nathan, in 1984 published his memoirs revealing his 'scandalous love life'. He wrote, "I was a tremendous success… leaping from bed to bed like a mountain goat… I was always convinced my father had won his spurs riding my grandmother's chambermaids."

"It is possible that Hitler discovered his Jewish background and his relation to the Rothschilds, and aware of their enormous power to make or break European governments, re-established contact with the family," wrote author Epperson. "This would partially explain the enormous support he received from the international banking fraternity, closely entwined with the Rothschild family as he rose to power."

There is no paradox as to why, with blood ties to the Rothschild family, Adolf Hitler should launch a pogrom against the Jews.

> **...if any States raise a protest against us it is only pro forma at our discretion and by our direction, for their anti-Semitism is indispensable to us in the management of our lesser brethren.** (Protocol 9)

Hitler was schooled by an Occult group in Berlin, linked to the Bavarian Illuminati. It is widely believed he decided on a pogrom against the Jews after reading the *The Protocols of the Learned Elders of Zion*. *Mein Kampf* was modelled on the Protocols. Those who funded him supported his anti-Semitism. Jewish international interests effectively engineered the Jewish holocaust. Hitler was the puppet. They pulled the strings. They instigated the process that led to the destruction of six million of their own people and Hitler served the 'Jewish Cause' on their march to world dominion:

> **We have got the gold in our hands, notwithstanding that we have had to gather it out of oceans of blood and tears. But it has paid us though we have sacrificed many of our people. Each victim on our side is worth in the sight of God a thousand Goyim.** (Protocol 1)

The holocaust has gained world sympathy for the Jews. Even today Jewish interests dredge the holocaust and through control of the media remind the world again and again of their 'victimisation' to ensure that none dare speak out against them for fear of being labelled 'neo-Nazi' or 'anti-Semite.' Hitler has given their Anti-Defamation League 'just cause' to protect them from criticism. It has provided a smoke screen as they accelerate toward the culmination of their dream to enslave humanity and gain complete dominion of the Earth. It has drawn their people around them and fanned the flames of hatred for the Gentile. It secured for them the return of their promised land.

...though we have sacrificed many of our own, but for that we have now already given them such a position on the Earth as they could not even have dreamed of. (Protocol 15)

We see the dark side of God exposed in the tragic history of the Jews. Historically, the traumatisation of the Jewish people by Gentile persecution created herd paralysis, national isolation and hatred for the Gentile oppressors. The victimised people turned to the only God that they knew. They found solace in their ancient religion and consolidated around their religious leadership. This process, occurring over millennia, created the extraordinary bondage of the Jewish people to their God and their ancient religion. Enmeshed in their culture, their religion become inseparable from their lives. This is how God kept his people subjugated. Then as now it is through fear that God keeps his people in bondage. This is clear from the threats made by Moses:

"If you will not observe to do all the words of this law that are written in this book, that you may fear this glo-

rious and fearful name, THE LORD THY GOD:
"Then the Lord will make your plagues wonderful, and
the plagues of your seed even greater plagues and of
sore sickness even longer continuance.
"Moreover he will bring upon you all the diseases of
Egypt, you were afraid of; and they will cleave to you.
"Also every sickness and every plague, which is not
written in the book of law, then will the Lord bring to
you, until you are destroyed.
"And you shall be left few in number, whereas you
were as the stars of heaven in multitude; because you
would not obey, the voice of the Lord your God.
"And it shall come to pass, that as the Lord rejoiced
over you to do you good, and to multiply you; so the
Lord will rejoice over you to destroy you, and bring
you to nought; and you will be plucked off the land,
wherever you go to possess it.
"And the Lord will scatter you among all people, from
the one end of the Earth even unto the other; and there
you will serve other gods which neither you nor your
fathers have known, even wood and stone.
"And among these nations shall you find no ease, nei-
ther shall the sole of your feet have rest: but the Lord
shall give you there a trembling heart, and failing eyes,
and sorrow of mind:
"And your life will hang in doubt before you; and you
will fear day and night and shall have no assurance of
your life." (Deuteronomy 28:58-66)

The features of the Jewish holocaust were clearly predicted by Moses and the sacrifice of six million of the
'holy people' was just a matter of expedience...

**And how far seeing were our learned elders in an-
cient times when they said that to attain a serious
end it behoves not to stop at any means or to count**

the victims sacrificed for the sake of that end. (Protocol 15)

Many people believe 9/11 was an 'inside-job'. Considering the American gains in the oil fields of central Asia through that 'catastrophe' I am inclined to believe this too.

In 'September 11, (2004)'Michael C. Rupert wrote:

The 9/11 attacks were the result of deliberate planning and orchestrated efforts by identifiable leaders within the US Government and energy and financial sectors to see a Pearl Harbour like attack which would provide America with the pretext for war, invasion and sequential confiscation of oil and natural gas reserves or the key transportation routes through which they pass.(Ref. www.from the wilderness.com

Osma Bin Laden was 'the patsy'. He has always served American interests in their march toward world supremacy. He claimed he 'didn't do 9/11'. He had no reason to lie. If he did it he would have crowed from the roof-tops. Why were there so few Jewish casualties in the Twin Towers? Were they tipped off? And what about the Born-again Christian, President George Bush? In the movie Fahrenheit 9/11 his reaction to the news of the disaster did not reveal shock. What was he hiding? Why did he let the Bin Laden family fly out of America immediately when all American aircraft were grounded and airports closed?

Every man aims at power, everyone would like to become a dictator if only he could, and rare indeed are the men who would not be willing to sacrifice the welfare of all for the sake of securing their own welfare. (Protocol 1)

Good or evil is always a matter of choice:

Again, the Devil took him up onto an exceedingly

high mountain and showed him all the kingdoms of
the world and the glory of them; and said unto him:
"All these things I will give you if you will fall down
and worship me.

"Then Jesus said to him, "Get thee hence Satan..."
(Matthew 4: 8-10)

Whereas Jesus Christ didn't take Satan up on the offer, it would seem that plenty of others have been only too happy to do so.

"Now the Passover of the Jews was at hand and Jesus
went up to Jerusalem, And he found in the temple
those who sold oxen and sheep and doves, and the
money changers doing their business. When he had
mad e whip of chords, he drove them all out of the tem-
ple, with the sheep and the oxen, and poured out the
changer's money and overturned their tables."
(John 2: 13-15)

Chapter 10

The Cults

"Question with boldness even the existence of a God; because, if there be one, he must more approve of the homage of reason than that of blindfolded fear."

(Thomas Jefferson)

When we come into our kingdom it should be undesirable for us that there should exist any other religion than ours...We must, therefore, sweep away all other forms of belief. (Protocol 14)

Judaism views itself as the only true religion and views all other religions and spiritual movements as false idolatry. Fundamentalist Christians and Muslims take the same view. The three religions rooted in the Old Testament or Torah, Judaism, Christianity and Islam are intolerant of each other and absolutely intolerant of other religions. Judaism and Christianity are especially clear in their intent. If ever they have mastery over nations they will take the opportunity to expunge other forms of belief as happened in the Albigensian crusade and would happen if the authors of the Protocols came into power because the Dark Lord commanded his people to do so:

> *These are the statutes and judgments, which you will observe to do in the land, which the Lord God of your fathers, gives you to possess, all the days that you live upon the Earth.*
> *You shall utterly destroy all the places, wherein the nations which you shall possess serve their gods,*

upon the high mountains, and upon the hills, and under every green tree: And you shall overthrow their altars, and break their pillars, and burn their groves with fire; and you shall hew down the graven images of their gods, and destroy the names of them out of that place. You shall not do so unto the Lord your God.
(Deuteronomy 12:1-4)

Deuteronomy is the foundation of the ancient Hebrew culture. For the Jewish people it has been the basis of their laws and their national identity for many generations. However, an unbiased reader, today, would be alarmed at the tone of the message of Moses to his people.

Take for example, the *Song of Moses*:

"For a fire is kindled in my anger, and shall burn unto the lowest hell, and shall consume the Earth with her increase, and set on fire the foundations of the mountains.

"I will heap mischiefs upon them; I will spend my arrows upon them.

"They will be burnt with hunger and devoured with burning heat and with bitter destruction: I will also send the teeth of beasts upon them, with the poison of serpents of the dust.

"The sword without, and terror within, shall destroy both the young man and the virgin, the suckling and also the man of grey hairs."
(Deuteronomy 32:21-25)

If in the *Song of Moses*, Moses were channelling his God and his channellings were published in a New Age magazine the readership would plummet. People would say that the entity he was channelling was very dark. If a religion forming around that entity, people would be even more concerned and would definitely describe it as a cult.

Devout Jews and fundamentalist Christians, who are

strongly attached to the Torah and Bible, proclaim all channelling to be evil and warn of the dangers of New Age cults. Reading much of the material channelled through Moses and other biblical prophets in the Bible it is clear that there is as greater danger in the 'Old Age Cults' based on the Bible than in any of the so-called New Age cults.

In the Talmud it says: *'We see the world, not the way it is, but the way we are'*. Advocates of the Bible denounce other religions, faiths and spiritual ways as 'Satanic cults'. We need to consider to what extent their judgements of others are a reflection of the cults to which they belong.

The Old Age cults of Jehovah are accepted as bona fide religions by humanity because they are as old as man himself and form the bedrock of our culture. They are respected by many millions of people throughout the world, because they are part of the establishment and most people have been indoctrinated with the belief that the 'God' of the Bible is beyond reproach.

The documents I have already cited make it abundantly clear that the Old Age Jehovah cults are exceedingly dangerous. These ancient cults are not just a bunch of religious fanatics. Over recent centuries they have consolidated colossal riches and universal power. They are enmeshed in all the establishments of our modern age. They create, own and control all money. Their tentacles reach into every aspect of civilisation through secret societies. Through cunning and secrecy they are having enormous impact on world affairs and are exceedingly difficult to identify and isolate.

In any sane society dangerous cults are not tolerated. Because the Old Age cult established by Moses considers itself to be at war with society, society has every right to defend itself, and use its best endeavours to expunge the cult. As the cult is Semitic in origin, to be anti-Semitic in reaction to this cult is no different to being anti-Nazi in reaction to Hitler, or anti-Communist in reaction to Stalin or Pol Pot. Yet we have to be clear that the most ancient cult of Jehovah is not the creation of the Jews. They are the product not the originators of the cult. They have been bred and brainwashed into it and fortunately many have succeeded in breaking free.

It is the cult not the members that pose a problem. It should be clear from what has been revealed so far, anti-Semitism plays into the hands of the cult as persecution of its members is a mechanism the cult uses to further its ends and for the most part, the Semites are not directly responsible for the activities of this ancient cult; even if their submissiveness and silence has led in part to its success. I know the vast majority of the Jewish people are good at heart; they are not fanatics or Zionists. Many are leading freethinkers, heretics and dissidents. I consider myself to be one of these. My sire and grandsire were circumcised Jews. My father was adopted outside of the Jewish faith into a Christian family. Though he escaped the childhood indoctrination of the Judaic religion he was brought up with the Bible. Though he became a Catholic he was never rigid and was more deeply spiritual than religious. He was a free thinker and taught me to question my Catholic indoctrination.

I did not receive the mark of circumcision but the blood of the Jewish people runs deep in my veins. I feel Jewish even if I am not accepted as such because of my gentile mother. I am just like my father and his Jewish genes have more bearing on me than circumcision. I feel a sense of belonging to both the Jewish and Christian traditions. Bridging the gap between Jew and Christian I have studied the Bible objectively and come to the conclusion that the 'God' portrayed therein is not a good god and I see more bigotry and intolerance amongst Christians than Jews.

Even in the faith there are many deeply religious Jews with good and generous hearts, and some of them are very poor. Also amongst them there are those who are truly enlightened, who are respectful of all other peoples, cultures and creeds — which is more than can be said of many fundamentalist Christians.

There are Jews who wander the Earth, taking only what they need to stay alive, who work for the greater good of the whole, out of unconditional love for all. Jesus Christ was one of these.

Jesus had the courage to confront the 'old age' cult of Jehovah. He warned the Jews that in their ancient cult they were enslaved to the Devil:

> "You belong to your father, the Devil, and the desires of your father you want to do. He was a murderer from the beginning, and does not stand in the truth, because there is no truth in him. When he speaks a lie, he speaks from his own resources, for he is a liar and the father of it." (John 8:44)

He endeavoured to show his people that the only way out of their cult was the way of love. At one time the mass of Jews followed him, welcoming him in triumph into Jerusalem:

> And many spread their garments on the way: and others cut down branches off the trees, and strew them in the way.
> And they that went before, and they that followed, cried, saying, 'Hosanna; Blessed is he that comes in

the name of the Lord.
'Blessed be the kingdom of our father David, that co-
mes in the name of the Lord: Hosanna in the high-
est.'And Jesus entered into Jerusalem...
(Mark 11:8-11)

Led by Jesus, the Jewish people were on the way of Love. It was the beginning of a New Age and they were so close to the Kingdom of Heaven on Earth. But the grip of their ancient cult was too strong. The people of that time were not sufficiently evolved in their understanding to overcome the pressure of their culture. They were still tightly bound to religious fear and superstition.

The Elders were in fear of the people:

And the chief priests and scribes sought how they
might kill him for they feared the people. (Luke 22:2)

They knew that without the acquiescence of the people, their cult would be dead and they would be finished so the Learned Elders, in Sanhedrin, manipulated the people to destroy Jesus...

But the chief priests and the elders persuaded the mul-
titude that they should ask for Barabbas and destroy
Jesus. (Matthew 27:20)

After the death of Christ, a cult rapidly formed around his person and within a few centuries this became the established religion of the Roman Empire. Just as the Jewish Elders destroyed Jesus Christ because he threatened their cult so, in the name of Christ, the Roman Catholic Church destroyed the Cathars who were more Christ like than the Catholics who persecuted them.

The Roman Catholic Church and all Christian religions that have stemmed from it are new forms of the old Jehovah cult. Like the chameleon it continually changes its form to adapt to different cultures. You can see this in the links between the Jewish and Roman priesthood. Roman Catholic priests wear the same vestments in the Mass as a Rabbi wears in the synagogue. They both wore a little black hat called the 'biretta.' Religious Jews wear a skullcap. Senior Catholic priests traditionally wore a skullcap called the 'zucchetto' and Catholic bishops and the Pope wear skullcaps to this day. The bread and wine of the Mass, attributed to Christ, goes back to Melchizedek (Genesis 14:18) and many other elements of the Roman, Greek and Russian Orthodox churches can be traced back to Judaic origins.

The policy of sons of Judaism becoming clerics in the Christian churches, in order to control them from within, is clearly revealed in the letter from the Sanhedrin or 'Grand Satraps' in Constantinople, to the Rabbis in Spain:

...make your sons canons and clerics in order that they may destroy their churches. ('La Silva Curiosa')

The hallmark of the cults of Jehovah is infiltration through deception and secrecy, taking systems over from within. At the same time the 'genuine article' has been discredited!

We have long past taken care to discredit the priesthood of the Goyim, and thereby to ruin their mission on Earth which in these days might still be a great hindrance to us. Day by day its influence on the peoples of the world is falling lower. (Protocol 17)

There is no doubt that established Christianity has degenerated from the original teachings of the founder and Christian intolerance and lack of love has led to wars and schism.

We shall force the Christians into wars by exploiting their pride and their stupidity. (Rabbi Reichhorn)

Christian churches are accepted as part of the establishment but the media and educational scientific establishment continually undermine them:

We shall not overtly lay a finger on existing churches, but we shall fight against them by criticism calculated to produce schism. (Protocol 17)

Modern forms of Christianity are based as much on the cult of Moses and adherence to the fear and intolerance of the Old Testament as on the love and universality of Christ taught in the New Testament.

...the German Reformation was based upon a crude Christianity; this kind of Christianity was invented, preached and propagated by the Jews... (Oscar Levy)

Christians think of themselves as sheep following the Good Shepherd:

The goyim are a flock of sheep, and we are their wolves. And you know what happens when the wolves get hold of the flock? (Protocol 11)

In the name of the Good Shepherd many self-righteous Christians proclaim Freemasonry as a cult of Satan. **Freemasonry** is a fraternal organisation founded on high principles of virtue, morality and brotherly love and is more tolerant of people's freedom of belief than Judaism or Christianity.

Freemasonry consists of independent Grand Lodges in most countries of the world. Unfortunately Freemasonry has been infiltrated and is manipulated from within through, 'elite' fraternities and chapters which are only open to Freemasons:

Until we come into our kingdom...we shall create and multiply free Masonic lodges in all of the coun-

tries of the world, absorb into them all who may become or who are prominent in public activity, for in these lodges we shall find our principal intelligence office and means of influence. (Protocol 15)

Freemasons pride themselves on their religious tolerance and Freemasonry welcomes members from every religion. The lodges only require belief in a supreme being and that a Bible be kept open in each lodge. Whilst Freemasonry is an important repository of ancient Hermetic teachings there is a predominant link Judaism through the **Temple of Solomon**. Each Freemason's lodge has two columns, one on each side of the master's chair; these symbolise the pillars at the entrance of King Solomon's Temple. The left hand pillar of the entrance porch is in the first degree for *Entered Apprentices*. The Temple of Solomon and the right hand pillar comes into the second degree for *Fellow Craftsmen* — along with the Greek temple with its five orders, Liberal Arts and Sciences. The setting of the third degree of Freemasonry is Solomon's Temple and the builder of the Temple, Hiram Abiff is central to the ritual for *Master Masons,* which includes the following vow of secrecy:

I − − − in the presence of T...M...H... and in the body of this Chartered and Right Worshipful Lodge of Master Masons, regularly assembled and properly constituted, of my own free will and accord, do hereby and hereon solemnly and sincerely promise and swear that I will always hele (hide), and never reveal, any of the secrets or mysteries of, or belonging to, the Degree of Master Mason, to anyone in the world...

Freemasons had to meet in secrecy because of Catholic intolerance and persecution by the Inquisition:

During the Middle Ages when any opposition to the Holy Roman Universal (Catholic) Church was forced deep underground, among the only organized groups able to move freely throughout Europe were the guilds of stone masons, who maintained halls or 'lodges' in every major city. (Jim Marrs, Rule by Secrecy)

The organisations of masons — and the secret schools of the Knights Templar — carried the mystery teachings from ancient Sumer, Egypt, Greece, including uplifting, inspiring and enlightening Gnostic, Hermetic and Cabalistic teachings at a time when the Inquisition was very active — under the cover of geometry and architecture:

One Masonic tradition claimed that Abraham, the patriarch of the Hebrews, taught the Egyptians special knowledge [Sumerian] predating the Great Flood. Later, this knowledge — reported as the work of the legendary Hermes Trismegistos — was collected by the Greek philosopher Euclid, who studied the work under the name geometry. The Greeks and later Romans called this discipline architecture. (Jim Marrs, Rule by Secrecy)

The masons opened their doors to non-masons in Tudor times. Although this was for survival at the time of the reformation it led to the growth of the organisation and expansion and proliferation of its esoteric teachings outside of the church and cathedral building guilds:

King Henry the VIII, in breaking with Rome, not only discontinued the church's building programs in England, causing widespread unemployment, but looted the assets of the Masons under the guise of taxes and tribute. To survive the lodges began opening their memberships to non-Masons. These outsider merchants, landowners, and others — many with Templar backgrounds — became known as 'Speculative' Masons. They embraced a mystical and esoteric doctrine based on traditions predating Freemasonry and brought to the order by Knights Templar members fleeing persecution by the church. (Jim Marrs, Rule by Secrecy)

Unfortunately, the need for secrecy left Freemasonry wide open to infiltration by the agents of Jehovah seeking dominion of the Earth. Eventually a perverted form of Masonry became a predominant means for the Learned Elders of Zion to maintain control of modern society.

...the basis for our organisation of secret masonry which is only known to us, and aims which are not even so much as suspected by those Goy cattle attracted by us into the 'show army' of Masonic lodges in order to throw dust in the eyes of their fellows. (Protocol 11)

The original 'Blue Lodge' of Freemasonry does not have a degree higher than the third degree, nor does it recognise the higher degrees. Degrees, up to thirty three, occur in the 'exclusive' orders, chapters and lodges which are open only to Master Masons who are naturally attracted to these by ambition and their own sense of self-importance and superiority over others:

You cannot imagine to what extent the wisest of the Goyim can be brought to a state of unconscious naiveté in the presence of this condition of high conceit of themselves, and at the same time how easy it is to take the heart out of them by the slightest ill-success, though it be nothing more than the stoppage of the applause they had, and to reduce them to a slavish submission for the sake of winning a renewal of success. (Protocol 15)

In the 'Red Lodge' of Masonry, Jehovah features very strongly. In *An Encyclopaedia of Freemasonry*(1871), Albert Mackey states:

> *'Jehovah is, of all significant words of Masonry, by far the most important... (being) the basis of our dogma and of our mysteries'.*

The 'all-seeing Eye' of Jehovah features as a Freemasonry symbol:

> *Brethren, let us remember, that wherever we are, or whatever we do, He is always with us, and **His all-seeing Eye** observes us; and while we continue to act according to the principles of the Craft, let us not fail to discharge our duty to Him with fervency and zeal.* (Ceremony of Closing the Lodge in the Second or Fellow Craft Degree. The "Standard" Ritual of Scottish Freemasonry).

Freemasonry became predominantly Judaic in the eighteenth century:

> *The fact remains that when the ritual and constitutions of Masonry were drawn up in 1717, although certain fragments of the ancient Egyptian and Pythagorean doctrines were retained, the Judaic version of the secret tradition was the one selected by the founders of the Grand Lodge on which to build their system.*(Jim Marrs, Rule by Secrecy)

The roots of Freemasonry are uncertain. Some believe they go no further back than the church, castle and cathedral builders of medieval Europe. Others, like author and Cambridge historian Andrew Sinclair in *The Secret Scroll*, trace the passage of Judaic wisdom through the Templars to the Masons:

> *"My researches had told me that candidates of the Royal Arch in modern Masonry were also initiated into the Order of Melchizedek. The candidate for the Higher*

Degrees was anointed with oil and proclaimed forever a priest according to the order. As a medieval Knight Templar, he now had the power to speak with the Word of God as Christ did, and to understand the divine purpose.

There is overwhelming evidence that Masonry has its roots in the confraternity of masons involved in the building of the Temple of Solomon. This is clear in the *Explanation of the Tracing Board of the Second Degree* in which even the corn and oil wages of the Entered Apprentices are detailed.

The rites of Freemasonry can also be traced back to the mystery teachings of ancient Egypt and Babylon. In the Explanation of the Tracing Board of the First degree, the Scottish Rite states:

*The usages and customs of Freemasons have ever borne a near affinity to those of the ancient Egyptians. Their philosophers, unwilling to expose their mysteries to vulgar eyes, concealed their peculiar tenets and principles of polity and philosophy under certain hieroglyphical figures, and expressed their motions of government by signs and symbols, which they communicated to their priests or **Magi** only, they were bound by oath never to reveal them.*

Many of the mysteries and rites of Freemasonry appear to have been the same as were absorbed by the Hebrews during their periods of exile in Egypt and Babylon. That is when their higher echelons took full advantage of the periods of Jewish dispersal:

God has granted us, His Chosen People, the gift of the dispersion, and in this which appears in all eyes to be our weakness, has come forth our strength, which has now brought us to the threshold of sovereignty over all the world. (Protocol 11)

The Judaic bedrock of Freemasonry is abundantly clear. It is in their rites and rituals:

"...the spirit of Freemasonry is that of Judaism in its most fundamental beliefs; its ideas are Judaic, its language is Judaic, its very organisation, almost, is Judaic. Whenever I approach the sanctuary where the Masonic order accomplishes its works, I hear the name of Solomon ringing everywhere, and echoes of Israel. Those symbolic columns are the columns of that Temple where each day Hiram's workmen received their wages; they enshrine his revered name. The whole Masonic tradition takes me back to that great epoch when the Jewish monarch, fulfilling David's promises, raised up to the God of Abraham, Isaac and Jacob, a religious monument worthy of the creator of Heaven and earth..." (La Verite Israelite [1861]; Vol.V. p.74)

In the Ceremony of Raising to the Third Degree under Exhortation, there is a ritual of re-enactment of the death of King Solomon's Master Mason, Hiram Abiff. Did the original order of Masons come into being under Hiram Abiff at the time of the building of Solomon's temple? When the temple was destroyed did the temple masons go underground during the exile in Babylon? What did the temple masons absorb from the Babylonian culture during captivity? When the temple was rebuilt, were the Babylonian rites preserved in the Judaic sub-cults of Sadducees and Pharisees? When this second temple was destroyed by the Romans, did the 'temple confraternity' go underground again to resurface in the middle ages through the order of the 'Poor Knights of Christ', renamed the 'Order of the Knights of the Temple of Solomon', commonly known as the **Knights Templar**? Did the Knights Templar go underground again due to persecution and then re-emerge in Freemasonry? To what extent were medieval masons in touch with the traditions of the ancient Temple masons? Who was responsible for maintaining the link? Did the cult of masons survive the dispersal of Rome and re-emerge as the medieval church and cathedral masons invigorated by Templar discoveries? There are many un-answered questions regarding the lineage of Masonry back into the ancient past but I am certain of the links be-tween modern Masonry and the ancient cult of Jehovah. There is no doubt in my mind that the Dark Lord with his all-seeing eye, controls every aspect of the modern world through his Judaic, Christian, Islamic and Masonic cults, but most especially through Masonry and affiliated secret societies.

Many people believe that the 'hidden influence' in our society originated in the Knights Templar and passed into Freemasonry. I believe this is an oversimplification. I also believe the 'Priory of Sion' linking the mysteries back to a bloodline of Christ is a red herring that serves to throw people off the scent of who is really at work behind the scenes. Many people who are awake to conspiracy theories believe that the Knights Templar were the original culprits. Others implicate the cult of Rosicrucians, or the cults of Theosophy. I look for footprints. There was an enormously powerful hidden influence behind the 'Order of Knights Templar' and the Roman Catholic Church that had Christendom fighting the Crusades, to secure the Holy Land for the rebuilding of Solomon's Temple. When this attempt failed the influence turned elsewhere and the Order of Knights Templar collapsed. Within a very short period of the Knights Templar being forcefully disbanded by King Philip IV of France, the first Masonic lodges appeared. In the proliferation of Masonic lodges and chapters, Zionist tentacles have reached out to every 'crook and cranny' of society:

In the most important and fundamental affairs and questions, judges decide as we dictate to them...for the administration of the Goyim...even senators and the higher administration accept our counsels...the Goyim enter the lodges out of curiosity or in the hope by their means to get a nibble at the public pie...(Protocol 15)

Through Freemasonry the Learned Elders of Zion exercise their secret control:

Gentile Masonry blindly serves as a screen for us and our objectives. (Protocol 4)

"Freemasonry has two doctrines, one concealed and reserved for the Masters, the other public..." (Albert Pike)

...those even who have occupied the Chair of the Master {Mason} for 50 years may yet be unacquainted with its mysteries. (Casanova)

The Learned Elders of Zion are able to covertly influence the most prominent people in society, through the social channels secured by the fraternity of Freemasons. Most Masons and certainly the majority of the public are unaware of what is going on:

The plan of action of our force, even its very abiding place, remains for the whole people an unknown mystery. (Protocol 4)

The vast majority of members look upon their affiliation with Freemasonry as little different from joining the Lion's Club, the Optimists, or the Chamber of Commerce. And from their standpoint, this is true. Even Masonic literature makes clear that only those initiates who progress beyond the thirty-third-degree status are educated in the group's true goals and secrets. (Jim Marrs, Rule by Secrecy)

Though most are oblivious of it, Freemasonry is ruthlessly influenced by the Learned Elders:

We execute masons in such wise that none save the brotherhood can ever have a suspicion of it, not even the victims themselves of our death sentence, they all die when required as if from a normal kind of illness...By such methods we have plucked out of the midst of masonry the very root of protest against our disposition. While preaching liberalism to the Goyim we have, at the same time, kept our own people and our agents in a state of unquestioning submission. (Protocol 15)

Freemasonry is a fraternity within a fraternity — an outer organisation concealing an inner brotherhood of the elect… the one visible and the other invisible. The visible society is a splendid camaraderie of 'free and accepted' men enjoined to devote themselves to ethical, educational, fraternal, patriotic and humanitarian concerns. The invisible society is a secret and most august fraternity whose members are dedicated to the service of an arcanum arcandrum [a sacred secret]" (Manley P. Hall; 33degree Mason)

Author Epperson made the interesting observation that every mason will deny that there exists an inner circle to the order because the 'average Mason' is truly unaware of this system while the 'Illuminated Mason' is pledged not to reveal it. "This second layer is protected by an oath of secrecy, which means that if they knew about its existence, you would be obligated by an oath not to tell anyone" he explained. (Jim Marrs, Rule by Secrecy)

And having used the Masons to secure their ends, the

'brotherhood of the snake' hidden within the 'brotherhood of Masons,' intend to discard them like a worn out glove:

When we at last, definitely come into our kingdom... Every kind of new institution of anything like a secret society will also be punished with death; those of them which are now in existence, are known to us, serve us and have served us, we shall disband and send into exile to continents far removed from Europe... (Protocol 15)

Freemasonry in its turn, gave rise to the **Jehovah's Witnesses**. The Jehovah's Witness cult was founded late in the 19th century by Charles Taze Russell as the 'Watchtower Bible & Tract Society' and Russell's original publication was known as *Zion's Watch Tower*, only later renamed *The Watchtower*.

Russell was a Zionist. On October 9th 1910, he preached his message of 'Zionism, Hope for the World' at the New York City Hippodrome. He repeated the message at the Albert Hall in London. He had a wide following amongst the Jewish people. In 1880 he predicted the restoration of Israel in Palestine, advertised Dr.T.Herzl's launching of the Zionist movement and published a Yiddish magazine, *Di Shtimme*.

Support for Russell's movement came from Jewish Masonry. Details of his finances revealed that The Watchtower Society received substantial funding from the **B'nai B'rith**. The B'nai B'rith are identified as the Jewish Masonic Lodge, I.O.B.B., (founded in 1843). In his translation of **The Protocols of the Learned Elders of Zion**, Victor Marsden identified the B'nai B'rith with the supreme council of the ancient cult of Pharisees, which dominated the Sanhedrin. This is, in my opinion, one of the most important clues to who is really pulling the strings behind the Masonry and other secret societies and cults which hold the Dark Lord Jehovah as 'God'.

Russell also received funds from the Zionist movement and other branches of Freemasonry. The financial holdings of C.T.Russell are covered in Fritz Springmeier's book *Be Wise as Serpents*. He argued the links between the Watchtower Bible & Tract Society in his book, *The Watchtower and the Masons*.

There is no direct evidence that Russell was a Freemason but there are clear links between the Jehovah cult he founded and Freemasonry. The early Watchtower conventions were held in Masonic halls. Many of Russell's beliefs were Masonic and some of these are still doctrine to Jehovah's Witnesses. For example:

> *Jehovah is the most important word being the basis of their dogma and the name of their god.* (The Watchtower and The Masons p.35)

Charles Russell identified Jehovah as God's distinctive personal name. In his biography, *The Laodicean Messenger, His Life Works and Character*(p.68) it states:

> *'The prime objective of Pastor Russell's life was to honour and magnify the name of Great Jehovah.'*

Russell frequently used the Masonic term 'Great Architect'. He also held the Masonic belief that The Great Architect yielded power to a lesser god and that Jesus was only a good man, not Almighty God. In his sermon, 'Desire of All Nations', Russell also voiced support for the Masonic belief in Hiram Abiff — the builder of the Temple of Solomon — as the Messiah. Like many Masons, he rejected the idea of hell and spoke of immortality in a future Golden Age, ideas which are cherished by Jehovah's Witnesses.

The Jehovah's Witnesses exist as an international confraternity, which offers mutual support and protection to fellow members. This pattern is modelled on the Masons.

Russell borrowed his logo of the 'Cross and the Crown' from the Knights Templar. This logo was also used by Mary Baker Eddy and the Mormons. Russell also used the 'Winged Sun & Serpent Disc' logo on his Watchtower periodical, a symbol used by Freemasons, Theosophists and Rosicrucians. This symbol appears frequently amongst the hieroglyphs in many ancient Egyptian temples and tombs. Russell was an Egyptologist and had a pyramid, built out of pink granite, as his tomb.

Charles Taze Russell was a brilliant man. He was a sincere seeker after truth and founded a movement to bring people into the light. However, he was heavily influenced by Egyptian and Judaic traditions, coming from Freemasonry, and created a cult, which has captivated millions of people to the Dark Lord Jehovah.

There is, of course, no evidence of a direct involvement between Pastor Russell and the highly secretive Learned Elders of Zion. Nonetheless, the *Watchtower and Bible Tract Society* was wide open to their influence. Because of Russell's inclinations toward Zionism and Masonry, the cult of Jehovah's Witnesses could be 'implicated by strong association' to have been used as yet another convenient front organisation by the Learned Elders of Zion. Certainly it has served as a bridge between Judaism and Christianity, supporting the worship of Jehovah as God.

Charles Russell was openly in support of Zion. However, support for Zionism does not prove a link with the Learned Elders. Charles Russell's Zionism stemmed from his pre-millennium outlook and his predictions of the New Jerusalem. In the time of Russell, Zionism was a popular movement concerned with the restoration of Israel in Palestine. Zionism came from the longing of many Jews to return to their ancient homeland.

The Zionism which created and supports the State of Israel should not be confused with the Zionism of the Learned Elders. The Learned Elders of Zion are not the Government of the Modern State of Israel. The Learned Elders of Zion are an international organisation involved in an illegal secret government, which through covert activity — mainly economic — controls the governments of all nations, including Israel.

The people and government of Israel are no more party to the clandestine activities of the Learned Elders of Zion than the people and government of any other nation on Earth. The majority of modern Israelis are people with little or no affinity for Jehovah or his cults. Only a minority are 'devotees' and are safer within those borders than without. Zionists and even Zealots in the international Jewish nation should not be mistaken as Learned Elders.

The Sanhedrin of Learned Elders is a group of seventy-one, with immense power, surrounded by a group of three hundred. Bankers, billionaires and industrial and media barons then surround these. Prominent public figures are rarely included in the inner core groups. These always remain hidden and operate from behind the scenes. Leading rabbis and the most influential Jews, the Elders' belonging to the ancient cult of Pharisees, who, by tradition, have steered the Jewish culture and the Jewish thought, dominate the Sanhedrin itself.

I believe the **'Cult of Pharisees'**, is the Secret

Government; the innermost core steering secret societies toward the goal of dominion of the entire Earth and enslavement of humanity, on behalf of the ancient Sumerian god Enlil, otherwise known as Jehovah. I believe the **'Cult of Pharisees'**, are the Elders of Zion that have manipulated and exploited the Jewish people as they have exploited and manipulated other peoples of the Earth. They manipulated the murder of six million Jews at the hand of Hitler as they manipulated the murder of Christ at the hand of Pilate. I believe they allowed the leak of *The Protocols of the Learned Elders of Zion* — the proceedings of their meeting in the nineteenth century — to fan the flames of anti-Semitism.

The **'Cult of Pharisees'** came into ascendancy during the Jewish exile in Babylon when many Judaic priests assimilated the 'Chaldean' science. The Pharisee cult can be dated back to 606BC when it was a confraternity of restricted membership amongst the Jews. Its members were bound by secrecy. In Jewish society they were the equivalent of the Masons in modern society. At the time of Flavius Josephus they numbered 6,000. At the time of Christ there was bitter rivalry between the Pharisees and the more orthodox sect of Sadducees.

The Pharisees hijacked the Sanhedrin — the ancient Jewish Parliament — when the Babylonian Pharisee, Hillel, was elected president. They were responsible for fomenting the revolt against the Romans under Hadrian, which led to the dispersion of the Jews in c.132. Amongst their number was the great magician Simon ben Yohai, father of the '**Cabala**' and Judah the Prince who compiled the **Babylonian Talmud**. It was under these powerful intellects that the influence of the Pharisees was consolidated in the Sanhedrin. With the destruction of the Temple by the Roman Emperor Titus, in c.70, the Sadducees lost their power and in the course of time they became dissidents, who contested the Talmud. Control of the Sanhedrin fell to the Pharisees. Through that council, rule of the Jewish nation and thereby, eventual conquest of the World, has always been the avowed intent of the cult of Pharisees. They are the zealots who use the word Zion to mean the Jewish people, the Temple mount in Jerusalem, and Heaven. They are committed to the rebuilding of the Temple in Jerusalem, whatever the cost, and fervently await the coming of the Messiah, their 'King of the World.'

Jesus Christ had strong words to say about the cult of Pharisees:

> "Woe unto you, scribes and Pharisees, hypocrites! For you are like white sepulchres, which indeed appear beautiful outward, but are full of dead men's bones, and of all uncleanness." (Matthew 23:27)

The Pharisees carried the age-old Babylonian cult into Freemasonry. Through Freemasonry the Babylonian cult has had such an enormous influence on modern civilisation that it could be described as 'Babylon the Great.' In the *Book of Revelation* the references to Babylon the Great (Revelation 17:3-5), the great but corrupt civilisation in the last days of this present world order, could be alluding to our own modern materialistic civilisation. For example, William Cooper documented the assassination of President J. F. Kennedy in November 1963, in the *Exposure Documentary* film *Did Secret Societies Kill J.F.K.(Exposure Magazine)*. Cooper said the assassination was a ritual regicide carried out in the Babylonian cult tradition. The choice of Dallas for the murder was not coincidental. The Masons had laid out that city along the lines of a Babylonian temple. It would seem that the cult of Pharisees that murdered Christ also murdered JFK.

> *"Wherefore, behold, I send unto you prophets, and wise men, and scribes: and some of them you shall kill and crucify; and some of them shall you scourge in your synagogues and persecute them from city to city."(Matthew 23: 30-34)*

I believe the cult of Pharisees, operating as the secret government in control of all governments in the world corresponds to the Beast of the Apocalypse. The ancient cult of Pharisees has received power and authority; the throne of the modern world and the crowns of many nations; from the Dragon of Old:

> *Then I stood on the sand of the sea. And I saw a beast rising out of the sea, having seven heads and ten horns, and on his horns ten crowns, and on his heads a blasphemous name.*
>
> *Now the beast which I saw was like a leopard, his feet were like the feet of a bear, and his mouth like the mouth of a lion. And the Dragon gave him his power, his throne, and great authority.(Revelation 13:1-2)*

Jehovah is Enlil, dragon amongst the serpent gods. His cults are dinosaurs heading for extinction. Humanity needs to let go of attachment to them because dinosaurs in their death-throes are dangerous things. If we hang onto them we may end up becoming extinct

Chapter 11

The Myths in Christianity

"As I understand the Christian religion, it was, and is, a revelation. But how has it happened that millions of fables, tales, legends, have been blended with both Jewish and Christian revelation that have made them the most bloody religion that ever existed."

(John Adams)

Christianity is one of the greatest religions in the world because of the teaching and examples Jesus Christ set of unconditional love and selfless service as portrayed in the Gospels. Jesus as a man set standards for other men and women to follow which are universal in their truth and timeless in their real value.

The idea that Jesus was God appeared three centuries after his death and can be traced back to Roman origin. It is common for myths, such as this, to grow around charismatic religious leaders and Christianity has not been immune from this tendency of history. If the myths are stripped away a simple teaching of compassion remains which is so inspiring it matters not if the source is fact or fable.

The central tenet of Christianity is that Jesus suffered and died on the cross to redeem us of our sins, was resurrected from the dead and then ascended into heaven. So important is this belief that St Paul, the founder of Christianity, said the faith is unfounded without it:

"If Christ has not been raised, your faith is in vain"
(1 Cor. 5:17)

Theologians argue that for the resurrection claim to be

acceptable there would have to be reliable records of people seeing and meeting the resurrected Christ. These occur in the Gospels of Matthew Luke and John but not in Mark.

The concluding verses of Mark 16:9–20 which profess eyewitness accounts are unreliable. The verses reporting the appearances of Christ after his resurrection and the ascension in the modern Bible Gospel of Mark (Mark 16:9 – 20) did not occur in the earliest Bibles i.e. the 'Sinai Bible' nor the 'Alexandria Bible', neither were they in the 'Vatican Bible'. They are not found in an ancient Latin manuscript of Mark code-named 'K' by analysists and they are absent from the old Armenian version of the New Testament and also from the Ethiopic version:

> The resurrection is the fundamental argument for our Christian belief yet no supernatural appearance of a resurrected Jesus Christ was ever recorded, nor any reference to an ascension into heaven, in the earliest Christian Gospel. The resurrection and ascension of Jesus Christ is the 'sine qua non' of Christianity, 'without which nothing'. (Catholic Encyclopaedia, vol XII, p792, 1911)

None of the early Church fathers including Irenaeus (115-202), Clement of Alexandria (160-215), Tertullian (160-210), Ammonius Saccas (175-245), Origen (185-251) or Eusebius (260-339) appeared to have knowledge of the concluding verses in Mark and St Jerome who translated the Bible into Latin from the Greek wrote early in the fifth century:

> "Almost all of the Greek copies do not have this concluding portion" (Jerome Epistle CXX.3, Hedibium)

The Catholic Encyclopaedia stated of the concluding verses of Mark:

None of the endings commands itself as original... the end of Mark (16:9-20) is not authentic.(Catholic Encyclopaedia, vol XII, p792, 1911)

The Council of Trent (1545-1563) approved of the added verses when all the received manuscripts and their substantial portions were declared sacred and canonical. However, this medieval imprimatur does not satisfy modern theologians. In the 1967 'New Catholic Encyclopaedia' the editorial committee stated that the earlier decision is:

...no longer sustainable in the view of the better knowledge gained concerning the Gospel's style and vocabulary...simply put, the last twelve verses in today's version of the Mark Gospel are not original to the story (New Catholic Encyclopaedia, vol XII, p 409, 1967) *and '...(the verses) differ so radically from the rest of the Gospel that it hardly seems possible Mark himself composed it'.* (New Catholic Encyclopaedia, vol XII, p 240, 1967)

Without the final verses, the Gospel of Mark ends with three women reporting the tomb of Jesus was open, the body was missing and a young man dressed in white sitting in the tomb said Jesus had risen from the dead. If the reports of Jesus appearing after the resurrection, as recorded in Mark, do not stand critics would argue the body had simply been stolen from the grave; as intimated in Matthew (**Matt 28:11-15**).

Whilst the Gospels of Luke and Matthew refer to the resurrection appearances, they do not carry the same weight as the Gospel of Mark which was *'the first of them in sequence of composition... and inevitably it set the standard for the later Gospels'.* (Catholic Encyclopaedia, vol IX, pp 674, 1910)

Modern critical analysis concludes that the Gospels of

Luke and Matthew were derived from the Gospel of Mark with 606 of the 661 verses appearing verbatim in Matthew and sixty nine percent in Luke so many people believe these two 'Synoptic Gospels' (synoptic meaning similar content) were derived from Mark. Critics argue that what was not in the original Gospel of Mark is suspect as additions to the original story.

The Gospel of John appeared later and is different from the Synoptic Gospels. But with the Gospel of Mark being the original Church writing anything that is in John, which is not in Mark is treated as unreliable.

Maybe Jesus was crucified by the Romans but the story of his being crucified as 'King of the Jews' makes the crucifixion story suspect. Jesus Christ was the illegitimate son of a carpenter. He may have had a lineage back to King David via Joseph, his foster father but that would not make him King of the Jews. Thousands of Jews could trace their origins back to David without any rightful claim to the throne. Kings are crowned and there is no mention in the Gospels of Jesus being crowned King of the Jews that would warrant I.N.R.I being inscribed on his cross by the Roman procurator.

In 37BC a claimant to the kingship of Jerusalem by the name of Antigonus was crucified and scourged by Mark Antony who then handed the kingship over to his ally, Herod. (Dio Cassius, bk. Xlix, p.405) The sympathy for the 'Crucified King of the Jews' was widespread along with understandable hatred for Herod. It is possible that in the passage of time the folklore associated with Antigonus became attributed to the popular and charismatic figure of Jesus the Nazarene.

I find it particularly hard to believe that the crucifixion of Jesus Christ never occurred. Perhaps the Romans crucified so many people, the execution of yet another Jewish rebel was not considered worth mentioning in the records in 'The Case for Christ' by Strobel, Tacitus is cited from Annals 15.44:

> *Nero fastened the guilt… on a class hated for their abominations, called Christians by the populace. Christus, from whom the name had its origin, suffered the extreme penalty during the reign of Tiberius at the hands of… Pontius Pilatus, and a most mischievous superstition, thus checked for the moment, again broke out not only in Judaea, the first source of the evil, but even in Rome.*

And in 'Jesus Outside the New Testament' by Yamauchi (p212) Josephus is quoted from Antiquities 18.63-64:

> *About this time there lived Jesus, a wise man, if indeed one ought to call him a man. For he…. wrought surprising feats… He was the Christ. When Pilate …condemned him to be crucified, those who had… come to love him did not give up their affection for him. On the third day he appeared…. restored to life… And the tribe of Christians… has… not disappeared.*

Critics have doubts as to the authenticity of this quote and there is no mention of the crucifixion of Christ in the early church records, even as late as the second century.

> *The cross didn't come into use until the sixth century* (New Catholic Encyclopaedia, vol. IV p.475)

The general use of the crucifix was endorsed at the Ecumenical Council of 680 when it was decreed in Canon 82 that the Church adopt the figure of a man on a cross. Pope Hadrian I ratified this between 772 and 795 (Origin of Religious Belief, Draper, p.252) but the early Church father, Bishop Irenaeus (115-202) denied the virgin birth, never mentioned the trial, crucifixion or resurrection of Jesus claiming rather that he declined towards old age:

'...although of crucial importance in the development of the Church's theology, Irenaeus presents problems of considerable difficulty in regard to details about Jesus Christ (New Catholic Encyclopaedia, vol VII, 1967)

Pope Leo X (1513-1521) is reported to have said:

"How well we know what a profitable superstition this fable of Christ has been for us" (Catholic Encyclopaedia vol IX, p163, 1910)

The theologian Dr Constantine Tischendorf commented

"We must frankly admit that we have no source of information with respect to the life of Jesus Christ than the presbyters' writings..." (Catholic Encyclopaedia, vol IV, p 583, 1908)

St. Jerome reported the presbyter Origen advising people in authority in the early church to resort to lying in order to win over disbelievers and convert them to Christianity (Adv. Rufin, Apol., 1,18.) and Jerome himself, author of the Catholic Vulgate Bible admitted to lying in his writing, justifying it on the basis that it was standard practice of writers before him. (De Viris Illustribus, 135, D.Vallarsi, vols. I-XI, Verona, 1734-42)

The Grecian Celsus complained that the early Church presbyters:

"... are forever repeating, 'Do not examine. Only believe and thy faith will make thee blessed. Wisdom is a bad thing in life; foolishness is to be preferred'. They teach men to believe without examination." (Contra Celsus, Origen, bk.I, chs. Ix;x)

The Epistles of St Paul confirm for Christians that by faith alone they will be saved. So much store is placed in the teachings of Paul in his epistles that many people feel the religion is more 'Pauline' than 'Christian'. However, theologians are aware that most of the Epistles attributed to St. Paul were not written by Paul but by a number of inconsequential individuals. An early edition of the Oxford Bible lists authors of the epistles as follows:

- Corinthians I: written by Stephanas, Acaicus and Timotheus (p.1164)
- Corinthians II: written by Titus and Lucas (p.1175)
- Ephesians: written by Tychicus (p.1186)
- Philippians: written by Epaphroditus (p.1190)
- Philemon: written by Onesimus (p.1209) (a servant)
- Colossians: written by Tychicus and Onesimus
- Hebrews: written by Timothy (p.1220)

Galatians and Timothy are attributed to Paul but even these Epistles are uncertain.

Even the genuine Epistles were greatly interpolated to lend weight to the personal views of their authors. (Catholic Encyclopaedia, vol VII, p.645)

Robin Lane Fox in The Unauthorized Version contends that whilst there was a local census under Governor Quirinius it was not decreed by Caesar Augustus for the Empire as a whole and it occurred in A.D. 6 after Herod's death, when Jesus was six! Fox puts the inaccuracies down to Luke's attempt to write the story so that it would appear to fulfill the prophecy of Micah. How could King Herod order the massacre of the innocents if he was already dead when Jesus was born?

There is no independent documentary evidence of the destruction of the innocents by Herod. Herod had many enemies amongst the Jews. Had he committed such an

atrocity it would have been widely repo
nounced yet there is no mention of the al
any of the Jewish or Roman records of th
many Jewish records were destroyed in the sacking
rusalem the lack of comment on an event of such cruelty
and barbarism against the Jews by their own King would
be remarkable if the atrocity had in fact occurred.

From the Jewish records there is no doubt Jesus was illegitimate but as it was common for girls to be raped in
the occupied territories the virgin birth, along with the
crucifixion, resurrection and ascension of Christ are more
articles of faith than historical fact.

The major article of faith in Christianity is that Jesus
Christ is God. Again, this was never part of early Christian teaching. It came into being at the Council of Nicaea,
convened in AD 325, by the Roman Emperor Constantine
when Jesus Christ was voted in as God by 161 votes to
157. The Emperor, who declared Christ to be the only begotten Son of God, one in substance with the Father, offi-
cially ratified his elevation to divine status. Roman law
allowed the Senate and Emperor to deify individuals.
The deification of Christ was not without opposition. It
caused a riot. Thousands of Roman soldiers were called
in to restore order. In the protest 1730 of the original 2048
delegates were evicted including Arius and his followers
who contended vociferously that Jesus was a man and
not a god. (Acta Concilii Niceni)

The Christian doctrine was summarised in the Nicaea
Creed, which has been repeated without question, to this
day, by Catholics throughout the world. Statements
without foundation are underlined:

*I believe in God the Father Almighty, creator of heaven and
earth and maker of all things visible and invisible and I be-*

.eve in Jesus Christ <u>the only begotten son of God</u>, <u>born of the father before time began, God from God, light from Light, true God from true God, begotten and not made, one in substance with the Father, through whom all things were made and he came down from heaven, was conceived of the Holy Spirit, born of the Virgin Mary and was made man and suffering under Pontius Pilate was crucified, suffered death and was buried.</u> He descended into hell and on the <u>third day he rose again from the dead and ascended into heaven where he is seated at the right hand of the Father from whence he will come again in glory to judge both the living and the dead.</u> I believe in One Holy Catholic and Apostolic Church, the communion of the saints, the forgiveness of sins and life everlasting in the world to come. Amen.

There is no doubt that Jesus Christ was a great prophet and an enlightened teacher but there is no reason to suppose he was 'God' any more than every human being is an aspect of the divine. Jesus was an exceptional human being and the Gospels carry an eternal message with the ring of truth. They tell the story of an individual with exceptional courage and love of mankind. His words of inspiration have touched hearts of millions down through the centuries and he showed by example that right living, courage and self-sacrifice and above all compassion for humanity to the point of a willingness to risk death was the way to enter the 'Kingdom of Heaven'. Whether he was crucified or stoned to death, by putting his life on the line, Jesus ensured his words would survive for posterity.

Much of what Jesus was taught was not intended to be made public. If we consider the chilling message from the Sanhedrin, in our day, for those who dissent…

We execute masons in such wise that none save the brotherhood can ever have a suspicion of it, not

even the victims themselves of our death sentence, they all die when required as if from a normal kind of illness...By such methods we have plucked out of the midst of masonry the very root of protest against our disposition. While preaching liberalism to the Goyim we have, at the same time, kept our own people and our agents in a state of unquestioning submission. (Protocol 15)

...And take into account a pointed reference to Jesus in the records of the Sanhedrin:

...thou shalt not have a son or disciple who burns his food publicly like Jesus the Nazarene." (Bablyonian Sanhedrin, 103a)

...We can begin to see why Jesus fell out with the Jews and why he was condemned to death by the Sanhedrin

The passage reveals Jesus as a member of the Nazarenes, a militant wing of the Essenes. The Essenes were an ascetic Jewish sect of healers and teachers — the name Essene is derived from the Egyptian equivalent of the Greek 'Therapeute' meaning healer. The Gospel stories of Jesus Christ suggest he was a very gifted healer and a teacher and it is known that many of his teachings and practices were standard in the Essene community. The passage also suggests that he made public that which was intended to remain private. He fed esoteric knowledge to the uninitiated, to sinners and servants, tax collectors and harlots, the poor and the oppressed.

In other passages the Jews complained that Jesus 'stole the Torah'. He took the power from the priesthood by revealing the teachings of Moses and religious mysteries to whomsoever would listen to him. Jesus taught the knowledge of God and the awareness that there is more to life than this material plane of existence, truths that had been secretly nurtured within the religions, mystery schools and esoteric societies, truths hidden to people who had not been cleansed; purified by strict initiation processes...

> *"For there is nothing that is covered up that will not be revealed, nor hidden that will not be known. Therefore whatever you have spoken in the dark will be heard in the light, and what was whispered in private rooms will be proclaimed from the housetops."*
> (Luke 12:2-3)

...For this the priests despised him and determined he had to die. There are a number records in the Gospels of attempts to stone Jesus or throw him over the edge of a cliff for his public teachings, e.g., John 8:59, Luke 4:29-30 & John 10:31-39.

It was rabbinic law, in the constitution of the Sanhedrin, that a man could not be condemned to death unless the offences for which he was guilty were fully recorded. Some authors suggest these records may have provided a transcript of the teachings of Jesus, for the original compilation of the Gospel of Mark. (Justin Martyr, Dialogue, Oxford Translation, 1861, Vol. II)

It could be argued that the Jews only recorded that the body went missing from the tomb because they wanted people to believe the body of Jesus was stolen and not resurrected (Matt 28:11-15). However, the Jewish records do go on to detail a very different final outcome of Jesus to the Bible. The Babylonian Sanhedrin (106b) recorded that Jesus the Nazarene was eventually captured and stoned to death at a place called Lud by a party led by a man called Pinhas. The details of his execution are recorded in both the Palestinian and Babylonian Talmuds appended by a passage from the Mishna:

...to bring him forward to the tribunal and stone him. And thus they have done to Jesus at Lud, and hanged him on the day before Passover. (Sanhedrin, 67a)

Though I still prefer to believe in the crucifixion the Jewish records of the death of Jesus Christ in his sixties by stoning are more tenable than the Gospel story of crucifixion in his thirties because the Jewish story is corroborated by the early Church fathers. Bishop Tertullian of Carthage (160-210) addressed the Jews:

"Ye stoned him" (Adv Judeaus, C. IX) and Bishop Clement of Alexandra (160-215) stated:

"In his sixty-third year of age (Jesus) was stoned to death." (Arethas Codex)

After stoning it was standard practice to hang the broken body on a tree or a stake as a warning to others. Jewish history recorded that this was done to the body of Jesus after he was executed. In the Acts of the Apostles Peter is reported as saying that Jesus was hung up on a tree (10:39). Original versions of the New Testament describe Jesus being hung up on a stake. Only in subsequent rewriting of texts was the word 'cross' substituted for the word stake. ('Crosses in Tradition', W. W. Seymour, 1898)

Jesus would have been hounded by the Jewish Elders and eventually executed by them because secret societies have, throughout the ages, retained hidden teachings available to their members only for whom the penalty of death is levelled on anyone who breaks secrecy. Jesus the Nazarene obviously broke silence and taught the hidden teachings of the secret societies to the masses out of compassion for their need. As such he could be regarded as a 'redeemer of mankind' risking his life for the welfare of others. In the end, whether you believe he was crucified or stoned, he paid the ultimate price for making the hidden truth available for the oppressed masses:

> 'No greater love has a man than he is willing to lay down his life for his friends'. (John 15:13)

Whilst many Christians have lived according to the example and teachings of their master, for the most part the failing of Christianity has been lack of love. It is not possible to have love and also to be right. Christianity proved this through centuries of self-righteousness, intolerance for other religions, and harsh cruelty to non-believers and dissidents, as displayed in the atrocities of the Albigensian crusade and Inquisition. Even today, fundamentalist Christians are renowned for their intolerance. The problem of Christian 'self–righteousness' stems from the belief that Jesus is God and the Bible is the 'Word of God' so everything in the Bible is absolutely true and every other religion and scripture and spiritual path not affiliated to the Bible is the work of the Devil. But critical analysis reveals the Bible to be a fallible document that has been tampered with over the centuries and Jesus was never recognised as God in his lifetime or for centuries after. He was elevated to the status of God by the Romans nearly three hundred years after his death.

If Christians were to accept that Jesus was a man and not a god and treat the Bible as the collection of Jewish scriptures no more or less true than the Hindu scriptures or the Gnostic scriptures then they might respect Buddhism and Hinduism and Hermetic Gnosticism as equally valid forms of belief for those who chose them.

Many enlightened teachers who have appeared in history have been elevated to the status of gods by their followers. In the wake of Hinduism, Buddhism and

Hermetic Gnosticism, Krishna, Buddha and Hermes have come to be treated as gods. It is common, in the passage of time, for folklore and fantastic tales to grow round the founders of great religions. If we can see past these to the purity of the teachings then we find that what Christ, Krishna, Buddha and Hermes were good men teaching almost identical eternal truths.

When followers believe that the founder of their religion is 'God' to the exclusion of all other 'gods' and their way is the only way to God then religious bigotry arises. This is why there is inherent danger in limiting 'God' to any person. The term 'God' belongs to a supreme intelligence underlying the Universe, not to any being or person within the Universe. Whilst everyone has the potential to be a full expression of God, saying any person is exclusively 'God' be it Jehovah in the Old Testament or Jesus in the New, is idolatry and cultism.

Religious cults throughout the ages have elevated their founders to the status of gods to justify their existence in the face of competition from other sects. To gain followers, money and power religions preach:

'Our God is the true God! Your gods are false! Only through our God will you be saved! Our way is the only way to God. God is on our side.' This is especially true of Christianity.

Like Hermes, Buddha and Krishna — Jesus Christ came, not to set himself above us as an object of worship but to reveal the birthright of every human being. As an equal he came to show us all how to become true human — god–man — beings.

Section III

My Testament

"None of this is meant to deny the existence of a universal creative force – God – the absolute All or Oneness of all energy and matter. The modern UFO contactees and abductees uniformly tell us that even the 'aliens' they have experienced claim awareness of a Supreme Being. The knowledge of this one God, who must have created the Anunnaki creators, plus the awareness that there is more to life than this material plane of existence, has been secretly nurtured within all the secret societies. Beyond any question, there are metaphysical –spiritual –aspects to this whole issue..."

(Jim Marrs, Rule by Secrecy, HarperCollins, 2000)

Chapter 12

The Understanding

The unconscious mind of man sees correctly even when the conscious reason is blind and impotent. The drama has been consummated for all eternity: Yahweh's dual nature has been revealed, and somebody or someone has seen and registered this fact. Such a revelation, whether it reached man's consciousness or not, could not fail to have far-reaching consequences.

(Carl Jung: Answer to Job)

The Hubble telescope looks out into a region of space the size of a grain of sand at arms length, and captures the light from untold thousands of galaxies, each containing hundreds of billions of stars and planetary systems beyond count. In that celestial population we are the equivalent of a bacterial infection that a little planet, on the outskirts of a modest galaxy, has contracted. Our importance to the Universe could be the threat that we pose to it. Infections have a habit of spreading through populations and they can cause epidemics.

On the Earth, humans are behaving as planetary pathogens or parasites. Stripping the host of vital resources and poisoning it with waste products, is characteristic of pathogenic or parasitic behaviour. The Earth is sick. From the air cities look like malignant tumours. Forests are diminishing or destroyed. Rivers, streams and oceans are polluted. Species are becoming extinct. The planet is warming as though she has a fever. She is dying of a life threatening disease called Man.

If you consider that the Earth is 4.6 billion years old and this whole process of planetary destruction has occurred over a few hundred years, you can see the parallel with a human disease which may only last for a short period of time, compared to the life of the body, but in that critical time it can be fatal. During that critical phase, when the population of the disease organism is at its greatest, there is the danger that it will spread to other bodies and infect them as well.

With the Earth dying beneath Man's feet, considering his current priorities and attitudes, can you imagine the havoc that human beings could cause if they were to embark upon inter-planetary travel? That day is not far off. With technology proceeding by leaps and bounds, mankind is all set to invade other stellar systems and treat the orbiting planets as we have treated the Earth. We have the capacity to rape and plunder them for resources. We have the potential to wage conventional or nuclear war on their surfaces. With our breeding potential, we could overpopulate and pollute them all. In time '*Homo-bacillus*'could infect the entire Universe and destroy it.

Consider human aggression linked to our intelligence and destructive capability. Consider the statistics of a single aspect of modern warfare — landmines. According to information released in 1996 by the International Committee for the Red Cross, more than 119 million active landmines have been scattered in 71 countries and as many again are stockpiled all over the world. Each mine has the capability to maim or kill an innocent person, all too frequently a child at play. There are 2,000 mine victims a month. Every 20 minutes a person is killed or injured by a landmine. These are usually civilians long after hostilities have ceased. Unlike other manufactured products, land mines don't have built-in obsolescence. Land mines have been built to last and inflict horrendous injury long after the time of conflict.

I have cited this as but one example of the madness of mankind, of our determination to needlessly maim and destroy members of our own species, through war and greed; of our wanton destruction of other species; of our capacity to render this beautiful planet uninhabitable. Consider the destruction caused to the Earth by pollution, nuclear waste, deforestation, roads, industrial and urban development, extinction of natural species and indigenous populations, and you will see why we could be viewed as a planetary menace. And it is not them — it is us. Many people have good intentions but when they are put to the test their primary concern is their own welfare and how much they can 'get out of the system' rather than 'how much they can do for others and put back into the system'.

Like any other living organism, the Universe has to protect itself from pathogens and parasites, from beings bent on destruction of themselves and everything around them, beings manifesting greed, selfishness and violence. We have plundered the Earth for power and money. Indigenous peoples have been murdered for possession of land. Plants and animals have been abused, tortured and exterminated. This is not just a recent pattern; it has been going on for thousands of years. Nowadays, through vivisection, these crimes continue in the name of science. As in the past, today we use skills and intelligence to destroy or exploit every living creature entrusted to our care.

Applying the Hermetic principle *'as above so below, as below so above'* I believe the Universe is a living organism in which galaxies are as cells in our bodies. In turn I envision, in the *fractal universe,* galaxies as living organisms in which stars and their planets are the equivalent of cells. Like our bodies, each galaxy would have its own intelligence. Many people believe in a centre of galactic intelligence. If galaxies were living bodies on a larger scale than us, then they would have immune systems just like our own. If we study our own immune systems we will see that disease organisms are first contained and then destroyed. This is also the way doctors treat epidemics. First they quarantine the people who are infected then they set about destroying the infective organism in the patients.

The plan of Jehovah – Enlil - to enslave us could be seen as a responsible effort to contain a deadly planetary disease. In giving us sexual potential, his brother Enki may have irresponsibly bio-engineered a potential planetary pathogen in his laboratory. Enlil could be endeavouring to prevent us breaking out and infecting the galaxy at large. The Universe might welcome us if we were synergistic (life enhancing). At least we would have to be benign. If we are pathogenic it might be containing us until we either choose to change or choose to destroy ourselves.

Another way to view our history is if the Elohim originally created us as slaves it is clear we have escaped. The Elohim Lord, operating through his agents and religious tyranny and indoctrination, could be working hard to recapture us. Alternatively now that we have broken free it could be that the Elohim are processing us to see if they can develop a useful organism for the Universe. Maybe that is what choice and free will is all about. Maybe it is a self-selection process whereby all sorts of situations are placed in our path to give us opportunities to exercise choice.

Personally I believe that Universal Intelligence is working through the Elohim team, now they have created us, to 'test and try us' before we are let loose on the Universe — much like a newly invented machine is tested for performance before it is launched on the market. The reasons why we were created and given sexual potential are incidental. Our origins are now irrelevant. The fact is we now exist as a sovereign species on a planet and the Universe has to contend with the situation as it is. Will we evolve into a life enhancing or continue as a life-destroying organism? Throughout human history all religions and 'spiritual ways' have addressed the issue of choices between 'good' and 'evil' and the word 'evil' being 'live' spelt backwards simply refers to human behaviour that destroys life.

Looking at religious history and the consistent messages coming through 'the teachers' — prophets, gurus, sages, rabbis and enlightened teachers like Buddha, Krishna, Christ, Mohamed, Lau Tzu, Nanak, Ghandi, Sai Baba, Maharaji and Amma, to name but a few. I am confident that the Universe is endeavouring to develop some useful 'synergins' in the human population. From the consistent message of 'end-time prophecies' I reckon this process is occurring within a given time frame – no machine is bench-tested forever. At the end of the processing human organisms that are life-enhancing could be harvested and human 'germs' that are life-destroying could be autoclaved.

And whosoever was not found written in the book of life was cast into the lake of fire.(Revelation 20:15)

Every human has the potential to transform from the path of planetary parasite to the path of planetary guardian. I honestly believe the Universe offers individuals opportunities to take personal responsibility for their lives. I believe we are evolving. I reckon we haven't come to the Earth on holiday. My sense is that we have been born into a boot camp.

If you have a problem in coming to terms with the 'Satanic' manifestation of 'God' then consider soldiers undergoing training. They usually figure the regimental sergeant majors that put them through their paces to be 'fiends out of hell' until they come under fire. Only then are they grateful for the toughness of their training. For warriors, tough but thorough training is a blessing in disguise. Look at the processes of initiation in native tribes. Do they not put their boys through tests of fear before they are accepted as men?

Universal Intelligence isn't stupid! A creature as potentially lethal to the Universe as Homo Sapiens is not to be let loose to roam the galaxies until it has learnt to live up to its name, the 'Wise Hominid' and wisdom comes through experience.

In *The Only Planet of Choice* (Schlemmer, P.V) the Earth is described as a unique free will zone; the only planet on a physical level where a species is given complete freedom of choice. In this book, humanity is presented as a 'unique experiment' in which the Semites are key participants. Schlemmer suggests we have a tendency to get stuck in comfort and complacency on this plane of existence. The followers of Jehovah are intended to keep us moving; hopefully onto higher planes.

From my perspective humans are trainee gods. With our individual free will and ability to create and destroy, we correspond to the 'gods' in ancient mythology, but on the physical level. We are in a safe situation — exercising the gift of free will and making our choices to determine our destiny — where we cannot do harm beyond the planet. It may look as though we are making a terrible mess on Earth but that is only because we are practicing. We are exposed to the full spectrum of good and evil on Earth because, to graduate as a full-blown god, the human being must experience hell as well as heaven.

The Cathars, who were exterminated as heretics, believed that on Earth we are in hell, and that *Rex Mundi*, the god of this world, the god responsible for our genesis, is Satan. From an impartial analysis of the biblical God and the behaviour of his Chosen People, it would appear that there is some truth in their belief! Certainly the Roman Catholics fulfilled their expectations.

So why does evil exist? Why is there so much evil in the world? Why would the god of this world be Satan? Why is Satan evil?

Accounting for evil has been one of the greatest philosophical challenges in human history. Some people stick their heads in the sand and try to pretend there is no evil. Others accept the traditional religious view that there was a rebellion in heavens and now there are evil spirits that have turned against God causing a battle between good and evil. My view on the matter is different.

I believe everything in the Universe is perfect and everything happens for a purpose and; that includes evil. I contend there is a divine purpose for evil and that it is as important in the evolution of humanity as good. I believe good and evil are two sides of the same coin; they are opposite but essential aspects of the same God.

In my opinion evil exists to increase the potential of spiritual charge in the Universe. Let me explain this by analogy of a capacitor. A capacitor is a component in an electric circuit for raising electrical potential. It consists of a non-conducting sheet of material against a conducting sheet. Electric charge on the conductor meeting the resistance on the non-conductor builds up until it overcomes the resistance. Imagine the resistance is a dam in a river. The water in the river builds up against the dam until it is high enough to flow over it. The high water creates pressure, which can be used to generate electricity in a hydroelectric turbine or turn a water wheel in a mill.

In the capacitor analogy the non-conductor represents evil. This is pressed up against a conducting sheet of metal, which represents good. Spiritual charge, like electricity, builds up on the metal because of the resistance of the non-conductor. This creates a high spiritual potential. In electrical engineering the word 'tension' is used for the build up of charge in a capacitor. This word is apt for the reaction of good to evil. It is appropriate for the good to overcome the evil as it is appropriate for the charge on a capacitor to overcome the resistance or for the water in a full reservoir to flow over the dam. What matters is that in the process of overcoming evil the spiritual potential of the good is increased.

The greater the resistance of the non conductor, the greater the potential that builds on the conductor; a higher dam leads to higher water, which produces more pressure and a greater power output. It follows that the greater the degree of evil the greater will be the spiritual potential of good.

If this perspective on evil is correct, the reason why there is so much evil in the world and why 'God' orchestrates the evil can only be because the Universe wants a huge potential of good 'spiritual charge' to come out of this world.

In order to create gods out of mere mortals, human beings need to charge up to a 'million volts' spiritually. This occurs in the process in which persons have to endure and overcome every type of evil. God requires us to endure the full experience of pain as well as pleasure. We have to know misery as well as joy. The furnace of mortal torment is where the base metal of mankind is transmuted into the 'gold of the gods'.

If the Universe harvests 'the good' and autoclaves 'the evil' that is not a judgement against evil beings it is simply honouring their choices. Evil means 'life destroying' so if an evil being experiences the destruction of there own life that is entirely appropriate to their chosen reality. Meanwhile they will have served their purpose as part of the 'perfect plan' for humanity.

The Bible story is full of metaphors to support my view of evil. The Bible tells of Eve choosing to come into the knowledge of good and evil in order to gain wisdom; it is only through living knowledge that we attain to wisdom:

> So when the woman saw that the tree was good for food, that it was pleasant to the eyes, and a tree desirable to make one wise, she took of its fruit and ate. She also gave to her husband with her and he ate.
> (Genesis 3:6)

'God' responded by manifesting the face of evil. As such he honoured the choice of Adam and Eve to grow in wisdom through the knowledge of evil as well as good. From the moment of Eve's momentous decision, 'God' started to treat humans like army recruits. He was like the genii that warned, "I wanted to be nice to you but you did what I warned you not to do so I have to be nasty!" As for the warning, telling Adam and Eve not to eat the fruit of the tree of good and evil was tantamount to telling children not to put beans in their ears. To me the 'Garden of Eden story' was the story of a setup.

In the Bible we also see Jehovah acting as a 'mirror for mankind'. The more evil humans became, the greater the evil projected back at them by 'God'. In the role of tempter or tester I see 'God' acting as an amplifier of evil. First souls are exposed to every kind of evil and then their choices and responses are monitored to see how they perform under stress? In the ancient 'Book of Enoch', Enoch describes the forces of evil as 'the Watchers'. This is an interesting description because it suggests that the 'Tempter' is also the 'Watcher' which fits with my model of a tester who also monitors the systems under test.

The Book of Job in the Bible is interesting the way it portrays conversations between 'God' and Satan as though they are working some sort of partnership. This doesn't correlate with modern idea in Christianity that Satan is the enemy of God.

At Medjugorje, in the former Yugoslavia, the young people claiming to be receiving apparitions of Mary, reported her as saying that a long time ago Satan asked God for permission to test the faith of humanity to the limit. God agreed and offered Satan any century of his choice. Apparently he chose the 20th Century. More precisely it was a 100-year period between 1914 and 2013. Whilst this story supports the idea that Satan and God are working as a team in the 'processing of humanity' it appears to contradict the idea that Satan is an aspect of God. This conundrum is easily resolved from the Bible:

And the Angel of the Lord appeared to him in a flame of fire in the midst of a bush. So he looked, and behold, the bush was burning with fire, but the bush was not consumed.... God called to him from the midst of the bush and said, "Moses, Moses." Moreover he said, "I am the God of your father, the God of Abraham, the

> *God of Isaac, and the God of Jacob." And Moses hid*
> *his face; for he was afraid to look upon God.*
> (Exodus 3:2-6)

In the burning bush, the 'God of the Bible' is revealed as an angel who, by definition, is extraterrestrial. The Elohim means gods in plural so the lord of the Elohim appearing to Moses in the bush and speaking as 'God' would correspond to one of the gods, an extraterrestrial or an angel, coming as a mouthpiece of universal intelligence. This picture figures closely with Sir Fred Hoyle's idea. In the *Intelligent Universe,* Hoyle favours the Greek idea of a pantheon of gods acting as managers in the Universe.

Conversations between Satan acting as a planetary manager and 'God' representing a higher level of universal intelligence would correspond to discussions between a local manager and a regional manager in industry.

Satan is associated with Archangel Lucifer. It would make sense of the Bible if the entity that appeared to Moses in the burning bush was Archangel Lucifer avoiding disclosure of his name:

> *And God said to Moses, I AM WHO I AM* **(YHWH).**
> *And he said "Thus you shall say to the children of Is-*
> *rael, 'I AM has sent me to you.'"* (Exodus 3:14)

Identifying Jehovah and Satan as one and the same is only a problem for people who do not understand the role of evil. Humans judge from a human perspective, not a universal perspective. Fortunately Christians, Jews and Muslims will have no problem in accepting that God can be evil as well as good, dark as well as light because the Bible, which they believe to be the 'Word of God' confirms that this is so:

I am the Lord and there is none else, I form the light and create darkness; I make peace and create evil; I, Lord, do all these things.(Isaiah 45:7)

Pilots are not given their wings until they have been put under test and duress in flight simulators. I like to think of planet Earth as a flight simulator for pilots of consciousness. If you want your wings as a galactic pilot you have to serve your time in Satan's flight simulator; and he will not spare you!

I used to wonder what the Chosen People were chosen for. If Mary's message at Medjugorje is true then maybe they were chosen to set up 20th Century civilisation as the great test Satan has been planning for millennia. Maybe they were chosen to set up the 'flight simulator'; the bench test for humanity. I honestly believe that *The Great Work of Ages* of the Learned Elders is nothing more nor less than 'systems testing' for Homo Sapiens. This is obvious from *The Protocols*. Every evil tendency in mankind has been exaggerated and reflected back. Every form of anger, greed and war, selfishness, conceit and stupidity, blind faith and faithlessness has been exploited to the full in the process. If we were wise we would honour the Chosen People of God for the great service they have performed for humanity down through the ages. They have been truly dedicated to their mission and the tests and temptations they have 'set up in modern civilisation — especially in the 20th Century — have been masterful and very effective. That cannot be denied. The wise would not be angry with the Jewish Elders and their agents, but would congratulate them, especially as we approach the time when the task of the Chosen People is complete; when we will see their power is finally broken:

When the power of the holy people has been finally

221

broken, all these things will be completed.
(Daniel 12:7)

I am not suggesting that we condone evil or the activity of the Illuminati. I am suggesting we go beyond judgement and understand the purpose behind evil. There is great danger in judging evil when we do not understand its purpose in the divine plan because in our judgement of evil we bring it upon ourselves:

Judge not lest you be judged, For as you judge you will be judged, with whatever measure you mete, It will be meted back to you. (Matt 7: 1-2)

To get into an issue of judgement of the great and manifest evil of the Chosen People is to buy into the duality of 'good versus evil' and play into their hands. That merely extenuates the endless cycle of conflict and achieves nothing. Look at recent history. The only revolution in the 20th Century that didn't play into their hands was the non-violent revolution in India lead by Mahatma Ghandi. The Indians did what most Christians only profess; they turned the other cheek. It was only religious intolerance and people resorting to violence that caused the revolution to turn sour.

If we stand in judgement of the evil, what do we intend to do about it? Pray that God will punish the authors of **The Protocols**? Hope they will roast in hell forever? Launch another pogrom? What if they are serving the highest good for the evolution of mankind, would they not deserve a place in heaven? The Elders of Zion earnestly believe they will be granted a place in heaven for their work. They are, after all, only obeying the command of the one that Christians, Jews and Muslims worship as God! Are they not ensuring that we experience to the full all the consequences of our choices - for good or for ill?

Are they not testing the quality of the human spirit? Would it not be true to say this process will be complete when we recognise it, own it with gratitude and then rise above it.

Hitler believed he had a divine destiny in setting up the most terrible war in history. George Bush believes he followed the will of God invading Iraq. Half a trillion dollars later people are wringing their hands in despair "If only Al Gore won the 2000 election that money might have been spend on the environment and attempts to reverse global warming!" However, 'Universal Intelligence' may be more concerned that we have war, war and more war until we are totally sickened and satiated by it and then decide, as a race, that it is unacceptable. In the East they would say this is an application of the 'Yin Yang' principle, when something comes to its extreme it switches to its opposite. Maybe all the money in the world would not avert climate change. George Bush may be serving our destiny better by squandering billions on a futile war than Gore's possible spending on a futile attempt to avert climatic catastrophe.

The Jehovah's Witnesses believe the Kingdom of Heaven arrived on Earth in 1914. That was the year the Great War began! They believe in the first hundred years of the Kingdom of Heaven on Earth things have to get a lot worse before they get better or we would never appreciate paradise when it finally dawns. Maybe everything in the world is working out exactly as it should and prior to 2013 we should cheer George Bush along rather than revile him. Maybe we shouldn't judge Hitler and Stalin, Pol Pot and Sadham Hussein either. Maybe the dark side of God is as 'good for us' as the light side. When we appreciate that then we would be worthy to use the word

'God'. Going beyond judgement and criticism we would appreciate that both good and evil serve the greater good.

If we have a problem with God being both good and evil maybe we should ask ourselves, " Am I perfect? Do I employ evil as well as good in my life?" Before we start throwing stones at Satan or the Devil, Jehovah or the Lord of Elohim and his chosen ones it has to be said:

> *"Let him who is without sin cast the first stone!"* (John 8:7)

Evil in the world is only a mirror reflecting back the inner state of being. Self-realised people recognise that they are manifesting the duality of the divine. They know as creator gods they need to work out the dilemmas of duality and to learn to balance good and evil. They appreciate everything that happens in their lives is serving in their evolution.

The wise appreciate they are aspects of God existing within the limitations of physicality, learning to balance opposites and resolve conflicts. Self-responsible people who embrace duality can claim to be hu(god)-man beings. Once they begin to make choices between what they perceive as good and evil they are exercising free will and acting as gods. They do what they do in the knowledge of who they are. They do what they do in the conscious knowledge of forging their destiny and the destiny of mankind.

If the Universe presents to us the polarity of good and evil, each person has to take responsibility for his or her own life. Many people blame the Devil for the state of the world. However, if the Devil is but God acting as a mirror of mankind the object of blame evaporates. We are left looking at ourselves. We are left having to take personal responsibility for our own thoughts, words and deeds.

If God is both friend and foe how can there be an enemy? If everyone is a God point on the spectrum of duality how can there be separation between good people and bad people?

Reading the Bible, Jesus and Jehovah appear as opposite faces of the same God representing our chance to choose. The Bible is the word of both Jesus and Jehovah; it preaches both love and hate. Most people who read the Bible, assuming that God is only good, miss the point that God manifests the full spectrum of duality. Their religious programming blinds them to the fact that God is dualistic and the Bible is a revelation of both the evil face and the good face of the Divine. The historical repercussions of blind faith in the biblical God calls into question the issue of authority. When under test, can we maintain our status as sovereign beings or do we surrender as slaves? To what extent can we follow our conscience and intuition even in the face of commands from the highest level? Take for example the events of World War II:

The German people behaved as they did under the authority of the Nazis because some believed that what they were doing was right. Others remained silent, being too frightened to do otherwise. Many followed mindlessly, like domesticated animals. They were obeying the orders of Adolf Hitler, their Father at the highest level.

During the horrors of the Jewish holocaust there were a few brave exceptions within the Nazi herd. Oskar Schindler, a member of the Nazi party, was certainly not a good man according to religious standards, but he rescued 1,100 Jews because he was capable of free thought and action. He followed his conscience against higher authority. He followed his heart instead of the herd.

No nation can be singled out for blame. Every race has

been the perpetrator or victim of holocaust. The Tibetans have suffered under the heel of China and Native Americans under the savagery of civilised Europeans.

The Milligan experiments show that the majority of people will follow orders without question, regardless of the apparent suffering they inflict on others. Most people, on joining a cult or a mob, will behave like herd animals. They will do as they are told or as others are doing, even if it involves inhumane behaviour. Whether they are in religions, corporations or armies, when humans accept orders without question, they abdicate their free will and their status as sovereign beings. Will we learn through the horrors of history the dangers of following the mob rather than acting and thinking for ourselves?

Animals herd through fear. Since ancient times, Jehovah has treated humanity as 'goyim' or herd animals. He has kept his Chosen People subjugated, isolated as a herd and loyal to him through fear. He has controlled them through dispersion and anti-Semitism. Hitler's anti-Semitism, fostered by the Jewish Elders, served to increase the chasm of isolation, suspicion and hatred, carved over the centuries, between the Jews and the other peoples of the Earth. Theirs was an awesome God who fanned the flames of hatred in his nation through the fear and terror of persecution. This Satanic Lord was reflected in the Russian Jew, Stalin herding millions of fellow Russians to the Gulag as cattle to slaughter and Hitler, grandson of Rothschild, herding millions of blood-fellow Jews into cattle trucks and shipping them off to their death.

Today in the aftermath of the holocaust, few will openly and honestly question the complex issues surrounding the persecution of the Jews over the millennia. As both victims and perpetrators in the play of history, it is for the Jewish people to open their eyes and take personal responsibility for their persecution. They need to address their own core issues if this terrible pattern of human history is ever to be broken.

In 1920, Oscar Levy, the respected humanitarian Jew, wrote about his people, saying:

> *"They are always inclined and that on account of their terrible experiences to denounce anyone who is not with them as against them, as tainted with 'medieval' prejudice, as an intolerant antagonist of their faith and of their race."*

The Jewish faith is their religion, their culture and their law is the glue that holds them to their fate. As Levy explains, it is woven into the framework of their history and the history of humanity:

> *"...There is no race in the world more enigmatic, more fatal, and therefore more interesting than the Jews....*
>
> *"...For the question of the Jews and their influence on the world past and present, cuts to the root of all things, and should be discussed by every honest thinker, however bristling with difficulties it is, however complex the subject as well as the individuals of this race may be....*
>
> *"...But first of all I have to say this: There is scarcely an event in modern Europe that cannot be traced back to the Jews."*

Levy, even as one of the Chosen People, was courageous in his questioning of his nation...

> *"For the Jews, as you are aware, are a sensitive community and thus are very suspicious of any Gentile who tries to approach them with a critical mind..."*

...and he had the honesty to speak strongly of his own people:

"We (the Jews) have erred, my friend, we have most grievously erred. And if there was truth in our error 3,000, 2,000, nay 100 years ago, there is now nothing but falseness and madness, a madness that will produce an even greater misery and an even wider anarchy. I confess it to you, openly and sincerely, and with a sorrow whose depth and pain an ancient Psalmist, and only he, could moan into this burning universe of ours...We who have posed as the saviours of this world, we who have even boasted of having given it 'the' Saviour, we are today nothing else but the world's seducers, its destroyers, its incendiaries, its executioners. We who have promised to lead you to a new Heaven, we have finally succeeded in landing you into a new Hell..."

He also questioned the spiritual ethics of his people:

"I look at this world and I shudder at its ghastliness; I shudder all the more as I know the spiritual authors of all this ghastliness."

Levy understood the role of the Judaic religion, and knew one day it would be held accountable:

"The great day of reckoning is near. It will pass a judgment on our ancient faith, and it will lay the foundations to a new religion. And when the great day has broken, when the values of death and decay are put into the melting pot to be changed into those of power and beauty..."

And yet in these statements Levy judges his people because it is not easy to come to terms with evil on the level we have witnessed in the 20th Century, or understand it as part of the 'divine plan'. The answer lies in the blind spot the Jewish people — as well as peoples of other religions — have around God.

There is enormous danger in people placing unquestioned faith in an external God rather than taking personal responsibility for their individual growth. Seduced by religion, people have blindly followed the 'Great Original Deception' as 'God. They have followed 'the Book' and 'the preachers' without question. They have placed their faith in a 'God' created by men in the image of man, because indeed there is no certainty that any of the Bible is true. There is huge danger in following our primitive forebears in their worship of extraterrestrials as gods. Humans should stand before extraterrestrials without fear, look them in the face and challenge them. We should not give our power away as Moses did:

> *And Moses hid his face; for he was afraid to look upon God.* (Exodus 3:2-6)

Nonetheless as a race we have grown in wisdom through the experience of good and evil. The purpose of evil needs be understood in order to be forgiven:

> *Under Heaven all can see beauty only because there is ugliness, all can know good as good only because there is evil.* (Lao Tsu)

Through suffering individuals learn compassion. People who have been victims of evil, who have known hardship and deprivation, are usually compassionate. Maybe this is why there has been so much suffering in history:

> *As many as I love I rebuke and chasten...*
> (Revelation 3: 19)

The Chosen People have been a major catalyst for change. But for them, Europe would still be a feudal society. Over recent centuries the Learned Elders have broken the power of the aristocracy, the church and many traditional institutions. Their revolutions and foments have shocked society into transformation. They have created the atmosphere of freedom in many areas of life, which have enabled an enormous expansion in human consciousness to occur. They are instruments of awakening and accelerators of human evolution. With their overriding influence there has been little opportunity for society to stagnate.

> *The Lord made everything for a purpose, even the wicked for an evil day.* (Proverbs 16:4)

More than anyone else, Jehovah's people have broken the hold of ancient cultures, which have caused stagnation in many societies throughout the world. The question is, who will break the hold that their own ancient culture has on them? Only if the grip on the Judaic culture is broken will the Jewish people find freedom. Their attachment to their ancient faith, to power and to money will continue to cause them to suffer because attachment is the greatest source of suffering. The same applies to Muslims, Masons and Christians. The Jews have the genius. They have the ability to lead change from cruelty to compassion; to foment the final revolution; the revolution of love:

> *"And yet there is hope, great hope, that this same race which has provided the evil will likewise succeed in supplying its antidote, its remedy the good.*

> *"...A new good as new love, a true love that calms and heals and sweetens, will then spring up among the great in Israel and overcome that sickly love, that insipid love, that romantic love which has hitherto poisoned all the strength and nobility of this world. For hatred is never overcome by hatred: It is only overcome by love, and it wants a new and a gigantic love to subdue that old and devilish hatred of*

today. That is our task for the future a task which will, I am sure, not be shirked by Israel, by that same Israel which has never shirked a task, whether it was for good or whether it was for evil...

"Yes, there is hope, my friend, for we are still here, our last word is not yet spoken, our last deed is not yet done, and our last revolution is not yet made. This last revolution, the revolution that will crown our revolutionaries, will be a revolution against the revolutionaries. It is bound to come, and it is perhaps upon us now." (Oscar Levy)

The final revolution is the revolution of awakening through the power of the creative spirit. In their genius the Illuminati know this and hence fear it most:

*The power of the personality has to be fought, as there is nothing more dangerous. If it is endowed with **creative spiritual forces**, it can effect more than millions of people.* (The Testament of Satan: Bavarian Illuminati)

The answer, as always, is the spiritual one. The paradox of the Jews can only be understood from a spiritual perspective. Understanding their God as Satan makes sense of everything. It makes sense of the cruelty of Zionism and the madness of Illuminized Masonry. It makes sense of Christian bigotry and hypocrisy and Islamic fanaticism.

Satan, the dark face of God, is traditionally viewed as the tempter and tester of mankind. As 'God' is an aspect of each and every one of us, so is Satan. Satan is that aspect of the mind that entices us to do something and then reprimands us for doing it. Satan is the thought of anger and revenge; the cruelty of rage and the wellspring of fear and guilt harboured in the human mind.

Satan is the mirror of humanity, the test of our divinity

and the harbinger of change. Satan is the aspect of universal mind, reflected in the human mind that stretches a being to the limits of being. Satan tests the power of individual personality, tempting people through fear to give their power away to others or through greed to disempower others. Responding to Satan with fear or revenge, with self-righteousness or anger is simply reflected back a hundredfold in this 'mirror of mankind'. Christians have lost their way if they focus on Satan and the evils of the world and judge others as being ensnared by the Devil. By the law of projection 'that we see the world not the way it is but the way we are' this is their reality. The only antidote to evil is love:

> *"But I say unto you, Love your enemies, bless those who curse you, do good to those that hate you, and pray for them that despitefully use you and persecute you."* (Matthew 5:44)

Compassion, understanding, detachment are the effective tools of response to the activity of the Sanhedrin of Jewish Elders, the Illuminati and the World Secret Government.

This is the time of awakening for the whole of humanity especially those of us in the Judeo–Christian–Islamic–Masonic traditions. We need to open our eyes to see the Hebrew god for what he is and understand his terrible role in history. Jews, Christians, Muslims and Masons have released a very destructive force on the world through idolatry of 'God'. Idolatry is worship of any beings outside of us. In worship we relinquish our sovereignty to others. Worship of 'the gods', of Jesus or Jehovah as 'God' is dis–empowering and dangerous. That is a vital lesson of history. As children we idolised our parents and treated them as beyond reproach. Then as we grew up and matured we began to see them in their true colours. As we come into racial maturity, we need to see the 'heavenly father' for who he is, as he is reflected within us and in everyone else around us. We need to know as much as we can about the 'God' that came to Abraham and Moses, where he figures in other cultures and if he were Satan as the Cathars, Templars and Masons have contended. We also need to find out more about the one who came as Jesus the Christ. Does he figure in the records of non-Judaic cultures? He has had an enormous impact on Western society. Does he appear in the scriptures of other societies, albeit with a different name? What was the link between him and Jehovah? Finally, what is the origin of the name 'Satan' that conjures up so much fear in so many? There is a clue in that name that unlocks the mystery around the Bible 'God'. The clue lies in the Vedic scriptures of ancient India.

Chapter 13

The Brothers

"There is no position on which people are so immovable as their religious beliefs"

(Senator Barry Goldwater)

The ancient Vedic scriptures tell us that Brahma, the creator, had four sons. The first-born Son of God was called **'At'**. The second was called **'Anda'**, the third was **'Atana'** and the fourth was **'Aka'**. These brothers were known as the **'Kumaras'**, which in Sanskrit meant 'princes'. In the Indian tradition the prefix **'San'** was added to each name as a sign of respect. The word 'San' means sacred or holy. The word persists today in its original form and meaning in Spanish. We are all familiar with it in San Francisco, named after St Francis. So in the Vedas the four sons of God came to be known as **Sanat, Sananda, Sanatana** and **Sanaka** Kumara. If we cross-reference the Indian legend to the Hebrew we find the first four born of God are the primary Archangels, **Lucifer, Michael, Gabriel** and **Raphael.** I assume that Lucifer corresponds to Sanat Kumara, Michael to Sananda, Gabriel to Sanatana and Raphael to Sanaka. If we track back to the Sumerian legend we hear much the same story, the father **Anu** with his sons **Enlil** and **Enki.** Are Sanat, Lucifer and Enlil the same person? And can we assume that Sananda, Michael and Enki are the same person?

There is the story in Greek mythology of the sons of Zeus descending from Mt. Olympus. Apollo was the elder son of Zeus. Apollo was also a 'sun god' or 'god of the light', hence his title *Phoebus*, the brilliant one. This would correspond to Sanat.

> *And they had a king over them, which is the angel of*
> *the bottomless pit, whose name in the Hebrew tongue*
> *is Abadon, but in the Greek tongue is Apollyon.*
> (Revelation 9:11)

In Hinduism, Sanat is revered as one of the sons of Brahma but also as 'Skanda', son of Shiva. He is portrayed as ever youthful and ever pure and is also considered to be one of the progenitors of mankind. According to a number of sources, including Mark Prophet, Sanat Kumara is known as the ***Ancient of Days.*** If that is true then we see a link between Sanat and Jehovah. In a vision, Daniel (Daniel 7:9) saw the Ancient of Days seated on the 'throne' as the 'God' of his fathers, Abraham, Isaac and Jacob, the one who appeared to Moses in the burning bush and described himself as YHWH sounded by some as 'Yahweh', or 'Jahveh' now commonly pronounced Jehovah. Sanat Kumara is also known as the 'Planetary Logos', which means the 'God of this world.' According to the Sumerian texts, Enlil held that position. But many — including the Cathars and Christians — consider the 'God of this world' to be Satan. Is there a link between Satan and Sanat? Indeed there is if we look at the names; Satan is an anagram of Sanat!

William Blake perceived Jehovah as having fallen from an original state of virtue and dignity as did Yeats:

> *...He is recognizably the 'Elohim' of the Old Testament in*
> *his 'aged ignorance', carrying the books of the Law, and*
> *yet Blake's Creator is not wholly evil; for as the 'Ancient of*
> *Days' on the frontispiece of 'Europe' (1793) we see the*
> *Creator with his golden compasses, who, though in part*
> *fallen, 'derived his birth from the Supreme God; this being*
> *fell, by degrees, from his native virtue and his primitive*

dignity' (W.B.Yeats). *(The Gnostics, p.147)*

Jesus made it quite clear that the god of the Jews was the Devil:

> *"You belong to your father, the Devil, and the desires of your father you want to do. (John 8:44)*

The Bible reveals that the Old Testament God and his 'Elohim' team made their descent to Earth. It is also clear from everything that has been written in this book so far that through the Jewish patriarchs, Abraham and Moses, Jehovah has deceived the whole world:

> *And the dragon was cast out, that old serpent, called the Devil and Satan, who deceived the whole world: he was cast out onto the Earth, and his angels were cast out with him.* (Revelation 12: 8-9)

If all this is true then the Elohim, 'Lord of the Bible' would be a fallen angel. Embarrassing to say the least for Bible believers! Worse still, if Jehovah is Satan then Judaism, Christianity, Roman Catholicism, Masonry, Mormonism, Islam, Jehovah's Witnesses and any other religion that promotes worship of Jehovah as 'God' would qualify as a satanic cult. Perhaps there is need to review the position of Satan.

The idea that Satan is archenemy of God emerged in late Judaism and early Christianity. This is contradictory to the Book of Job. Gnostics, like William Blake, believe in the fallen state of the Old Testament God but in the Gnosis there is the understanding that neither the fall of God or of man was a disgrace. Somehow it was all part of a greater plan.

In the Hindu tradition all the sons of 'the Father' were driven out of heaven and descended to Earth which fits with the ancient scriptures of the Bible that revealed the descent of the 'Elohim' — the descent of a group of gods rather than a single God — from the heavens to Earth.

"Come let us go down... (Genesis 11:7)

I would see the 'sons of God' driven out of heaven more as a father kicking his overgrown boys out of the nest to force them to fend for themselves. It is tough for kids when they first leave home but that is often their making. No father hates his sons forever because they were rebellious and he had to kick them out into the wide world. Few sons hold it against dad forever because he brought out the big stick. More often than not it engenders respect.

The Vedas of ancient India taught that Brahma called on his sons to leave heaven and go out into the universe to create life. He asked them three times and three times they stubbornly refused to leave the comfort and security of heaven to journey into the unknown Universe as co-creators. In rage, Brahma drove his sons out of heaven. That rage was Shiva. The destructive rage of Shiva needed to be balanced against the creative impulse of Brahma and thus Vishnu came into being as the preserver. In the Hindu trinity, the three personalities of God, Brahma, Vishnu and Shiva — creator, preserver and destroyer — are more moods than persons. Whereas Christians speak of 'three persons in the one God' Hindus would speak of three attributes of God; which are essentially attributes of the Universe. Creation, preservation and destruction are cycles to the endless changes and transformation that we witness in the heavens and on Earth. Birth, life and death; morning, day and night and the seasons, witnessed in the upward flow of sap in the spring, the sap sustained in leaf and branch through summer into autumn and the downward flow of sap into the roots from autumn into winter.

Christians believe from the Bible; that one son of 'God' drove the other out of heaven:

> *And there was a war in heaven: Michael and his angels fought against the dragon; and the dragon fought and his angels, and they prevailed not; neither was there a place for them any more in heaven.*

(Revelation 12: 7)

The Vedas tell us that 'God' drove all his sons out of heaven because they all rebelled against him. The Sumerian records that pre-date the Bible corroborate the Vedas. They describe conflict in heaven between the sons of God, their subsequent descent to Earth, and ongoing conflict down here.

A Stuart Wilson channelling on the Elohim threw a lot more light on the subject for me. Contemporary channellings never carry the weight of channellings recorded in ancient scriptures, such as the Bible, but they are often a lot clearer. According to the channelling, the Elohim were truly awesome light beings involved in the creation of life in the very first galaxy. They went through immense difficulties, challenges and adversity in the process and have never been surpassed in their abilities as co-creators. The Universe is expanding and spirits of the calibre of the original Elohim team are needed to establish life in the new galaxies. The Elohim are now responsible for training spirits and bringing them up to their own standard as 'universal managers'.

When I heard this channelling my mind went back immediately to 'The Intelligent Universe' where Sir Fred Hoyle imagined 'the gods' — the Elohim — as managers in the Universe. If it was the adversity, difficulties and challenges the Elohim met in the first galaxy as co-creators of life that made them what they are today, top managers in the Universe, then in training spirits to match them they would obviously put them through difficulty, challenge and adversity.

The image in the allegories of many religions is of the primordial children of God losing paradise. First angels and then mankind fall from innocence. The sin is not in the fall from grace but man's interpretation of the descent from paradise.

No pain no gain! Growth comes with change and comfortable people don't go anywhere. Success comes through successful duplication. Great leaders train leaders as good if not better than themselves.

As above so below, as below so above…

The Universe is a fractal. It runs on duplication. All protons are identical to all other protons; the same goes for neutrons; primary particles are duplications of an original template. The same goes for stars and galaxies, atoms and molecules. They are all repeating patterns. The allegory of God and the Archangels the hosts of angels and multitudes of mortals are images of the Universal fractal. God births the Archangels, and the Archangels birth the angels. Angels in turn birth human souls as God-man or Hu-man beings — **B**orn to **E**xpand the **I**nfinite **N**ature of **G**od

People will generally succeed only if they are willing to leave their comfort zones. More often than not successful people are those who, by circumstances, got kicked out of their comfort zones. Success comes with personal growth, which comes with a willingness to leave the comfort and security of the known and embrace the insecurity, change and challenge of the unknown. Few people do this willingly. Those who do are generally forced by circumstances to make the break for freedom.

If the Sumerian records are to be believed, gold was the driving force in the creation and evolution of mankind. In the 'Universe network' the up-line leaders came to Earth in search of gold. As in all networks there is a mixture of competition and cross-line support. This was the pattern between Enlil and Enki in the Sumerian records. Sometimes they were cooperating. At other times there was competition if not downright conflict between them.

To begin with the leaders came with their own down-line organisation and started digging for gold. The going got tough and down-line dropouts dried up the flow. One of the leaders — Enki — was resourceful and built a new organisation of down-line gold diggers from the indigenous population. The leader in competition – Enlil — poached some of Enki's group. Enki responded by transforming Enlil's stolen hybrids into a self-replicating species with the potential to cause him a huge amount of trouble.

Enlil seized the opportunity of climatic changes to rid himself of the problem Enki has created for him but Enki tipped off Noah. The Noah group survived and multiplied, threatening to usurp Enlil so Enlil responded by dispersing them and confounding their ability to communicate. As numbers built again he took a leaf out of Enki's book to train a leader to control and re-enslave the human species.

We would expect Enki to respond as he always responded. We would expect him to appear amongst the humans threatened by Enlil's schemes and lead them to freedom and safety; we are, after all, the creation of Enki not Enlil. It is Enki who loves us as his children. Enlil's only interest in us is as a domesticated species for exploitation whilst we are tame, and extermination if we go out of control. From this pattern we could expect Enki to appear amongst the chosen people of Enlil, to break their loyalty to him and lead them out of bondage into freedom. The appearance and behaviour of Jesus the Christ fits our expectation of Enki precisely.

Masons, Jehovah's Witnesses and Seventh Day Adventists, from their analysis of the Bible, believe that Jesus Christ was an incarnation of Michael Archangel. The 'Ascension' channellings of Eric Klein support this and go further by indicating Jesus Christ is an incarnation of Sananda which links Sananda in the Vedas of India with Michael in the Hebrew tradition. I have already suggested that Sananda, Michael and Enki were names for the same person in the Hindu, Hebrew and Sumerian traditions respectively. Was Jesus Christ an incarnation of Enki? Were the two gods of the Bible, Jehovah and Jesus the ancient Sumerian gods, Enlil and Enki? I believe they were.

The competition between Enlil and Enki, from a human perspective, is the duality of good and evil but from a Universal perspective there is no evil. The ongoing contest between Jesus and Satan, Enki and Enlil has served a higher purpose. It has set up the all-important process for the testing and transformation of mankind. If Enlil wins the contest then humanity will either destroy itself or be enslaved. If Enki wins the contest then the human family will attain freedom and enlightenment and evolve into fully empowered gods.

Chapter 14

The Ascension

"True religion is real living; living with all one's soul, with all one's goodness and righteousness."

(Albert Einstein)

As well as 'Ancient of Days', Sanat Kumara is known by the title; **'Gatekeeper of the Beyond the Beyond'**. This appellation can help us understand the duality of the Bible God that has traumatised our history.

In my new physics of consciousness I predicted the Universe is divided into a number of levels of energy and that we live on one, delineated by the speed of light. Beyond our physical level of reality I believe there is a hyper-physical level and 'beyond the beyond' a super-physical level of quantum reality. I imagine each of these three major levels of reality could be subdivided into planes based on different speeds of energy.

My speculations of the division of the Universe into physical, hyper-physical and super-physical levels of reality accords with traditional metaphysics, in which the seen and unseen reality is described as physical, psychic and spiritual. Mystics perceive man as body, mind and spirit and in new-age parlance these three levels correspond to the third, fourth and fifth dimensions, respectively.

In metaphysical writings – such as Theosophy and the teachings of Alice Baily – there is mention of a barrier between the psychic and spiritual; between the hyper-physical and super-physical; between the fourth and fifth dimensions; between the beyond and the beyond the beyond. In line with my own thinking, this makes sense. It would make sense to me that an intelligent Universe would have a planet housing a potential planetary pathogen confined in quarantine. I call the barrier between the beyond and the beyond the beyond, the 'quarantine barrier' or 'Q-barrier'. In terms of the sky-god involvement in the history of humanity it would make sense that Enlil is responsible for the quarantine of our species; that he would be 'the gatekeeper of the beyond the beyond'.

If the super-physical fifth dimension, the beyond the beyond is the realm of spirit it would correspond to the Christian heaven and if the Ancient of Days — Sanat/Enlil/Jehovah — is Satan then the guardian of the gates of heaven would not be St Peter, it would be Satan. Maybe Satan's job is not to keep people in hell but to keep them out of heaven. That's something to meditate on in Church!

My own attitude to heaven is more in line with the Hermetic heavens than the Christian image. According to Hermes we look at heaven when we gaze into the night sky. I speculate that we are in a 'zone – of – density' a region of space time where the speed of energy is suppressed to the speed of common light. I contend that our solar system was contained by a zone-of-density when we were released by Enki as a self-replicating species. This would correspond to the idea of the 'fall' at the time of 'Adam and Eve'. This may sound far-fetched but if the Universe is a living organism in which stellar systems are the equivalent of cells, it would make sense that the Universe would have an immune system for containment of endangered planets. Just as a diseased cell in our body can be engulfed by white blood cells so a planet would be engulfed by a zone-of-density in space time which depresses the speed of energy. This would have the effect of trapping the beings on the planet to the dimension delineated by the low speed of energy, barring them access to the dimensions formed of higher speeds of energy; higher dimensions enjoyed by residents of other star systems outside the zone-of-density. We see these stars because the speed of their lights drops as it enters our zone-of-density and reverts to its original value as it leaves the zone on the other side. These ideas could account for the anomaly that Uranus and Neptune have been estimated to be older than the Universe. Space-time measures would be affected by the change in speed of energy and so all our estimates of the size and age of the Universe, taken relative to the speed of light, would need to be reconsidered if ever this hypothesis were proved true.

To understand the zone-of-density concept, the effect on light and the legend of 'the fall' imagine a pond full of goldfish. One of the fish contracts a bacterial disease. Rather than leave it in the pond to infect the other fish you lift it out and drop it in a goldfish bowl where it can recover or die as the case may be. As light enters the glass and water of the bowl its velocity is depressed. As it leaves the bowl on the other side, the light reverts to its original velocity. In this analogy the bowl represents the zone-of-density, the goldfish is the planet Earth and mankind is the infective organism.

Just as the vet you call in to treat the fish is the enemy of the bacteria so Enlil/Satan is the enemy of mankind. Now we don't make a habit of decrying doctors and vets as evil because they destroy disease so why should we judge Satan as evil because he endeavours to contain us in slavery and ignorance through religious fear and superstition. The last thing he would want is for us to develop the science and technology to reach for the stars.

Don't get depressed about being a disease organism the Universe is trying to destroy. The pattern with pathogens and parasites is they start out as harmless little organisms until they multiply in masses and destroy their host by consuming it and choking it with toxic waste. It is human selfishness and greed which causes the disease that is destroying the Earth. As we become selfless and caring towards others, all creatures and the Earth, we transform from malignant to benign and qualify as galactic citizens by becoming planetary guardians rather than planetary parasites.

The role of Enki/Christ is to guide us in the ways of unconditional love to give us the opportunity to heal ourselves and the Earth. Should that occur then just as the goldfish can return to the pond, so the zone-of-density can be lifted and the intrinsic speed of energy of the Earth can ascend to its original value. This is the ascension which is almost upon us.

The Omega point for evolutionary completion fast approaches as the cycles of human incarnation on Earth come to a close. The time of the harvest has arrived and the ascension is the gathering of the good fruit of humankind. Ascension is the imperative of our time. All other issues pale beside the clarion call to all nations and peoples on the Earth. As the planetary timepieces approach the twelfth hour, the winds of change blow upon the Earth, calling everyone to awaken from slumber and make their final choices. For each the choice is stark and clear, love or hate, faith or fear, joy or despair, the spiritual or the material.

Ascension is not for the chosen few. It is offered to everyone regardless of class, colour or creed. The only requirement for ascension is unconditional love. Ascension is not for those seeking an escape from the Earth. Planet Earth is about to take a quantum leap in Her evolution. She is about to ascend into a new age of peace, enlightenment and super-physical consciousness. If you wish to stay with this, the Beloved Planet, you also must choose to take the quantum leap into higher consciousness.

Ascension is passage through the gate in the Q-barrier between the beyond and the beyond the beyond. The super-physical fifth dimension is atomic matter, just like the physical third dimension but with a higher intrinsic-speed of energy. The hyper-physical fourth dimension is a world of psychic non-reality. It is a domain of projected fantasy, fears, dreams and mental imaginings. Between incarnations the individualised human mind returns to its psychic domain to integrate what it has accrued in a lifetime before reincarnating to manifest in another time or culture. Rarely in the cycle of incarnations does the mind ascend into the fifth dimension. Only when the individual mental and emotional being has outgrown its attachment to physical existence and learnt the lessons of detachment and unconditional love taught by all the great spiritual teachers in history – Christ, Buddha, Krishna, Nanak, Maharaji, Sai Baba & Amma to name but a few – is it ready to pass through the Q-barrier and ascend into super-physical existence in the fifth dimension and beyond.

The people of the Earth are now being activated to their higher calling. A new light is emerging as never before seen on Earth, even in ancient times. Religious fanaticism will implode and the falsehoods of modern science will collapse into their very foundations. Esoterica will pass as a fleeting shadow and the middling New Age phenomenon will just dissipate. There is no middle ground. There is either total commitment to the Light and corresponding action or a holding to shrinking money, shallow comforts, greed, violence and half truths.

Modern civilisation is a test for people. It sorts those who are ready for ascension from those who are not. It is the means whereby the sheep are sorted from the goats, the wheat from the chaff. People who are not ready to ascend will be too distracted by the toys and games of the modern world to hear the voices from the wilderness calling for personal change in preparation for transition. Those who hear about ascension and apply themselves to personal growth have the opportunity to make a choice because indeed all are invited to ascend but it is a matter of individual choice whether a soul chooses to ascend; whether a soul gives the opportunity for eternal life priority over everything in their temporal life.

Many are preparing for ascension as they 'awaken' and undergo personal change and learn their lessons of compassion and unconditionality, responsibility and forgiveness, priority and self-mastery. As we surrender attachment to people, places and things, beliefs and agendas, books and bibles, theories and opinions, judgments and addictions, religions and sciences and everything else that we all cling to, we release our ties to the Earth as it is at present.

The way each individual responds to the ascension call depends not upon this one lifetime but upon their many lives in the cycle of their incarnations on the Earth. Some resist and heap scorn. Others rejoice at the news of a lifetime. They won't question how it comes to them or judge its presentation. Many are embracing a spiritual path and are sincere seekers of truth. Of these many are now ready for completion and a lighter body of eternal joy and immortality. Others are not. People will decide for themselves and their decision will not be made according to who they are in the world or what they think but what they are in the heart.

We are in the end times. Deep in their hearts many people know that they are living in the last days. However, this is not news of doom and gloom. As birth follows death, day follows night, as spring follows winter so all ends lead to new beginnings. An alpha point breaks through the omega like the dawn in the deepest dark bringing with it renewal, regeneration and reestablishment of the universal law of love. The old age with its false values will crumble into dust. This is bad news only to those who are attached to it. For those who let go, this is the advent of the long awaited Golden Age of peace and love, truth and freedom.

This is the time of the long awaited time when an accounting is due, for all are indeed held accountable for their actions and attitudes. Scriptures have predicted an outpouring of gifts of the Spirit in the end times in those who are committed in service to Light, Love and Truth. So hold fast to your truth, the truth you know in your heart to be real. As the Earth is rocked to its very foundations and the shell of materialism is shattered, those who abide in the truth of the heart, in defiance of external appearances and increasing adversity, will shine with a radiance only dimly remembered and an authority such as the Earth has scarcely known. As the Earth passes through her birth pangs into paradise men and women everywhere will rise to their true hu-man potential. This is the time when we are called to return to our home. If you choose to respond, rejoice and be glad for though the darkness may deepen your deliverance is at hand.

No one is barred from ascension because of his or her religion. All people from all faiths, including open minded and good hearted agnostics and sincere truth seeking atheists. The primary requirement for ascension is the ability to love all beings unconditionally. Beliefs are unimportant.

When the moment of ascension arrives, which is known only at the highest level of the Universe, qualifying participants will be offered a doorway or opening of light. That will be their moment of choice; to stay with the world they know with its security and attractions, addictions and attachments or step into the void of the unknown. The opportunity to choose will only last for a few moments. Wavering or hesitation or a thought of fear and the door will recede and vanish. The opportunity for ascension and immortality will pass. James Twyman at the end of his book 'Emissaries of Light' gives a description of the appearance of the ascension doorway of light and it's slipping away in response to a thought of fear and hesitation entering his mind. In reality ascension requires priority for the Spirit over all things in this world with a high degree of faith and fearlessness. The commitment of the emissaries of light in their selfless service to humanity and their degree of detachment was exemplary. When it comes to the mass human ascension the collective effect will make it easier for the rest of us to pass through the gate.

It requires an ability to follow the irresistible pull of the heart despite the defiant resistance of the head. Those who decline the ascension opportunity will go through the normal death process whilst the Earth is cleansed prior to its ascension. Those who have ascended prior to the Earth will rejoin it at that point. Beings in the fourth dimension who are prepared for ascension but died prior to the opening of the gateway to the beyond the beyond, pass through from the beyond. Many who miss the opportunity of ascending from the physical plane during life will have the opportunity to do so from the hyper-physical after death. No one will miss the opportunity of passing through the gate into super-physical reality if they have an open and a loving heart and displayed compassion and selfless service in their lifetime.

If the majority of people were 'awake' and prepared for ascension then it would be possible for the entire human family to ascend with the Earth. However, this is unlikely as it would force the process on unwilling participants and people who are not loving.

"Many are called but few are chosen"
(Matt. 22:14)

Whilst many are invited to ascend only a few will choose to do so because few have the courage to leave the known for the unknown, security for insecurity, and voluntarily surrender their attachment to people, places and things for the void.

"In ascension you don't die... you become aware of your body as light. Then you're able to pass through the Void totally consciously... to the higher dimensions aware the whole time. You simply walk out of this life without going through the death process... When a person ascends he/she disappears from this dimension and reappears in the next, passing through the Void. (Drunvalo Melchizedek)

It has to be difficult for a being to choose ascension because once a soul goes through ascension; the Universe is stuck with it.

"Ascension is the process whereby the soul, having bal-

251

anced its karma and fulfilled its life plan, merges first with the Christ level of consciousness and then with the life-source of the I AM. Once the ascension has taken place, the soul, that once impermanent aspect of being becomes the immortal one, an incorruptible atom in the body of God." (St Germaine)

There needs to be obstacles and challenges for us on the path to ascension and we need to balance our experiences of good and evil and complete our Earth missions of becoming Homo sapiens (wise hominids) before the momentous event of becoming immortal can occur in our lives.

I appreciated why the Ancient of Days had to bar mankind from **The Tree of Life**, at the alpha point of our evolution. If **The Tree of Life** represents immortality through ascension it was obvious first a process of learning and maturation needed to be completed by as many humans as possible. It seemed obvious to me that the last thing the Universe would want is a fresh lot of immortals using their powers to rape and plunder the planets.

It became clear to me that Enlil and Enki thought they could plunder the Earth for gold, and get away with the bioengineering of some useful slaves but now they are tied inextricably to the destiny of this little planet on the outskirts of the modest Milky Way galaxy. When Enki transformed Enlil's docile hybrids into a major self-replicating threat to the Universe he put Enlil on epidemic alert. Sexually potent humans are powerful, with immense potential to create or destroy yet awakened and immortalised they have the potential to be truly glorious beings. But in terms of the Elohim agenda, I often wonder if the mining for gold and bioengineering of slaves and conflict between Enlil and Enki was not a 'front' to keep the 'Will of the Father' a closely guarded secret. For the purpose of training and testing spirits, for 'Operation Terra' to be authentic the divine plan and 'way out of the maze' had to remain in esoteric rather than exoteric knowledge. Enki broke the code by making the 'secrets of immortality' known to the masses. As Jehovah, Enlil barred the way to **The Tree of Life**, Jesus/Sananda/Enki has opened the way up for us again.

As a scientist I am aware of the laws of nature. Only a few acorns make it into oak trees, only a few tadpoles make it to frogs. The billions of humans on Earth at this time are provision, by the laws of statistics, that a good number are harvested in ascension. If only 5% make ascension and 95% of the population perish in ignorance that would still be equivalent to 100% harvest of the entire world population just a few centuries ago. However, I think Enki has in mind a bumper harvest!

There is no judgement in the Universe. Every being has to receive the same opportunity of ascension and immortality regardless of who they are or what they have become. We humans have the gift of 'free will'. To be punished for exercising it is an affront to the gift. We are free in this world to do whatever we want, to inflict or indulge in pleasure or pain, as we choose. Each and every human makes his or her own choice of destiny, free and unimpeded. At the same time there is the need for the Universe to protect itself from humans intent on greed and violence when the cost is destruction of planetary biospheres.

I love placing myself in Jehovah/Sanat/Enlil's shoes, wondering what I would do if I were gate-keeper of the beyond the beyond, guardian of the gates of heaven — the portals to the 5th Dimension — and humanity was to be given the opportunity for mass ascension with freedom of the Universe, assess to the Tree of Life and immortality. I would construct a filter. A filter acts to attract or attach unwanted things to itself. For example, a water filter attracts and absorbs things you don't want to drink out of water. Only the pure water passes through.

It seemed obvious to me that an intelligent Universe would construct an **Ascension Filter** to attract people who are attached to greed and violence, fear and self-righteousness, selfishness and materialism. It would entice them to choose not to ascend. It struck me that twentieth century civilisation provided every thing conceivable to distract people from the spiritual disciplines that are obviously necessary to make ascension a priority and prepare for the faith and fearlessness necessary to step into the void, without hesitation, especially when there is no forewarning:

"No one knows the day or the hour." (Matt. 24:36)

When I read Oscar Levy...

"We (the Jews) have erred, my friend, we have most grievously erred. And if there was truth in our error 3,000, 2,000, nay 100 years ago, there is now nothing but falseness and madness, a madness that will produce an even greater misery and an even wider anarchy...We who have promised to lead you to a new Heaven, we have finally succeeded in landing you into a new Hell... I look at this world and I shudder at its ghastliness; I shudder all the more as I know the spiritual authors of all this ghastliness."

...the penny dropped. The Jews haven't erred. They are doing precisely what they were chosen to do. They have created the ascension filter. Their job has been to create modern civilisation with its industry and its commerce, its money and banking, its media and material-ism, its religious cults, its wars, its revolutions and technology, its capitalism and its communism. That is the ascension filter. That is God arranging every conceivable distraction for us as we are poised for the greatest opportunity of our evolution.

Every form of addiction is available to keep us attached to the Earth plane. The priorities in the civilised 'sensible' world keep our attention focussed on money or the lack of it, sport and pastimes, relationships and careers, property and possessions, business and health or the lack of it, stress or apathy, religion and science, philosophy and technology, television and radio, newspapers and magazines, music and movies, studies and jobs, careers and craziness, war and peace. Everywhere there is conflict and confusion, contradiction and criticism. Everything exists to keep us confused and distracted, perplexed and preoccupied so that when the call to ascension comes we are unlikely to hear it, less likely to believe it and even if we do it is highly unlikely we will be prepared for it.

When I realised that the authors of the global civilisation were the Chosen People of Jehovah, the Ancient of Days, the Gatekeeper of the Beyond the Beyond then my hunch about the filter became more solid. It was obvious to me that the Gatekeeper was setting up hurdles between humanity and the gate. When I came across the stories of Enki and Enlil in the ancient Sumerian records and linked them to the Bible stories, then a clear pattern of obstacles and obstructions between men and women and the 'Tree of Life' emerged.

By analogy imagine us all as flies emerging on mass from pupating grubs abandoned in a fish bait tub in the corner of a room. We are heading for the wide open world through an open window - gateway to the fifth dimension. Suddenly rolls of sticky flypaper unravel in front of us - Judaic-Christian civilisation with all its distractions and delicious addictions. Can we resist the tempting odours emanating from the glue and negotiate the tacky maze to freedom? Can we escape Enlil's carefully laid flytraps and help as many other flies as he can make it through the window.

In terms of the fly paper analogy, anything that causes a breakdown in civilisation and increases human compassion is a boon. It is a fact that people are more caring and courageous in wartime than peacetime, in catastrophe than in comfort. Disasters often bring out the best in people. In this context, evils like climate change, natural disasters and wars that make humanity more uncomfortable have their purpose in the evolution of mankind. I believe the predicted mass ascension is timed to coincide with a disaster — the word means death star –akin to the event that destroyed the dinosaurs. This will cleanse the Earth of the current global civilisation that has its roots in antiquity, as foretold thousands of years ago in the famous dream of King Nebuchadnezzar and recorded in the Bible:

> "You O King, were watching; and behold, a great image! This great image, whose splendour was excellent, stood before you; And its form was awesome.
>
> "This image's head was of fine gold, its chest and arms of silver, Its belly and thighs of bronze, its legs of iron, Its feet were partly of iron and partly of clay.
>
> "You watched while a stone, cut without hands, struck the image on its feet and broke them in pieces.
>
> "Then the iron, the clay, the bronze, and the silver,

and the gold were crushed together, and became like chaff from the summer's threshing floors; the wind carried them away so that no trace of them was found.

"And the stone that struck the image became a great mountain and filled the entire earth.

(Daniel 2:31-35)

Daniel interpreted the dream to symbolise a series of civilisations that would dominate the Earth after the Babylonian represented by the gold head of the statue. There is no doubt in the minds of Bible scholars that the legs of iron represent the Roman civilisation right through to the modern age.

To my mind, the feet of clay mixed with iron represent reinforced concrete. The strike of a stone, 'cut without hands', on the feet, that destroys them - a stone that fills the Earth like a mountain - that I interpret as an asteroid strike in our time, bringing the current world order to an end. Our concrete civilisation has grown out of the previous civilisations e.g. our systems of finance (represented by the image of gold) can be traced back to the ancient Babylonian civilisation. The destruction of the concrete civilisation by an asteroid would cleanse the Earth of the influences of all the previous civilisations.

Ascension is an alternative to death to the extent that it offers us a choice. With death a person leaves the planet without choice. With ascension people choose to leave when the opening of light is offered to them. If they choose not to ascend because of their fears or attachments, they automatically choose death. When and how they die is irrelevant. At death everything a person holds dear on the Earth is lost to them. It follows that it is a mercy for circumstances to take away everything a person holds dear on the Earth if they are destined to choose the ascension, because with the unavoidable alternative they are going to lose everything anyway. Any loss of people or property is a boon in disguise because if people had any comprehension of what is in store for them on ascension, they would endure anything and forego everything that this world has to offer.

"For what will it profit a man if he gains the entire world and loses his own soul?"

"Or what will a man give in exchange for his soul?"
(Mark 8: 36-37)

Chapter 15

The Awakening

"Give the world the best you have and it may never be enough but give the world the best you've got anyway."

(Mother Theresa)

The story of humanity is the story of Universal Intelligence finding its way to a greater light by going through the deepest darkness. We represent the evolution from innocence, through the experience of every facet of good and evil, into discernment, wisdom and maturity. Paradise was only lost so that it would be appreciated when re-found.

The Earth is the place where 'God' — Universal Intelligence — learns lessons through limitation. In the state of division, separation, amnesia, relative impotence, locked in a single consciousness point in space and time, the All Knowing, All Powerful, Omniscient, Omnipresent, One has through us all a powerful learning experience in the hu-man (God-man) form on Earth.

> *His state was divine, yet he did not cling to his equality with God but emptied himself to assume the condition of a slave and became as men are.*

(Philippians 2:6-7)

Jesus Christ was a man like the rest of us but he was a way-shower. The only difference between him and us is he woke up to his innate divinity. He let go of his limitations and became a fully enlightened human being – as did Krishna, Buddha, Hermes and many others. The Catholic Church contends Mary did the same. And why not! Are women to be excluded from the awakening? Of course not! Kuan Yin of ancient China went through an awakening to the enlightened state through a life of difficulty and adversity, selfless service and compassion — as has Amma in our present time.

We are all gods and goddesses who have divested ourselves of equality with God and emptied ourselves of power and knowledge to take on the limited, slave like nature of mortal man and woman. We are God evolving through the human state:

For God omniscience and omnipresence are as nothing. For the unlimited the ultimate adventure is to experience limitation; separation, constraint, powerlessness and the state of forgetfulness.

Divested of power and knowledge God plunges into matter and passes into amnesia... the newborn baby, helpless and vulnerable, opens its eyes and cries.

God looks out onto a strange new world. The adventure had begun...

Collectively, I believe we are God learning, evolving and resolving the schisms inherent in duality. We each, in our many lives, choose between heaven and hell. To quote Krishna speaking to his disciple, the Prince Arjuna millennia before Christ :

"Freedom from fear, purity of heart, constancy in sacred learning and contemplation, generosity, self harmony, adoration, study of the scriptures, austerity, righteousness;

"Non-violence, truth, freedom from anger, renunciation, serenity, aversion to fault finding, sympathy for all beings, peace from greedy cravings, gentleness, modesty, steadiness;

"Energy, forgiveness, fortitude, purity, a good will, freedom from pride — these are the treasures of the man who is

born for heaven.

"Deceitfulness, insolence and self-conceit, anger harshness and ignorance - these belong to a man who is born for hell

"The virtues of heaven are for liberation but the sins of hell are the chains of the soul. Grieve not Arjuna for heaven is thy final end.

"There are two natures in this world: the one is of heaven, the other of hell. The heavenly nature has been explained: hear now of the evil of hell.

"Evil men know not what should be done or what should not be done. Purity is not in their hearts, not good conduct, nor truth."They say: 'This world has no truth, no moral foundation, no God. There is no law of creation: what is the cause of birth but lust?

"Firm in this belief, these men of dead souls, of truly little intelligence, undertake their work of evil: they are the enemies of this fair world, working for its destruction.

"They torture their soul with insatiable desires and full of deceit, insolence and pride, they hold fast their dark ideas, and they carry on their impure work.

"Thus they are beset with innumerable cares which last long, all their life, until death. Their highest aim is sensual enjoyment, and they firmly think that this is all.

"They are bound by hundreds of vain hopes. Anger and lust is their refuge; and they strive by unjust means to amass wealth for their own cravings."(Bhagavad Gita 16: 1-12)

Evil exists so that we can rise above it. Hell exists so that through the experience of it we will strive for Heaven and appreciate that which maybe we once took for granted. Evil exists so we can grow through it and beyond it. Ignorance exists so we can awaken from it into enlightenment. Every being is on a journey. Eventually all will awaken. How long that will take and how much suffering must be endured is up to each individual. The awakening occurs in a moment and can occur in any moment.

It is not for us to judge between good and evil because our judgements pull us deeper into the mire of duality. It is for us to shift from being right to being love. This is the awakening to live our lives in the knowing of whom we are and our innate potential for goodness.

Life just keeps on going, free of feelings of suffering, joy, sadness, pity; like a river it tumbles each day into the next. How you wake up and perceive the day is up to you. How you choose to perceive others and yourself is also up to you. But notice how judgement and anger leaves you feeling inside; notice how when you don't communicate with people you are left feeling suffocated, blocked — even sick. Is the feeling of being right or better than others worth your own suffering? Notice then how when you give with love and understanding you are left with the feeling of joy and wholeness.

There's no right or wrong, no good or evil, only a fresh new day with every sunrise. Finish each day knowing that everything is complete; there is nothing more to do or worry about. Relax into sleep in the knowing that there is nothing more important than the day that will awake you.

(Rebecca Ash ~London ~ 14/03/04)

There is no absolute evil as all evil serves the greater good. If we want love and light, joy and laughter, peace, truth and highest wisdom to prevail on the Earth we have only to cross the line between selfishness and selflessness. If we are all incarnations of God why aren't we all like Jesus or Amma? The answer is simple:

When we are selfish we pull things toward ourselves from others possessions, people, attachments and property. These are accompanied by fearful thoughts and emotions of greed and jealousy, possessiveness and anger, control and manipulation which build a shell around our hearts which prevents the expression of our innate divinity.

When we are selfless we push things away from ourselves toward others. As we give rather than take our deeds of charity are accompanied by loving thoughts and emotions of compassion, joy and courage. With generosity of spirit comes an outpouring of spirit and an expression of our innate divinity in its longing to love and serve and help others in their journey through life.

"If you want something, give it away!" (Tony Budell)

It all begins with an attitude of loving and caring, giving and sharing. Attitude shapes our thoughts which then shape our lives and we can enhance our attitude by affirming our 'I AM' divine status.

Jesus affirmed as the I AM when he said:

"Before Abraham was, I AM"(John 8:58)

"I AM the way the truth and the life"(John 14:6)

Krishna spoke as the I AM:

I AM the Father of this Universe, and even the source of the Father. I AM the Mother of this Universe and the Creator of all. I AM the Highest to be known, the path of purification, the holy OM, the three Vedas.

I AM the way, the Master who watches in silence; thy friend and thy shelter and thy abode of peace. I AM the beginning and the middle and the end of all things: their seed of Eternity, their Treasure supreme. (Bhagavad Gita 9: 17-18)

I AM the soul, prince victorious, which dwells in the heart of all things. I AM the beginning, the middle and the end of all that lives.(Bhagavad Gita 10: 20)

Krishna was speaking here fully self-realised, awakened human being, aware of his at-one-ment with 'God'. Each one of us is an incarnation of the I AM consciousness, the one indivisible source of all because the Universal Consciousness is indivisible:

Time and space, particles and motion, vortices and waves, are all acts of consciousness. The principle of division so essential to these building blocks of the Universe does not necessarily apply to the creative consciousness that brings them into being. All protons have identical characteristics. This suggests they come from the same consciousness. Consciousness is one and it is indivisible. You and I are conscious. The consciousness in us is indivisible. We are essentially the same being in different bodies. If you call it 'God' then every human is the One God in a different body. (The New Physics of Consciousness)

So each human being can speak as Krishna or Christ spoke because each one of us is an embodiment of the same One divine essence. The same conscious awareness lives in us all. We are the One life in the many bodies. We are the I AM awareness in physical incarnation. Collectively we are God. We have infinite power, knowledge and wisdom locked away within us.

We have nothing to fear and every reason to rejoice and be happy. All we have to do is wake up. Awaken to who we are. We do not need to be redeemed or found. We do not need to be saved because we were never separate.

We are God. We just forgot. We fell asleep to learn through the experience of limitation and forgetfulness.

If we declare ourselves as God, because we are God, the Universe is bound to obey. We are only powerless because, as God, we have chosen a state of denial and powerlessness. If we decide to reverse that decision — which we can do at any time —we can step back into our full power again. And that is truly awesome!

The thing about Jesus, Jehovah and Krishna is that they didn't go round denying that they were God whereas most people do. If you are God in human form, and you deny it, because you are God your denial becomes an instruction for the Universe, which the Universe is bound to obey. If you believe you are a poor, powerless, insignificant little person then the Universe will deliver you goods and services appropriate to your specification and expectation.

Collectively, as a result of thousands of years of religious indoctrination — to the effect that human beings are all miserable sinners — humanity has programmed the Universe to this effect — which explains why so many people find themselves in a miserable, sinful state.

We do not have to suffer. We choose to suffer. Indulging in selfishness, apathy and ignorance we inflict the experience of suffering upon ourselves and upon others. There is another way. We could stop blaming, stop complaining and start making I AM affirmations:

I AM *beautiful*
I AM *wonderful*
I AM *in love with life*
I AM *at peace with my neighbour*
I AM *in a positive mood today*
I AM *feeling good today*

I AM *at harmony with all that is*
I AM *truth incarnate*
I AM *the living knowledge*
I AM *a wellspring of joy in this world*

Dr. Masaru Emoto of Japan has shown that water crystalises differently when exposed to positive affirmations against negative affirmations. We are 90% water living on a watery planet where all life depends on water. Positive affirmations have a very beneficial impact on our bodies and the world around us. Negative affirmations have the reverse effect.

Love and light, joy and laughter, peace, truth and highest wisdom can prevail in each one of us and the whole of humanity if we choose that to be so. We could affirm for healing to occur in every heart and home, in every family, community and nation on Earth. If we wanted to, we could reconcile the duality of good and evil, now and forever. There is nothing to prevent us from resolving conflict in ourselves then project this resolution to the world at large. This is our destiny and our opportunity. A positive attitude and affirmations are invaluable in the preparation for ascension, both individually and collectively.

We can have the millennium of peace, joy and enlightenment if we collectively affirm for it because in truth the ascension is people coming into their own power and choosing the reality they want to live. We can choose life over death, peace rather than war, love instead of hate.

We can enact our intent in our daily lives. There is much we can do. If we begin on the inner planes with prayer and affirmation, our action on the outer planes will be immensely more powerful and effective. We are the gods in an expanding and evolving Universe. With our collective intent we can achieve any target we set. All misery and suffering can be averted. We are Universal playwrights. We can be the directors and producers in a new drama.

> ...and they shall beat their swords into ploughshares
> and their spears into pruning hooks:
> nation shall not lift up sword against nation, neither shall
> they learn war any more. (Isaiah 2:4)

There are many things we can do to bring about the ascension of the Earth and humanity. We could use personal initiative:

There is nothing more dangerous than personal initiative; if it has genius behind it, such initiative can do more than can be done by millions of people among whom we have sown discord. (Protocol 5).

Networking important and inspiring information can be a huge service to humanity. Recommending inspiring websites can spread 'The Word'. Books gather dust on bookshelves, they need to be read. If you are inspired by a book read it then pass it on. It is also important to give copies of inspiring books to students. Young people represent the future and students have a right to be informed of the influences in their world. When they are questioning they have a right to a broad spectrum of opinion and information so that they can make considered choices for their future and the future of their world.

Gifting time, energy, abilities and a small percentage of income for the upliftment of humanity is important. Vast sums of money lie stagnant whilst many worthwhile projects flounder for need of funding. The vast majority of the world's population are unable to lift themselves out of poverty. The 'negative karma' associated with money can be shifted by the act of giving.

Money leads nowhere unless it is used for good:

"For what will it profit a man if he gains the whole world, and loses his own soul?" (Mark 8:36)

Grace is worth more than gold. Support those who inspire you. If you have read *The Celestine Prophecy* by James Redfield, you will notice that the section on the *Ninth Insight* — which predicts the ascension — also states that the world will only move from darkness into light when people give money to those who inspire them spiritually. If the focus in this world is on material rather than spiritual gain then the world will never rise above materiality and self-interest. Whatever a person says or believes, their priority lies in their purse.

"Do not lay up for yourselves treasures on earth, where moths and rust destroy and where thieves break in and steal. But lay up for yourselves treasures in heaven, where neither moth nor rust destroys and where thieves do not break in and steal. For where your treasure is your heart will be there also."
(Matthew 6:19-21)

We can help people in need. We can all be the source of a miracle in another person's life. There is always the opportunity for spontaneous acts of giving and compassion for others who are less fortunate than ourselves. The poor provide us with an opportunity for spiritual growth through service. They should be respected as such. Only small amounts are required to meet their basic needs, bringing dignity and creativity into their lives. Small interest-free loans can lift people and communities from poverty to prosperity. Many prefer an interest-free loan without undue pressure for repayment. Microcredit, pioneered in India by Ella Bhatt, and championed by Hillary Clinton, is transforming the lives of millions of people in the third world, especially women. Small amounts of money, in the hands of women, are mostly used with integrity for the welfare of the family and the community at large. The bulk of money in the hands of men has been used as an instrument of power and control. Large sums of money generate greed in most people and people unable to share their money and possessions demonstrate impoverishment of spirit. In the hoarding of money, and material things, they obstruct their own soul growth and withhold resources from others who need them.

The poor of the Earth are a source of spiritual wealth, offering humanity the opportunity to strengthen the spirit through good works and acts of care and compassion. If everyone was giving, loving and caring for everyone else, imagine how rich and happy we would all be. If everyone was sharing what they have with everyone else there would be no need for money. There is plenty for everyone. Money has allowed the wealth of the many to amass in the hands of the few, who use it to further their own ends. If we cannot solve global problems by the fair distribution of money, the end of money will solve global problems.

Selfless service to others is the fast track to ascension because it demonstrates our compassion, our care; our ability to love unconditionally.

"The beauty and charm of selfless love and service should not die away from the face of this Earth. The world should know that a life of dedication is possible, a life inspired by love and service to humanity is possible"

Amma

One story that touched my heart was of a girl who

trained to be an actress — drama was her passion. However, she was called to nanny two small children for a mother who wanted to devote herself to business. Two years later her father asked her when she planned to stop being a nanny and start her acting career. She replied "When the Universe makes it clear to me to leave the children!"

Nine years later she was still mothering the two children —having long since given up on acting — when suddenly the mother committed suicide. Where would those two children have been if that girl had put her career before her calling? A mother sacrifices herself for her children. She sacrificed herself for another woman's children. Through her selfless service the young woman was expressing the love of the Divine Mother. And her attitude was so humble. Asking me not to mention her name she wrote; "...*there are many people who enable my life and the choices to be the way they are. The whole web is what's important; the shimmering vortex of family...*"

As each individual awakens to integrate the entire web of the human family they become a shimmering vortex of light that illumines the way for others to follow. Amma is an outstanding example. As a girl she sacrificed security and family life to devote herself, in love and selfless service, for the welfare of the entire family of humanity:

"*The opportunity to love and serve others should be considered a rare gift, a blessing from God.*"

Amma

We can learn to trust that the Universe will provide for us in our times of need. A great deal of stress in modern life occurs because people lack faith and trust in the providence of Spirit. If we give away what we don't need and then intend and affirm for what we do need and want in our life we make room for a miracle. It is important to allow time for the manifestation to occur and not be attached to how it occurs. Total trust in the unfolding miracle of life is a way of self-mastery and ascension.

We can choose to share our lives with people who inspire us. We can also read books, visit web sites and listen to recordings, which uplift and inspire:

Words which give peace, words which are good and beautiful and true, and also the reading of sacred books: this is the harmony of words.(Bhagavad Gita 17: 15-16)

The best way to learn is to teach and, as unique incarnations of God, every human has a unique lesson for everyone. Everyone has something to share. When two or more gather with a common intent, the effect is more powerful than an individual on their own. There are groups that meet on a regular basis for sharing inspiration and uplifting experiences, prayer, meditation and affirmation. They work as a battery to send love and light, peace and healing wherever it is needed in the world.

We can envision the world and the future, as we would like to see it, then use affirmation and visualisation processes to put the vision into the collective consciousness.

A great deal of inspiration can be gained from channelling — especially if you allow yourself to be the channel. Most channelling is highly informative, inspiring, encouraging and uplifting. Nonetheless, treat channelling more as a source of inspiration than information because specific information, especially in regard to predictions and dates, is rarely accurate. Exercise discrimination and do not feel you have to believe everything the channel has to say. All channelling includes a varying degree of the channel's mindset and the entities being channelled are not especially greater or lesser than we. They may be 'the gods in heaven' but we are 'the gods on Earth'. They need us for their evolution as much as we need them.

Daily meditation to connect with our Source is vital for ascension:

Quietness of mind, silence and self-harmony, loving -kindness, and a pure heart: this is the harmony of the mind. (Bhagavad Gita 17: 15-16)

The Knowledge of God exists in the stillness when mind and activity cease. In that moment of relaxation, of complete stillness within and without, when we are totally in the breath and the body, then our real divine presence fills the void; but first we must embrace stillness:

Be still and know I AM God (Psalm 46:10)

Another key to meditation is relaxation. When we relax the divinity within us can expand into the stress-free space and fill us with infinite grace.

"Learn to be relaxed in all circumstances. Whatever you do and wherever you are, relax and you will see how powerful it is. The art of relaxation brings out the power that exists within you. Through relaxation you can experience your infinite capacities."

Amma

If you can't meditate just breathe! Conscious breathing or centering your attention on the breath is the simplest and most valuable form of meditation. Allow your breath to go slow and deep of its own accord. Have no expectation of an experience, because expectation blocks experience. Allow your connection to the source of your life to gift you with whatever is most appropriate, as you surrender thought and activity to stillness, that allows peace into your life.

This is the Holy Spirit, the Great Spirit but also your

Spirit because there is no division or separation in the Spirit. As you grow in communion with your Spirit, every breath will become a meditation and every act a service. This is the traditional way of yoga, the way of union with the Divine through meditation, the communication of truth and good works. Meditate on your truth. Envision and speak your truth. Serve your truth. This is the threefold way of truth:

Some by the Yoga of meditation, and by the grace of the spirit, see the spirit in themselves; some by the Yoga of the vision of Truth; and others by the Yoga of work.(Bhagavad Gita 13:24)

People on the path to ascension do whatever they can to serve others and the welfare of the whole. Many people make the excuse: 'I am far too busy' or 'I will do it tomorrow'. Never put off until tomorrow what you can do today. Beware of the trap of the 'busyness of modern life'. If you are entirely devoted to your business or your work know that...

...Businessmen and merchants will not enter the places of my Father!

(The 'Gospel of St. Thomas' from 'The Gnostics' p.32)

I love to serve the Earth. I enjoy collecting litter from a road side or cleaning a stream, clearing trash from a seashore or planting trees, especially those that bear fruit. These are ways of honouring and respecting beloved Mother Earth. We can all do something for the environment. If we had the will we could transform the Earth into Paradise.

It's not just what we do but how we do it that counts. Whatever you do can be transformed by mindfulness.

"It is the art of making your mind still and focussing all your energy on the work you are doing, whatever it may

be, that will enable you to bring out your full potential. Once you learn this art everything happens effortlessly and spontaneously."

Amma

The vibration of the flower will open your heart chakra and help you plumb the depths of your being. 'Stick your nose in a rose', or any other flower — but watch out for the bees — and fill your lungs with the fragrance, the frequency of the flower.

Doing whatever makes your heart sing. Follow your spirit and your truth. Follow your joy. Live in laughter. Do what makes you happy. Don't let others discourage you. People with singing hearts rarely stop to criticise. Leave those who find fault with you and allow others, with singing hearts, to dance into your life. Welcome those who share your vision. However, if your heart sinks, don't do whatever it is you were about to do, even if others think you should. Only you know what is right for you. Meditate and feel into the 'direction of joy', moment by moment, day by day and allow your happiness to lead you.

Just as a room full of darkness can be dispelled by a single candle of light, so a life full of emptiness, despair and negativity can be transformed into happiness, contentment and positivity by a minimum daily practice of prayer and affirmation, service, meditation and a good dose of laughter and sex.

Unhappiness is 'soul pain'. It tells us when we are 'off track'. If we feel depressed we need to either surrender to our situation — or change it. The choice is always ours. Happiness will indicate when we are in the state most conducive to our personal growth.

If you are full of joy, fun and laughter you will serve

others by bringing happiness into their lives. You can do this simply by your abundant state of being. This will also help you to release addictions. Alcohol, smoking and drugs are not the only addictions that destroy people, their initiative, state of freedom and soul evolvement. Negative thinking, judgements, criticism, gossip, anxiety and small talk are addictions. Money and material things can also be addictive. Sex can be another common addiction. Any compulsive patterns of thought, talk or behaviour denotes lack of self-mastery.

Certain foods — refined carbohydrates for example – are also addictive and destructive to health. If our metabolism is toxic and out of balance this will affect our moods, attitudes and thinking. Nutrition and lifestyle changes are all part of the awakening.

Without addictions we can have real fun and make merry. The pleasures of life are there to serve us, not enslave us. When we awaken to self-mastery we can enjoy everything because nothing has a hold on us: and the hallmark of an awakened soul is a sense of humour.

Many people heal with their hands and their minds. This brings relief to those who suffer. It also brings soul growth to those who heal. During times of meditation we can also visualise the beloved Earth and send her healing.

Sound and dance can be a powerful form of healing. Enjoy music that inspires and uplifts you. Sacred music can be as powerful as meditation and prayer in uplifting the soul and connecting it to the Divine. Dance allows the energy of the Divine to flow through the body, releasing tensions and stimulating circulation and the flow of oxygen to every cell in the body. A dancing body stays young and healthy. Song and dance help to fill life full of joy.

Take confidence in yourself, in your abilities and what

you are able to do, no matter how small and insignificant it may appear to be. Love, dedication and intent matter more than results. Nonetheless, stretch yourself. Be courageous. Speak out for what you believe in. Act decisively with a willingness to learn from your mistakes. Take the leap of faith and follow your heart. Allow for your own flow of inspiration but don't take yourself too seriously. Learn to laugh at yourself, have fun and play:

"Verily I say to you, unless you accept the Kingdom of God as a little child you will not enter it.
(Mark 10:15)

Let your light shine. Don't hide your light under a bushel. Share your gifts, insights and enthusiasms with others:

"You are the light of the world. A city that is set on a hill cannot be hid.
"Neither do men light a candle, and put it under a bushel, but on a candlestick; and it gives light to all that are in the house.
"Let your light shine before men, that they may see your good works, and glorify your Father who is in heaven." (Matthew 5:14-16)

It only requires a certain critical mass of people to awaken for the mass consciousness of humanity to shift. That is when the mass awakening occurs. We are fast approaching the omega point of human evolution in this present cycle of incarnations. Ours is the opportunity for awakening to our unlimited divine selves if we can let go of attachment to limitations, especially limiting thoughts and beliefs, that hold us back

There may be a degree of material deprivation and physical discomfort, before the present saga finally comes to an end. We can prepare by learning to trust and make do with the minimum.

Amma sets an example. Although millions pass through her hands in aid of her charities and she is treated like royalty in India, when she sleeps at all, she still sleeps on a bare mat on the floor. This builds strength of spirit and resourcefulness. Learning to be content with what we have rather than hankering for what we don't have, learning to care and share, these are the keys to survival, contentment and lasting happiness.

I wish you courage in your final 'sprint for the stars'. Every blessing under heaven will be yours as you are about to graduate from this terrestrial school, as a god amongst the gods, so rejoice and be happy. Know that everything in this world is but a test of your spiritual worth. Earth is the place where souls come to undergo initiation into godhood. Forgetting this during incarnation is part of the initiation. We are here for personal growth so we may as well accept whatever comes gracefully. Be prepared for anything. Guard your freedom and your truth with your life, because without freedom and truth, life isn't worth living. However, true freedom can come when the body is imprisoned or trapped through disability or disease. Truth and freedom are states of the Spirit more than physical circumstance.

Young people especially may feel discouraged by what they see in the world. They may have a sense of hopelessness, degradation and lack of a positive future. They are being subjected to unremitting stresses in the home and classroom, with external pressures being brought to bear on them by market forces and the mass media. At home they are often burdened with parent's relationship problems when they have their own to contend with. At school, college and university they are placed under further stress, as they have to contend with an ever-increasing burden of work coupled with a dubious future. Diet is deteriorating and the media blasts them with unrealistic images, concepts and goals. They are often left with a sense of failure and despair. Violent movies, television and computer games, drugs, and alcohol present themselves as a means of escape when in fact they accelerate the spiral of destruction.

Young people are being tested to their limits in the final days of materialistic civilisation. They need to learn to take their personal power before the soul-less forces within society enslave them. They can trust the future because they hold the key to the future in their hands. They are the future. If they grow in the Spirit, the Earth will be theirs and the fullness thereof.

For a gentle transition to occur from the old age to the new, there is a need for people to be informed. If you feel some of the information I have shared with you shocking, my reply is that the truth can often come as a shock. But if it motivates you to take positive, responsible action for personal evolution and the evolution of the human race then it has served its purpose. Many will already be aware of much of what I have said. If that is the case, I hope this book will have helped tie up loose ends and fill in some gaps.

I want to leave you with words of inspiration from 'Tomorrow's God' by Neale Donald Walsch (Hodder & Stoughton 2004).

I love the Bible. I continually draw inspiration from it. I have it beside me at this moment. But it is the 'Word of God' no more and no less than the writings of Walsch and many other 'God' inspired authors, channellers and teachers of today. For me 'Conversations with God' and

'Tomorrow's God' are as inspiring and uplifting as the Bible, the Gita or any other scripture from the past. I don't believe every word of it because all sacred books – including the Bible — convey the personality and opinions, attitudes and mindset of the human authors through whom God speaks.

Even the atheists have their part to play. I consider *The God Delusion* by Richard Dawkins to be an important book the subject of God. Though I don't agreed with everything he says I admire Richard Dawkins immensely and see a very similar underlying warning in *The God Delusion* to that in *Tomorrow's God* (Neale Donald Walsch, Hodder & Stoughton 2004) of the danger in *Yesterday's God* and the religions this misconception has spawned.

So why is there a dark side to God? The reply from Walsch's 'God' is that God is Life. Life is both good and bad. Life creates and it destroys, it births and it devours, it gives life and brings death, it is the source of joy and suffering. Life is everything. The problem with 'God' is not God but man's concepts around God. Religions have separated God from man and make God their exclusive domain. This has brought the world to where it is today. Through Walsch, 'God' is asking us to ditch the name 'God' and replace it with the word 'Life'. Should we do this in a stroke religions would be rendered obsolete and, with universal respect for Life, the world would be restored to Paradise:

"When you believe in Life, you do believe in God, whether you say it in so many words or not. You can be an atheist or an agnostic or anything in between, and it will not matter to Tomorrow's God.

"It does not matter today, but tomorrow all of you will know this. Tomorrow every human being will understand.

*And that understanding will be good, because it will elimi-
nate much of the conflict that has resulted from each of you
believing in your particular God in your particular way.*

*"You have not been able to agree with each other on this
topic when you have used the word, 'God' or 'Allah' or 'Jehovah', 'Brahman,' or the many other names you have
given to the Essence and the Being, the All and the Only.
Now I suggest that there is another word for God, the
meaning of which you may all agree upon. When this word
is exchanged for the word 'God,' everything suddenly becomes simple and clear.*

*"Yes, 'Life' is the one word in your many languages that
comes closest to carrying the meaning that some of you are
seeking to express when you use the word 'Allah' or 'God'
or 'Brahman,' 'Vishnu,' or 'Shiva,' and that you hope describes or can be a container for 'the stuff that God is.'*

"In one word, LIFE is the 'stuff that God is.'

*"Life IS. Life is that which IS. It has no shape, no form, no
gender. It has no color, no fragrance, no size. It is ALL
shapes, all forms, all colors, fragrances, and sizes. It is both
genders, and that which is genderless as well.*

*"It is the All and the Everything, and it is the No Thing
from which Everything emerges.*

*"There is nothing Life creates that is not Life Itself. All that
you see everywhere around you is Life, expressing. Life is
everything. It runs in, as, and through everything. YOU
are Life, expressing, and Life is you, expressing itself as you.*

*"Everybody else is Life expressing. There is no one, not a sin-
gle living being, who is not an expression of Life. Even those
you consider the worst among you are an expression of Life.*

*"None of these statements seems controversial. Not many
people would seriously argue with them. The truth of these*

statements seems obvious on the surface.

"Now play a little trick on yourself. Play a little game. Exchange the word 'Life' for the word 'God' and see what happens. Watch you mind go crazy. Make the same statement, as above, but use the word 'God' in place of the word 'Life' and watch what your mind does with it."

(Neale Donald Walsch: *Tomorrow's God*)

Index

Index

About the author

As a child protégé David declared he would prove the existence of God through science. Following in his father's footsteps, he became an amateur pioneering scientist in the Victorian mould. But the story really began when he discovered a lost knowledge from ancient Yogic philosophy that brings together the ancient science of the East with modern science from the West. Could it be David stumbled on the key to the Universe!

On Jan 15, 1975 David delivered the inaugural lecture on his new physics from the historic rostrum of Michael Faraday at the Royal Institution of Great Britain. In 1985, under the direction of Sir George Trevelyan, David started teaching his vortex physics and science of ascension in lectures and seminars throughout the UK. Since then he has travelled the world with his new easy-to-understand physics linking science, spirituality and consciousness. His compassionate approach to evil and the way he combines cutting edge science with sacred songs makes him an unusual but fascinating and uplifting teacher. David has nine children and eight grandchildren.

To contact David or book him as a speaker email: **davidash333@btinternet.com**

If you enjoyed this book (and naturally we hope that you did) we recommend the following title for your further reading enjoyment.

This book introduces a new paradigm which integrates science and religion. With an easy rewrite of physics there is a profound philosophy. Clear analogies and simple diagrams make the science understandable and enthralling. A theory for everything emerges which is simple and brilliant! Supernova explosions in distant galaxies provide proof for the theory.

A new vision of matter sits with a fresh understanding of God. Science and religion reconciled; the Universe will never be quite the same again!

ISBN: 978-0-9802561-3-0

Kima Global Publishers, is an independent publishing company based in Cape Town. We specialise in *Books that Make a Difference to People's Lives*.

We have a unique variety of Body, Mind and Spirit titles that are distributed throughout South Africa, the U.K., Europe, Australia and the U.S.A.

Among our genres you will find non-fiction — healing, wellness, philosophy, parenting, business coaching, personal development, creative workbooks, spiritual, fantasy and visionary fiction titles.

www.kimaglobal.co.za

Universal Creative Intelligence - 7
No. of stars + grains of sand - 25
David accepts the Bible/Old Test. as "gospel"!
Masons + Jews started French Revolution →
   Led to Communism (Marx + Lenin were Jews)
               Stalin
                                          121|123|136

Jewish influence - 149|150|155|157

Jewish banks - 162

Nazis + Jews - 164 (Hitler - Jewish)

9/11 - Inside jobs - 168

Fundamentalist Jews|Christians|Moslems - 170

David's Jewish roots - 173

Jews + RCs - 175/176   And, Masons - 180
       And, Jehovah Witnesses - 189

Christian myths - 195, 198, 201 (Vote on Jesus +
                            God - Nicene Creed)
Man destroying Universe - 210/212/246
Universal Intelligence watching us - 214
Energy - 243   We are God - 260   ↓ Nucleus!